Madam Chief Justice

Madam Chief Justice. John Seibels Walker's portrait of Chief Justice Jean Hoefer Toal. Photo courtesy of Lucas Brown, Kickstand Studio.

Madam Chief Justice

JEAN HOEFER TOAL OF SOUTH CAROLINA

EDITED BY W. Lewis Burke Jr. and Joan P. Assey

Foreword by Sandra Day O'Connor

Introduction by Ruth Bader Ginsburg

THE UNIVERSITY OF SOUTH CAROLINA PRESS

© 2016 University of South Carolina

Published by the University of South Carolina Press
Columbia, South Carolina 29208

www.sc.edu/uscpress

Manufactured in the United States of America

25 24 23 22 21 20 19 18 17 16
10 9 8 7 6 5 4 3 2 1

Library of Congress Cataloging-in-Publication Data
can be found at http://catalog.loc.gov/.

ISBN 978-1-61117-692-6 (cloth)
ISBN 978-1-61117-693-3 (ebook)

Contents

Illustrations

SANDRA DAY O'CONNOR,

Associate Justice (Retired), Supreme Court of the United States

Foreword

WE OFTEN CELEBRATE "firsts," and for good reason. Firsts are important. They mark the end of one era and the beginning of another. Once a threshold is crossed, it becomes much harder to go back. But we often forget that being a first is not always easy. It can take a long time, a lot of work, and at least a few false starts.

I know a little about being a first. In 1981 I became the first woman to serve on the Supreme Court of the United States when President Reagan nominated me to the seat left open by Justice Stewart's retirement. I was the only woman to serve on the Supreme Court until 1993, when President Clinton nominated Justice Ginsburg to the seat left open by Justice White's retirement. I was thrilled when I heard about Justice Ginsburg's nomination. At last I knew that while I was the first woman to serve on the Supreme Court, I would not be the last. Today there are three female U.S. Supreme Court Justices. A new era has certainly begun.

Jean Hoefer Toal has been a lot of firsts. In 1988 she became the first woman to be elected to the Supreme Court of South Carolina. In 2000 Jean became the first woman to serve as that court's chief justice. She is also the first native Columbian and the first Roman Catholic to serve on South Carolina's highest court. Prior to her judicial service, Jean became the first woman in South Carolina to chair a standing committee in the state House of Representatives. Jean is truly a trailblazer in her home state.

This book discusses Jean's firsts. But it also does so much more. The book begins with Jean's early days as a lawyer, describing her path from researching in the basement of a law firm to representing clients in the courtroom. You will learn about the important cases Jean tried and their impact on the law and the lives of people in South Carolina. The book will then take you through Jean's campaign for public office and her days in the state legislature. And you will of course learn about Jean's groundbreaking election to the Supreme Court of South Carolina.

The book also discusses Jean's contributions to the smooth and effective operation of South Carolina's courts. It describes how Jean embraced technology, recognizing the essential role it plays in a modern court system. You will learn about how she used technology to connect the state courts to one another and to make them more efficient and accessible. You will learn too about the good business sense Jean brought with her from years spent running her family's sand mine and how it influenced her leadership style and views on judicial administration. And the book also guides you through the valuable programs Jean developed to introduce students and teachers to the appellate process and the Supreme Court of South Carolina.

In discussing Jean's life and career, this book will take you on a journey through South Carolina's history as well. The book describes the lay of the land when Jean began practicing law, a time when women did not even serve on juries. You will learn about the important legislation Jean helped to enact against the backdrop of South Carolina's evolving economy. And you will read stories from women lawyers about what Jean's election to South Carolina's highest court meant to them and to women throughout the state.

My retirement from the Supreme Court of the United States in 2006 marked the end of one chapter in my life and the beginning of another. It allowed me to spend more time with my family and to embark on new projects. One of the projects that I am most proud of is iCivics, an interactive, web-based civics education program for students and teachers. You can find it at www.icivics.org. iCivics has a rich array of curricular materials, including curriculum units, lesson plans, online forums, web quests, and video games. Its purpose is to help restore civics education to our nation's schools and to teach the next generation the fundamental knowledge and skills of citizenship. We must ensure that the next generation will be ready to take up their civic responsibilities, for the very health of our democracy depends on an informed and engaged citizenry.

When I was looking for people to join the iCivics team and to help introduce the program to students and teachers across the country, I knew that I could count on Jean. As with everything she does, Jean took the project all the way. Under her leadership South Carolina became one of the first states to incorporate iCivics into its classrooms. Jean helped make my vision for iCivics a reality. And in doing so, she became yet another first. In 2011 Jean was the first recipient of the National Center for State Courts' Sandra Day O'Connor Award for the Advancement of Civics Education. I am also proud of Catherine Templeton and Molly Craig, my two national iCivics coordinators, who helped implement iCivics in South Carolina and in every other state in the country.

I am delighted to know Jean Hoefer Toal. We both came of age in a time when women were not lawyers and were certainly not judges. We both served in our state legislatures and on our state appellate courts. We both are as dedicated to our families and our friends as we are to our profession and our communities. And we both can hit a golf ball and host a great party.

I know that you will enjoy learning about Jean Hoefer Toal's life and about her beloved South Carolina. I hope that her story inspires you as it inspires me. Jean's story serves as an important reminder that being a first is just the beginning.

Acknowledgments

THIS BOOK HAD ITS genesis in the South Carolina Supreme Court Historical Society. U.S. district judge Joseph F. Anderson Jr. proposed the idea of
a biographical volume on Jean Hoefer Toal to the society, and C. Mitchell
Brown, president of the society, wholeheartedly endorsed the idea. It is
quite fitting that the society would choose to produce a volume on Jean
Toal because it was her leadership that led to the creation of the society.
Under her guidance the Supreme Court Historical Society has sponsored
colloquia on topics related to the South Carolina legal profession and supported three other books published by the University of South Carolina
Press. Two of the society's books grew out of these seminars. A third volume, *Matthew J. Perry: The Man, His Times and His Legacy,* was sponsored
by the society to be published with the dedication of the Matthew J. Perry
United States Courthouse in Columbia. Similarly this book about Toal will
also mark an important event, the retirement of Jean Hoefer Toal as chief
justice of the Supreme Court of South Carolina. Like the Perry book, the
Toal book will be followed by an appropriate colloquium.

Jean Toal's career has been a remarkable one. When she was admitted to
the South Carolina Bar in 1968, fewer than one hundred women had been
admitted to practice in the state's long history. As one of the few women in
the bar she became both a leader and a model for other women aspiring to
legal careers. In 1975 she was elected to the state House of Representatives
and quickly became a leader. In 1988 she was sworn in as the first woman on
the Supreme Court of South Carolina. In 2000 she was elected chief justice,
becoming the first woman ever elected to the highest position in the state's
judiciary. So it is certainly appropriate to produce a biographical volume on
Jean Hoefer Toal to memorialize her remarkable life and career.

For the editors this was a task of honor and friendship. We have been
fortunate to have the full cooperation of the chief justice in compiling this
volume. Dr. Joan Assey has been a longtime friend and colleague. As director
of information technology for the South Carolina Judicial Department, Joan

has been instrumental in Chief Justice Toal's projects to modernize the courts of the state. Lewis Burke has also been a friend of Toal's for many years. He recently retired as director of clinics (a position that Bill Toal held when Lewis was in law school) and professor of law at the University of South Carolina School of Law. He coedited the other three books sponsored by the society.

Much of Chief Justice Toal's career is recorded in her legal, legislative, and judicial speeches and writings. However, to pay appropriate tribute to her contributions to the state of South Carolina, we needed scholarly contributions from a variety of sources. We have assembled a stellar group of authors. We cannot fully express our appreciation for all their excellent contributions to this effort. This book was the brainchild of U.S. district judge Joe Anderson. Joining Judge Anderson in birthing this book was Mitch Brown, president of the South Carolina Supreme Court Historical Society. Judge Anderson helped recruit Sandra Day O'Connor and Ruth Bader Ginsburg to write the foreword and the introduction. We are especially appreciative of Catherine Templeton and Vickie Eslinger for their assistance respectively with the foreword and the introduction. Templeton was one of two South Carolina national iCivics coordinators for Justice O'Connor, and Justice Ginsburg was an advocate for Eslinger.

Bakari T. Sellers is a former member of the South Carolina House of Representatives and a practicing attorney in Columbia. His essay is an introductory biography of Toal, which Sellers cowrote with his law professor Lewis Burke while he was a third-year law student. Jay Bender practiced law with Jean Toal in Columbia and is now a professor of law and journalism at the University of South Carolina. He writes about Toal's early legal career. M. Elizabeth Crum, a shareholder at the McNair Law Firm in Columbia, details Chief Justice Toal's legislative years. During that time she served as director of research and staff counsel for the House Judiciary Committee. Mitch Brown worked for Toal's law firm at the time of her election to the state Supreme Court. He was one of her first law clerks and describes her early judicial career. Brown is an accomplished appellate lawyer at Nelson Mullins, Riley, and Scarborough law firm in Columbia. Richard Mark Gergel is a United States District Court judge and was one of the founders of the South Carolina Supreme Court Historical Society. He has contributed essays to all three of the society's prior volumes. Again, Judge Gergel has written an essay for this volume. Emeritus Professor Robert L. Felix of the University of South Carolina School of Law examines the tort law decisions of Toal. Third-year law student Jessica Childers Harrington has written a piece with Lewis Burke on the Abbeville County School District case. Former law clerk Tina Cundari, now a lawyer with Sowell, Gray, Stepp, and Laffitte in Columbia, recounts the remarkable impact the chief justice has had on modernizing the South Carolina court system. Jean Toal Eisen and Lilla Toal Mandsager, the daughters of Jean and Bill Toal, eloquently relate their story of growing up in the household of a remarkable woman, their mother. Sue Erwin Harper, of Nelson, Mullins, Riley, and Scarborough law firm in Columbia, and Elizabeth Van Doren Gray, of Sowell, Gray, Stepp, and Laffitte, chronicle Jean Toal's mentoring of South Carolina women lawyers.

Amelia Waring Walker, current law clerk, coordinated the personal reflections from the following friends and associates. The Honorable Richard W. Riley, former U.S. secretary of education and governor of South Carolina reflects on his long association with Toal and her contributions to the state. Sitting South Carolina Supreme Court justices John W. Kittredge and Kaye G. Hearn write of their experience serving on the state's highest court with Toal. Retired state Supreme Court justice James E. Moore also reflects on his service with Toal. U.S. District Court judge Cameron McGowan Currie reflects on childhood experiences with Jean Toal. Former South Carolina Bar president I. S. Leevy Johnson was Jean Toal's classmate in law school and law partner of her husband, Bill. He describes the chief justice as a mother and wife. Other contributors include: former Speaker of the South Carolina House of Representatives Robert J. Sheheen; Mary Campbell McQueen, president of the National Center for State Courts; Bradish J. Waring of Nexsen Pruet in Charleston and a former president of the South Carolina Bar; and Blake Hewitt, a former law clerk, now a litigator and appellate advocate with Bluestein, Nichols, Thompson, and Delgado in Conway, South Carolina.

Walter B. Edgar is a retired professor from the University of South Carolina. His works on the history of the state, including his book *South Carolina: A History*, establish him as the preeminent South Carolina historian. Dr. Edgar and Judge Joseph Anderson have written the concluding essay of our volume.

On any such project there are numerous people and institutions that provided assistance in a myriad of ways. We need to thank them all. John Seibels Walker's portrait of the chief justice is the basis of the dust jacket that Lucas Brown of Kickstand Studios photographed for the cover.

The contributors for this volume have been a dream. They really have produced a marvelous group of essays.

Molly A. Hunter with Equal Justice in Washington, D.C., was helpful in our preparation of the essay on the Abbeville School District case. We are also greatly indebted to Kathy Ellis of the South Carolina Judicial Department and Lisa Davis of USC School of Law for their assistance with so many tasks. Dr. Michael Mounter of USC School of Law Library prepared the index. Michelle Pinckney, executive assistant to the chief justice, has been an invaluable help. Katherine Heminger, Ashley Robertson, and Amelia Waring Walker, current law clerks for the chief justice, provided extensive editorial help. Keith McGraw of USC provided wise counsel and assistance with photographs and illustrations. Many members of the bar have been supportive in numerous ways.

The University of South Carolina Press has been generous in its advice and assistance. Alex Moore, Linda Fogle, and Jonathan Haupt cannot be thanked enough.

RUTH BADER GINSBURG,

Associate Justice, Supreme Court of the United States

Introduction

IN THE 1960S DEEPLY embedded traditional attitudes toward women, strengthened by years of unchallenged discriminatory actions, permeated American culture. Women faced many inequalities in the workplace as well as in other aspects of their lives. As the decade progressed, American citizens began awakening to the legal, social, economic, and political disabilities imposed on women and to the possibilities of improvement. By 1971 women and men in larger numbers than ever before were turning to the nation's courts to challenge the traditional stereotypes, restrictions, "protective" legislation, and attitudes employed by the state, society, employers, and institutions that served as roadblocks to women attaining full citizenship stature.

During this period South Carolina and the majority of its citizens had a deeply ingrained conservative culture with well-defined, traditional expectations of women and their role in society. Conformity with these cultural expectations, as was true in other parts of the country, was often enforced by codification, regulation, and "custom and usage," as well as social pressure. There were few women in positions of political power, nontraditional employment, or the upper echelons of educational institutions. Every path to power was controlled exclusively by males. South Carolina politicians were slow to embrace the dramatic changes taking place in society resulting from the civil rights and nascent women's rights movements.

State senator Walter J. Bristow Jr., a forward-thinking future judge, was not so slow. On November 18, 1970, he recommended Victoria LaMonte Eslinger, a first-year law student, for appointment to the highly coveted part-time position of page for the South Carolina Senate during the 1971 session of the General Assembly. Pages were temporary employees, working only from January to June when the Senate was in session. The position was offered generally to college students as well as law students at the University of South Carolina School of Law, who found the positions attractive because the working hours were flexible, and offered them the opportunity to view the lawmaking process as well as to meet state officials. The Senate had a custom and tradition of employing only males as Senate pages. Upon receipt of her application, the clerk of the Senate told Eslinger that because she was a "girl," she could not be a page and stated that as long as he could prevent it, there would be no female page in the Senate. He further expressed his fear that if he appointed Eslinger as a page, senators would recommend women of "doubtful virtue" for appointment as Senate pages and offered the suggestion that she apply for the job of tour guide. Eslinger declined.

Instead Eslinger sought legal representation from the Southern Regional Office of the ACLU Foundation, an organization that was controversial in South Carolina, to challenge the Senate's exclusion of women as pages by way of a class action sex discrimination suit. The ACLU, with which I had consulted on several sex discrimination cases while working as a full-time professor at Rutgers University School of Law and subsequently Columbia Law School, had long advanced the cause of women's rights and in 1971 had identified women's rights as its top legal and legislative priority. In the spring of 1972, I was hired to found and direct the newly created ACLU Women's Rights Project through which we worked with ACLU affiliates in every state to seek redress for gender-based discrimination through the court system.

Laughlin McDonald, an attorney with the ACLU, filed the *Eslinger* suit on February 11, 1971, and shortly afterward sought out Jean Hoefer Toal, a bright and energetic young lawyer who had graduated near the top of her class some three years earlier, to ask if she would join the trial team. It was during this time, from 1971 through 1973, as the *Eslinger* suit proceeded through the federal courts, that I first consulted with Jean. A 1968 graduate of the University of South Carolina School of Law, Jean was one of South Carolina's approximately ten practicing women lawyers, and one of only three who tried cases. She had just returned to Columbia, the state capital, and was employed with a well-known medium-sized defense firm. Long interested in civil rights and holding the firm belief that justice and fairness should apply equally to all, Jean unhesitatingly agreed and expanded her practice into the area of civil rights. She did so without concern for the potential controversy that might arise as a result of her association with the ACLU, the undertaking of a case that challenged the traditional southern view of women's position in society, or the fact that the named defendants were the most politically powerful men in the state at the time. The original named defendants included the clerk of the Senate of South Carolina, the president ex-officio of the Senate, the president pro tempore of the Senate, and all other senators of the state of South Carolina, jointly and severally.

The case was originally captioned *Victoria LaMonte Eslinger, for herself and for all other women similarly situated, Plaintiffs v. Lovick Oliphant Thomas, Jr., as Clerk of the Senate of South Carolina, Earle Elias Morris, Jr., as President ex-officio of the Senate of South Carolina, and as a representative of the Senators of South Carolina, and Edgar Allan Brown, as President Pro Tempore of the Senate of South Carolina, and as Senator of Barnwell County, South Carolina; and all other Senators of the State of South Carolina, jointly and severally, who are similarly situated, and their successors in each office, Defendants.*

In their answer to the complaint, the defendants admitted they did not hire females for the position and alleged, among other things, "that the performance by females of the functions of those attendants known as Senate pages would be regarded by the public as improper and indecent, and, . . . the contempt and ridicule encouraged thereby would tend to reduce the dignity of the Senate and could cause the Senate, and the members thereof, to be subjected to unwarranted accusations of moral impropriety." The function and duties of the Senate pages to which the answer referred included their "dispatch to hotel and motel rooms of Senators in the city of Columbia both in the day time and night time as well as their dispatch to the automobiles of the various Senators" and "the occasional requirement that they remain in the State House in the company of the Senators during entire nights when the Senate is in session . . . all of which would be regarded as improper should these services be performed by female pages for male Senators."

In an effort to render the case moot, on June 2, 1971, the South Carolina Senate passed Senate Resolution No. S. 525, which enumerated the duties that were "not suitable . . . for young ladies" and which "may give rise to the appearance of impropriety" and allowed females to be employed as "clerical assistants" and "committee attendants." The legislation prohibited females from, among other things, doing such things as cashing personal checks for senators at local banks, running errands to personal automobiles, on occasion driving such automobiles, and obtaining food and refreshments for the senators, and employment was conditioned on their providing a statement from a woman's parent or guardian "assuming responsibility for her transportation, safety and supervision" to and from her home. Incredibly even for 1971, the defendants did not even try to claim that the purpose of the resolution was to protect the young women employees but instead posited a defense that reflected only the desire to protect the senators from nonexistent evils such as ridicule and the hypothetical and improbable injury to their dignity.

Although Title VII of the 1964 Civil Rights Act protected women in private employment in 1971, it specifically excluded from its aegis state employment. Thus the only way to challenge the South Carolina's sex discrimination in public employment was to base it on the language in the Fourteenth Amendment to the United States Constitution at a time when the applicability of the equal protection clause to women had rarely been litigated and most past precedent had held that the clause applied only to race. The *Eslinger* suit sought to obtain a ruling that state-sanctioned discrimination against women was unconstitutional under the Fourteenth Amendment, which provides in relevant part: "No state shall make or enforce any law which shall abridge the privileges or immunities of citizens of the United States; nor shall any State deprive any person of life, liberty, or property, without due process of law; nor deny to any person within its jurisdiction the equal protection of the laws."

The lawyers in the *Eslinger* case knew they faced a formidable challenge because the Supreme Court had never before applied the equal protection clause to sex discrimination but had, instead, issued numerous precedential opinions based on generalized and antiquated stereotypes of women. Beyond the hurdle of persuading the federal district court that the equal protection clause applied to sex discrimination when there was little positive precedent for that argument, they urged the court to apply a strict standard of scrutiny where the legislative classification was based on sex as it was in Senate Resolution S. 525.

In determining if discrimination were prohibited or permissible under the Fourteenth Amendment, courts in 1971 employed two different standards. Where a legislative classification of citizens was involved, the usual standard for determining its constitutionality was whether there was a reasonable and rational relationship between the classification and a legitimate state interest. However, when the classification was based on race or the denial of a fundamental right, the Supreme Court applied a stricter standard of scrutiny for determining whether there had been a denial of equal protection and imposed on the state the heavy burden of proving a compelling state interest.

I conferred with Jean on strategy and on several briefs that were submitted in connection with various hearings, as well as the appellate brief submitted to the Fourth Circuit Court of Appeals. The briefs addressed novel constitutional issues related to the analysis of sexually discriminatory classifications under the Constitution and were part of a nationwide push to achieve full equality for women under the law. *Eslinger v. Thomas* was tried in January 1972. The United States Supreme Court had decided *Reed v. Reed*, 404 U.S. 71, on November 22, 1971, and found for the first time that a state had violated equal protection in a sex discrimination case when it declared unconstitutional a discriminatory Idaho statute that gave mandatory preference to a male over a female for appointment as administrator of

an estate when both were equally qualified and within the same entitlement class. *Reed v. Reed* made it clear that the equal protection clause
applied to the *Eslinger* case, but the lawyers still had to convince the court
to elevate gender-based classifications to the level of a suspect category (the
same high standard of scrutiny applied to race discrimination cases) for
review purposes.

When the district court issued its opinion on March 28, 1972 (*Eslinger
v. Thomas,* 340 F. Supp. 886 [D.S.C. 1972]), it applied the equal protection
clause to women and held the defendants had no justifiable reason for
refusing to hire women prior to the adoption of S. 525. It then used the
most lenient review standard to rule against Eslinger, holding that the
restrictions in S. 525 had a rational basis and were not unreasonable, arbitrary, restrictive, or unconstitutional. It declined to apply the stricter constitutional standard applicable to classifications of individuals based on
race or when a fundamental right is involved as urged by Eslinger, and
which would have, by the district judge's own admission, held the Senate's
resolution and action unconstitutional.

On appeal to the United States Fourth Circuit Court of Appeals, the
lawyers continued to urge the adoption of the strict scrutiny standard and
asked the court to treat sex, like race, as a suspect classification. The
Fourth Circuit did not apply the stricter standard but applied the test set
out in *Reed* and reviewed Senate Resolution S. 525 to determine if there
was a fair and substantial relationship between the restrictions on females
and the purpose of the resolution (to protect the Senate's dignity and to
protect it from the appearance of impropriety and from ridicule). The
Fourth Circuit held that the Senate's actions were unconstitutional and
ruled in favor of Eslinger. The court found that the rationale for restricting
the females' duties was unconvincing and rested on the implied premise
that "the female is viewed either as a delicate and vulnerable creature who
must be protected or as a 'brazen temptress,' from whose seductive blan-
dishments the innocent male must be protected." Of the requirement that
female employees submit a parental statement, the court said, "Adult
females or nearly adult females are no longer chattels of their husbands or
parents . . . [and] unwelcome special protections, especially denial of
employment opportunity, foisted upon them is counter to modern law and
modern social thinking."

Jean has continued to bring modern law and modern social thinking to
the forefront of South Carolina as she has broken almost every barrier to
women's success. She has been a warrior in the fight to allow women equal
opportunity to aspire, achieve, participate in, and contribute to society
based on their individual talents and capabilities. Her courage, innovation,
and determination, which were evident so early in her career, have continued

to flourish as has her commitment to seeing that women have the opportunity to excel. I am pleased that I was able to collaborate with Jean at the
very beginning of her career and to watch with admiration as she has risen
to the pinnacle of South Carolina's judicial system. Jean is a shining example
of the heights to which women can rise when their individual strengths
and abilities are unhampered by discrimination or barriers based on artifi-
cial stereotypes of the "proper roles" of women.

W. LEWIS BURKE JR. AND BAKARI T. SELLERS

"It's a Girl"

ON JANUARY 28, 1988, an "IT'S A GIRL" sign appeared on one of the ornate granite columns of the Supreme Court building in Columbia, South Carolina. The pink-ribbon festooned banner announced the arrival of the first woman on the Supreme Court of South Carolina.[1] It was the election of Jean Hoefer Toal to the state's highest court that was being celebrated. On that same day, Carol Connor achieved another South Carolina first when she was elected the state's first female circuit judge. The newspapers were full of stories and photos of the triumphant Toal. One included a shot of Toal and Connor celebrating together in the balcony of the House of Representatives.[2]

The gestational period of this achievement for women lawyers in South Carolina was centuries long. The story of Jean Hoefer Toal's election to the Supreme Court and her later ascension as its first female chief justice includes many elements of the American saga. Her great-grandparents were part of the nineteenth-century European migration to America. The Civil War was the direct cause of one of her ancestors moving to the state, while also igniting change in all aspects of southern society. Her grandparents and parents were part of the growing middle class in the Deep South, and as businessmen they played a role in moving the South away from an agriculturally dominated economy. These factors and many others are critical components of her story. But the long history of the struggle for civil rights for women and African Americans in this country and the state of South Carolina provide the main historical narratives within which the arrival of this "girl" on the high court should be told.

Women's Rights and the Civil Rights Movement

Jean Toal's climb to the chief justice's chair is remarkable when one considers how restricted women's rights had been throughout much of the state's history. In the nineteenth century, women had limited property rights and essentially no "political" rights. The 1868 Constitution of South

Carolina extended the right to own property to married women for the first time, but when a delegate to the 1868 constitutional convention moved to grant women the right to vote, his motion was met with derision and defeat.[3] Not until 1895 did the state constitution even grant women the capacity to contract.[4] As the twentieth century began in South Carolina, women could not vote, serve on juries, or be lawyers. But the women's suffrage movement was on the rise across the country. As the same time, however, African Americans were experiencing a dramatic decline in their rights. The United States Constitution had granted the right to vote to African American men after the Civil War, but by 1900 that vote had been wrested away in the state by lying, cheating, stealing, and murder.[5]

Twenty years later women obtained the right to vote in South Carolina. It was in this process that both the parallels and the dissimilarities between the rights of women and African Americans became even more evident. Congress had proposed the Nineteenth Amendment on June 4, 1919, granting women the right to vote, but the South Carolina General Assembly refused to ratify it.[6] By August 26, 1920, two-thirds of states had ratified the Nineteenth Amendment without South Carolina's help. On March 7, 1921, nearly seven months after the amendment had been approved, the South Carolina legislature begrudgingly enacted a statute granting women the right to vote in the state.[7] While the right to vote theoretically applied to all women, the Nineteenth Amendment's promise proved just as false for black women in South Carolina as the Fifteenth Amendment had been for black men. When well-educated black women sought to register to vote in the state in 1920, they were prevented from doing so and often humiliated as well.[8]

The right to vote for white women was also not without limitations. In a paternalistic maneuver, the all-white, all-male legislature immediately exempted women from jury service.[9] When this exemption was challenged in court, the state Supreme Court drew an analogy between the constitutional rights of women and blacks. The court reasoned, "It has been repeatedly held by the Supreme Court of the United States that the 15th amendment does not confer upon colored men the right of suffrage; it only forbids discrimination."[10] Therefore, citing the U.S. Supreme Court's decision in *U.S. v. Reese*,[11] the Supreme Court of South Carolina held that the Nineteenth Amendment did not confer on women the right to serve on juries. Consequently an exemption became a prohibition. Women did not obtain the right to serve on juries until 1967 when the legislature ratified a voter approved constitutional amendment.[12] This was two years after passage of the 1965 Voting Rights Act by the United States Congress, the legislation that finally assured African Americans the franchise in the South.[13]

Such parallels between the treatment of women and African Americans by the white male–dominated society are numerous and almost too well-known to require much discussion. However, the differences are significant. White women enjoyed more privilege in South Carolina than did any blacks during most of the twentieth century. This state of affairs was reflected in the different treatments of women and black men in the legal profession. Certainly both groups saw progress over the course of the twentieth century. But as women were rising in the profession by 1920, the black bar was rapidly declining. In fact not a single black person was admitted to the state's bar in the 1930s. This decline was not reversed until the civil rights movement accelerated in the late 1940s, and the number of black lawyers in the state climbed into double digits by the end of that decade. Knowing the state's progress on race and sex gives a context to understand the rise of the first woman to the Supreme Court in South Carolina. The progress on both issues was no doubt related; however, they were certainly not intertwined and did not proceed in lockstep.

As the twentieth century began, one lone black man still sat in the South Carolina legislature,[14] whereas no woman had ever served there. Black lawyers were still active during the first decade of the new century; four of them even appeared before the United States Supreme Court trying to save their clients' lives.[15] In fact African American men had been admitted to the bar as early as 1868.[16] By contrast, however, women were not allowed to practice law in South Carolina until 1918. Before even the first woman was admitted to the state's bar, over one hundred African American men had been admitted.[17] A black woman did not overcome the double handicap until 1940.[18] The state had had a black Supreme Court justice nearly fifty years before Miss James Perry became the first woman admitted to the bar. Jonathan Jasper Wright became the first African American to serve on any state supreme court in the nation's history when he was elected by the General Assembly in 1870. Not only would Wright precede Toal on the court by 120 years, another African American male was elected to the court before she was.[19] Toal was a candidate in that contest in 1985 but chose to withdraw, allowing Ernest A. Finney to be elected without opposition and become the second African American to sit on the court.

Jean Hoefer Toal

Jean Hoefer was born on August 11, 1943, to Lilla Farrell and Herbert Wellington Hoefer. Her mother was from Atlanta, the daughter of James Edward Farrell, an Irishman who had moved from Boston in the 1920s to start a successful plumbing business. Herbert Hoefer was born in Columbia, South Carolina. His father, Fredrick, was the child of German immigrants. In fact Jean Toal's great-grandmother had been born on a ship in route to the United States from Germany. Her great-grandfather Hoefer had arrived in

Charleston and worked first as a cobbler before moving to Columbia. Her great-grandfather Frederick Schmidt had come to the country from Germany during the Civil War as a hired substitute for an Ohio man who did not want to be drafted. Eventually Schmidt moved to Columbia with the Union Army units that occupied the city after the Civil War. Establishing themselves very well in Columbia, these families became solid members of the middle class. Frederick Schmidt served on the city council in the late 1890s. Toal's grandfather Frederick Hoefer was the manager of a cotton seed oil company and also a member of the Columbia City Council.[20] Her father was a graduate of Clemson College with a degree in engineering who also obtained a master's degree from Cornell. Eventually he would own a sand quarry and continue in the family tradition of being a successful businessman. Her mother followed the traditional life of a southern woman as a stay-at-home wife and mother. Jean was the oldest of five Hoefer children. They lived in Heathwood, one of the city's more prestigious neighborhoods.[21] She attended and graduated from the neighborhood high school, Dreher, in 1961. The family attended St. Joseph's Catholic Church, where Jean sang in the choir. Among family and friends, Toal has always been known for her toughness. Her sister recalled in an interview in January 1988, "When it came time to choose sides for teams, the boys demanded that it would take two girls to equal a boy—except for Jean."[22] This ability to command respect intertwined with her family's values certainly played a role in producing a chief justice of South Carolina.

The Influence of the Civil Rights Movement

Born during the height of World War II and at the commencement of the modern civil rights movement, Jean Toal grew up in a world in transition. During the war the United States struggled with multiple identities. One identity was a united nation drawn together by idealism and patriotism to defeat the horrors of fascism. Another more shameful identity was the hypocrisy and racism of Jim Crow. The eyes of many were opened as African American soldiers were asked to spread "democracy" in Europe while facing oppression and degradation at home. Southern black soldiers saw racism in a new light. One of Jean Toal's heroes, Matthew J. Perry Jr., had a life-changing experience traveling on an army troop train when it stopped in Alabama. He related that he was hungry, but wasn't allowed in the terminal restaurant because of his race. "I and other blacks had to go to a window outside the kitchen. . . . This was nothing strange; I had done this before. *I am in uniform, I am in uniform.* I am a United States soldier. I could look through [the window] and here seated inside . . . [are] these Italian prisoners of war. And of course, the young waitresses were smiling and literally flirting. . . . You have no idea of the feeling of insult that I experienced."[23] Perry would return to South Carolina, attend law school, and become the leading civil rights lawyer in the state's history. Civilian groups also reacted to racism. The NAACP organized on a statewide basis and entitled one of its first campaigns "Double Victory—Democracy at Home and Abroad."[24] Before the end of the war, the civil rights organization had its first legal victory in the state when it won a teacher pay equalization case for black teachers.[25]

Women were also reacting to and adapting to the changing world. Many women assumed traditional male roles. Best known of these were the "Rosie the Riveter" jobs in the defense industries. The legal profession also saw changes. At least twenty women attended the University of South Carolina School of Law during the war, and sixteen ultimately became members of the state's bar. One female graduate of the law school has said that the enrollment of the women students kept the doors of the law school open during the war.[26] While these women lawyers did not become activists for women's rights, many were ahead of their times. Some combined careers and families. For example Doris Camille Hutson married and had three children. She also has had a very successful career on the Texas Court of Appeals.[27] Sarah Graydon McCrory married and raised five children and then practiced law for twenty years after her youngest child went to college.[28] Hazel Collings Poe combined family life while serving as a municipal judge for many years.[29] Louise Wideman and Sarah Leverette held various public service positions, including both being worker's compensation commissioners, but did not have families.[30]

Toal was too young to have been aware of the civil rights activities in the state during the war or the fact that women were attending law school in increased numbers. But these people and their actions had sown a fertile field in which a Jean Toal could and would grow. As she started school, she soon became aware of the degree to which civil rights lawyers were changing the South. While she was in elementary school, the United States Court of Appeals declared Columbia's segregated public bus system unconstitutional in *Flemming v. South Carolina Electric & Gas Company*.[31] Also, the case considered by many the most important civil rights case ever brought, *Brown v. Board of Education*, actually originated in South Carolina as *Briggs v. Elliott*.[32] As Toal gained an awareness of these cases, she was influenced by the fact that her family was more opened-minded than most southern white families.

This is best illustrated by her father's relationship with Matthew J. Perry. Despite the fact that Perry brought cases like *Flemming*, Herbert Hoefer hired the young black lawyer, and they developed a personal relationship.[33] Although Perry had a private law practice, his major legal endeavors were on behalf of the NAACP. This meant that he represented student protestors across the state. While Toal was a high school student, she became involved in a biracial student organization to oppose segregation. As a result she was a witness to a demonstration at the state capitol building that resulted in the arrests of two hundred students.[34] Shortly thereafter she attended the trial of those black students and observed Perry in action in the courtroom. Perry lost that day, but the case was won on appeal and became the landmark First Amendment case of *Edwards. v. South Carolina.*[35] Toal was impressed. Her memory of Perry in action in the *Edwards* trial was captured in a short essay she wrote about him. She described him as "an imposing figure—tall, slender, conservatively and impeccably dressed, with a deep, melodious voice. His command of the language was a thing of beauty. His command of the law was complete and powerful."[36] The title of her essay was "A Life Changed."

In 1961 Jean Hoefer entered Agnes Scott College in Atlanta and majored in philosophy. She was on the debate team, the judicial council, and the varsity field hockey team. She was also drawn to activities off campus. She had opportunities to see Martin Luther King Jr., and she spent her collegiate summers on voter registration drives in South Carolina, Georgia, and Mississippi.[37]

The call of the law and the challenge of racial injustice were major influences on her postcollege choices. She has noted, "My personal conviction, my membership in student organizations, and my first hand witnessing of the civil rights struggle in Columbia and Atlanta inspired me to become a civil rights activist."[38] After a family friend encouraged her to attend law school instead of graduate school, in 1965 she enrolled at the University of South Carolina School of Law.[39] In a class of over two hundred, she was one of only four women. The school had no women of color and only two black male students. Although she faced discouragement during her decision-making process from those who felt "the profession was not open to women," Jean Hoefer was not deterred.[40] Her good friend and classmate Robert Sheheen later stated, "Law school was a different world for her, the women stood out then because there so few of them. But . . . I knew she'd be a successful lawyer."[41]

Toal made many friends and allies in law school. Her most important friendship became much more. During her second year Jean Hoefer married her classmate William Thomas Toal. They became quite a team, she as managing editor of the law review and he as editor in chief. The couple also developed a close friendship with I. S. Leevy Johnson, the only black student in their class. Johnson credits the Toals with making law school more bearable and at times even enjoyable.[42] That friendship resulted later in a law partnership between Bill Toal and Johnson, the first law partnership between a black man and a white man in modern state history.

Law Practice

When Jean Toal graduated from law school in 1968, the nation and the world were in turmoil. The Vietnam War was at its height. The *Los Angeles Times* that summer reported that the war's death toll had reached 25,068.[43] Death seemed to dominate American life. The assassinations of the Reverend Martin Luther King Jr. and Senator Robert Kennedy had thrown a pall over the United States. Riots occurred all across the country, and even the Democratic National Convention was marred by street violence. And in 1968 the civil rights movement suffered deaths in South Carolina. The bloodshed came when three college students were killed and twenty-eight wounded by shots fired by state highway patrolmen on the campus of South Carolina State College. The shootings have ever since been known as the Orangeburg Massacre.

But Toal did not head off to be the civil rights lawyer. Instead, she took a job in a unique place for women in the state, with the firm of Haynsworth, Perry, Bryant, Marion, and Johnstone in Greenville, South Carolina. This was "the" Haynsworth firm. Judge Clement Haynsworth, later to be nominated for the U.S. Supreme Court, had been a member of the firm.[44] Jean's husband, Bill, was a law clerk to Judge Haynsworth. With sixteen lawyers, the Greenville firm was the largest in the state. One of its founding partners was Miss James Perry, the first woman lawyer in the state. In 1968, with so few women lawyers in the state, the firm was unique not only because of its distinguished history but also because it had a woman partner, Jean Galloway Bissell, who had been mentored by Miss Perry.[45] Naturally Bissell became Toal's mentor. Under Bissell's tutelage she performed many tasks: research and assistance in drafting documents for the first public stock offering for Daniel Construction Company, pension and profit sharing plans for J. P. Stevens, Alice Mills, Hollingsworth on Wheels, Daniel Construction Company, and many other corporations; trusts and wills for many individuals and foundations; corporation certifications; and defense work in products liability, workers' compensation, automobile liability, and medical malpractice cases.[46]

When she joined the Haynsworth firm, only forty women were licensed to practice law in the state, and only ten were in active practice. Since women were not allowed to serve on South Carolina juries, it is not surprising that only two women lawyers were trying jury cases. Toal recognized very quickly that she was a rare bird and that she could use this fact to her advantage.[47] She soon found her way to the courtroom. The 1957 Civil Rights Act gave women the right to sit on federal juries, but not until 1968 did South Carolina allow women on state court juries.[48] This historic milestone created a great opportunity for Toal. Not only did the male litigators want this rare female lawyer to impress their new "feminine juries," these same lawyers discerned they had the makings of a great litigator in their midst. Also "because so many men had job-related exemptions and women did not, many juries were female."[49] Toal could use her sex to an advantage.

Her time with the Haynsworth firm prepared Toal for the next phase of her career. Toal and her husband returned home to Columbia, where she joined the medium-sized Belser law firm in 1970 and Bill became a law professor. The Belser firm was known primarily for its defense work, but Toal had broader interests. Toal has said, "I expanded our base to include more plaintiffs' cases, administrative law cases, domestic litigation, and employment cases."[50] By January 1974 she was a partner at the firm. She described her law practice in an interview:

"I was privileged to appear on a frequent basis in all levels of trial and appellate courts in this state, including trials, or appeals before the Magistrates Court, County Court, Probate Court, Master-In-Equity, Circuit Court, Family Court, South Carolina Court of Appeals and South Carolina Supreme Court. . . . I also had considerable administrative law experience in litigation involving environmental matters, federal and state procurement, hospital certificates of need, employment matters and election matters."[51]

But Toal did much more. In response to the changing world, she took on more cutting-edge cases and tried to expand into some civil rights areas. One of the most important cases of Toal's early career was that of Victoria Eslinger, a law student who brought a sex discrimination case against the state Senate. Eslinger had been appointed by her state senator as a page, but the clerk of the Senate denied her the job because of her sex. Toal recognized that neither law school nor her corporate and defense firm law practice had fully prepared her to handle such a case, and so she called on the Center for Study of Women for the expertise she needed. The center, a joint venture of the law schools at Columbia and Rutgers, was headed by law professor Ruth Bader Ginsburg.[52] Naturally Ginsburg was enormously helpful.[53]

Senior United States District Court judge Robert W. Hemphill initially heard the case. The South Carolina Senate clerk took the position that the duties of pages might require them to come to the senator's hotel rooms on personal errands and that such visits would create an appearance of impropriety. Toal had obtained affidavits from male pages that trips to hotel rooms were only a small part of the job. When Toal tried to present her evidence and arguments on this point, the *Eslinger* case took a disturbing turn. Toal was interrupted by Judge Hemphill, who stated, "Maybe that's the opportunity your client seeks." The shocked Toal responded that she thought the remark was unfair to her client and moved on with her argument.[54] But the next day the local newspaper excoriated the judge. The headline read "Impropriety by Judge." Toal's law firm was upset with her, and some of the male lawyers protested that they had warned her not to take such a case. But soon she and all the other parties were summoned before Judge Hemphill, who issued a weak apology and recused himself from the case.[55] Despite the assignment of a new judge, Eslinger lost. On appeal, however, the Fourth Circuit Court of Appeals reversed the district court and established the right for women to serve as Senate pages.[56]

During this time, Toal had other public interest cases. She handled some criminal appeals such as *Downey v. Peyton*,[57] a death penalty case (*State v. Larry Portee*),[58] and a large personal injury case (*Owen Martin v. National Railroad Passenger Corporation 'AMTRAK'*).[59] She also represented the Catawba Indian Tribe in the third largest eastern Indian land claim in the country (*Catawba Indian Tribe v. South Carolina*).[60] These cases reflected Toal's commitment to progressive change through the law. However, *Eslinger v. Thomas*[61] was the highlight of her early legal career and demonstrated Toal's commitment to helping other women in the profession.

Politics and Community Life

When she returned to Columbia, Jean Toal was determined to live more than just the life of a lawyer. During the *Eslinger* case, she gave birth to her first child, a girl. A second daughter was born in 1980, and both children attended and graduated from Columbia's public schools. Toal also returned to her home church, St. Joseph's Catholic, where she served as a member of the parish council and as a lector.[62] She and her husband also chose to live downtown instead of in the white flight suburbs that had grown up around the capital city during the 1960s. They bought a home in the Shandon area, located near the University of South Carolina campus and just a few blocks from downtown. Jean Toal was one of the founders of the Shandon Neighborhood Council and served as the first chairperson from 1972 to 1974. During this same period, she attracted the attention of Governor John West, who appointed her to the newly formed Human Affairs Commission.

Soon political life beckoned. As Toal tested the waters of the political scene in 1974, the currents and crosscurrents of state, regional, and national politics were creating both opportunities and dangers. Richard Nixon had been elected and then reelected president in 1968 and 1972 using the so-called Southern Strategy.[63] South Carolina was represented in Washington by a Republican senator and a Republican congressman. In 1966 Carolyn Frederick had become the first Republican woman ever elected to the South Carolina legislature. In 1970 the first African Americans in the modern era were elected to the state House of Representatives.[64] However, in the Republican landslide of 1972, two of the new black representatives were defeated while three Republican women and one Democratic woman were elected to the House.[65] But significant change came in two years. The election of 1974 was dramatically altered by litigation brought by civil rights attorney Matthew Perry. In *Stevenson v. West*,[66] the Supreme Court of the United States reversed a lower court order and caused South Carolina to elect its legislature using single-member districts.

Aided by the nationwide bipartisan "Win with Women '74" campaign, sponsored by the National Women's Political Caucus, Toal made the decision to run for the state House of Representatives.[67] As a woman and a Democrat she would have both advantages and disadvantages. In the newly created House district, she would face a Republican male incumbent, Roger Kirk.[68] But the smaller, single-member districts did offer her an advantage. The district encompassed many downtown neighborhoods where she was already known because of her activities on behalf of the community. With this advantage and her tireless campaigning, she won in November. That fall three Republican women had been returned to the House, along with four Democratic women, including the first African American woman, Juanita Goggins.[69] Also elected was Toal's law school classmate and friend I. S. Leevy Johnson. In addition to Johnson, eleven other black men were elected to the legislature. The women's movement, the increasing power of black citizens, and single-member districts had combined to produce the most diverse legislature in the state's history.

In her first year, Toal was appointed as a member of the House Judiciary Committee. She was also the floor leader for the successful fight to pass the Home Rule Act, which gave counties more control over their budgets and other aspects of local government. The fight for this bill was difficult and complex. South Carolina had always been a legislatively controlled state. The new scheme reduced the power of the county senators and representatives who had previously made most local government decisions.[70]

Following the passage of the Nineteenth Amendment in 1919, the Equal Rights Amendment became the most significant women's rights issue of the twentieth century. The proposed Twenty-Seventh Amendment was approved by the U.S. Congress in 1972. Even before her election, Jean Toal had been an advocate for ratification of the Equal Rights Amendment (ERA) because it would make "women first class citizens."[71] Early in her first term in the legislature, debate on ratification was stifled and then cut off by the bill's opponents using the House rules. While thirty-three legislators were still away for lunch, opponents of the amendment quickly tabled approval of the ERA, which meant that it could not be considered again in that session. In response to the tactics, Toal calmly responded, "they played it very well. Some of our key people had not gotten back from lunch. We were simply caught short—which is perfectly legal."[72]

After reelection to the House in 1976, Toal was appointed to the Rules Committee. She introduced another ERA Resolution in 1977[73] and again in 1978 and 1982.[74] She debated with local opponents of the legislation as well as Phyllis Schlafly, one of the nation's leading anti-ERA figures.[75] However, after ten years women's efforts across the nation to obtain ratification of the ERA failed, and the period for approval expired. South Carolina was one of fifteen states that failed to ratify the amendment.[76] Toal later recounted, "regardless of passage of the ERA, the impact of its debate is evident in the increased opportunities available to women today."[77]

In 1983 Toal was the chief advocate and floor leader as Judy Bridges endeavored to become the first woman family court judge in South Carolina. After she succeeded, Bridges stated that "Jean Toal's energy was boundless, and her ability to persuade and cajole her male colleagues to vote for a woman (who at the time was pregnant) as a family Court Judge turned the tide." Bridges won by a single vote.[78]

Toal eventually chaired the House Judiciary Committee. She was the first women to head a standing committee in the General Assembly's history and was "generally regarded as an expert on constitutional law and state finances."[79] Dwight Drake, chief political aide to Governor Richard Riley, stated, "If you ask every member up there to list secretly the five leaders in the House, she'd be up there on everyone's list. She's one of the brightest people I've ever come across."[80] Toal's persona, intelligence, and success demanded respect from friends and foes alike. When asked about her style, Toal simply said, "I do my homework on the issues and I know each of the other 123 members of the House. I know their names. I've had conversation with them. That's how you get legislation passed."[81] Toal was often criticized for her brashness and her language.[82] However, her ability was never questioned. As one state House observer noted, "Even on one of her bad days, she's one of the best legislators here."[83] However, her work ethic and her manner would test Toal, the legislature, the press, and the public as they adjusted to a woman in power.

Associate Justice, South Carolina Supreme Court (1988–2000)

Toal's participation in national Democratic Party politics, particularly with the Carter presidential campaign in 1976, opened up the possibility of appointment to the federal bench.[84] To the surprise of many, however, Toal did not want to be a federal judge; instead she wanted to sit on the South Carolina Supreme Court.[85] Her journey to that court certainly required breaking the "glass ceiling" for women. Again Toal faced opportunities and pitfalls. Judicial offices are elected by the legislature in South Carolina. As a member of the legislature, she knew all the members. But the vast majority of these voters were men. The legislature had chosen only one female judge before—the family court judge Toal helped elect.

In 1984 Jean Toal began her first campaign for the Supreme Court. However, the time was not yet right for her. Toal was seeking to be the first female justice, but at the same time circuit court judge Ernest Finney was seeking to be the first African American justice since Reconstruction. Circuit judge A. Lee Chandler was also a candidate. The two nontraditional candidates were not successful, and Chandler won.[86] In 1985 Toal and Finney both tried again. With very strong support from the Legislative Black Caucus and other Democratic leadership, Finney emerged as the choice of the legislature. He was both senior in age and experience to Toal and had also been the first African American ever to serve as a circuit court judge in South Carolina. As House Agriculture chairman John Snow, a Democrat from Williamsburg stated, "I'd like to see a woman on the court and would like to see a black. My choice right now is Finney. My next choice would be Toal."[87]

On January 29, 1985, Toal withdrew her name for consideration, thus clearing the way for Finney. Upon her withdrawal Toal said, "Ernest and I represent the dreams and aspirations of many South Carolinians who have previously had only limited opportunities for public service in our state. These factors make it even more difficult for us to be pitted against each other."[88]

In late 1986 Toal again sought a seat on the court. Again she faced a sitting circuit court judge. Based on his connections and his experience, Judge Rodney Peeples appeared to be the front-runner. But for one of the first times in state history, a judicial election was being closely examined by the press and the public. Early in the process, the Judicial Screening Committee failed to recommend Peeples but unanimously found Toal qualified.[89] One newspaper even endorsed her because of her "squeaky clean" record.[90] Ultimately Peeples's ethical problems forced him to withdraw from the race.[91] In fact Peeples was publicly reprimanded for his ethical misconduct in 1988.[92] Toal's election was unusual for more reasons than her sex. She was the first justice elected to the court without judicial experience since Representative Lionel K. Legge in 1954, she was more than a decade younger than her fellow members of the bench, and she was Catholic.[93] She did have at least one thing in common with the rest of the court, as all the other justices had also been members of the South Carolina House of Representatives.

Jean Toal was sworn in on March 17, 1988. Her former client Columbia lawyer Victoria Eslinger noted how times had changed in the sixteen years since Toal represented the law student in her case against the state Senate. Eslinger recounted that she had recently been in a courtroom where the three lawyers, the law clerks, the clerk of court, the court reporter, and the judge were all women.[94] Eslinger concluded that "the face of the court system in South Carolina was changing."[95] In celebration Toal simply confided, "My prayer at Mass this morning was that I might ultimately prove worthy of this great trust and heavy responsibility."[96] Toal also announced that "I will also hope to be known as a strict constructionist of the constitution with a high regard for individual rights."[97]

Three decisions from early in her tenure as an associate justice demonstrated that Toal would be the type of justice she promised. In *South Carolina Department of Mental Health v. State*, Toal wrote for a unanimous court, "It is impermissible . . . to confine children in a mental institution just because an adequate detention facility is unavailable. . . . The practice of committing juveniles to DMH for safekeeping prior to adjudication has developed because of the lack of better alternatives. It is the responsibility of the Legislature to designate an appropriate place."[98] In *State v. De La Cruz*,[99] again writing for a unanimous court she found that the legislature had not violated the state's constitution's separation of powers doctrine by imposing a mandatory twenty-five-year drug sentence of which no part could be suspended by a judge. In another case she demonstrated her judicial sympathy for victims of crimes and found that the testimony of the lingering emotional pain suffered by a rape victim was appropriate evidence to present to a jury.[100] Toal was certainly willing to push the legislature on behalf of confined juveniles. The *De La Cruz* decision shows judicial deference to the legislature, but taken together the two later cases showed her conservative approach to getting tough on crime.

While Toal was certainly no liberal justice, she was an activist in other ways. As an associate justice, she was assigned many administrative projects by the chief justice. In 1989–90 Toal was chair and codrafter of the new South Carolina Appellate Court rules that were the first major revision in twenty years. She supervised the renovation of the Supreme Court building, which required her to make budgetary presentations to the legislature. Toal also was chair of two task forces. One was the Juvenile Justice Task Force created by Governor Carroll Campbell and U.S. district judge Joseph Anderson to study the Juvenile Justice Department. The other was the Task Force for Adoption of South Carolina Rules of Evidence patterned on the Federal Rules of Evidence. The Juvenile Task Force resulted in a report asking the General Assembly for $32 million as "an investment in the future." As a result of the evidence task force, in 1995 South Carolina became the thirty-sixth state to adopt a form of the Federal Rules of Evidence.

Reelection: The Double Standard

Over the last two decades of the twentieth century, the scrutiny of public figures has grown more intense. Justice Toal has not escaped such attention.

While she had benefited from the troubles of circuit judge Rodney Peeples in her successful run for the court in 1988, she faced a strong challenge to her reelection to the court in 1996, in the person of circuit court judge Tom Ervin of Anderson. Judge Ervin's candidacy was apparently encouraged by Republicans.[101] Newspapers and the Associated Press reported that "Republicans had started a quiet movement to oust Justice Toal."[102] Many conservatives, especially Republicans, had long considered Toal a "liberal."[103] It is true she had been a Democrat, but a doctrinaire liberal she was not. In 1987 when she was running against Peeples, one newspaper interviewed numerous legislators and bar officials about the judicial philosophy of the two candidates, and none seemed to think that Toal would impact the conservative philosophy of the court.[104] In fact one newspaper reported that Toal was a death penalty proponent like her opponent and more probusiness than her opponent in 1988.[105] Another newspaper stated that the liberal label was "diluted in more reasonable minds by her opposition to abortion, her supports of the death penalty, and her fight against pornography."[106] In 1996 the press reported that Toal responded to the "liberal" label by stressing her conservative credentials in her testimony before the legislative screening committee.[107]

But a Republican challenge was not surprising. In 1988, even after half of the members of the screening committee declared the circuit judge unfit, the Republican chairman of the Judiciary Committee continued to support Peeples.[108] Despite the issuance of the screening committee's report on the Peeples's ethical breach, one newspaper poll found that sixty-two Republican legislators were still favoring him.[109] Since the majority of the legislature in 1996 was Republican, the challenge to Toal was certainly threatening. But her record simply did not warrant a challenge based on her judicial philosophy. Were other motives behind the challenge?

The *Greenville News* quoted a local woman lawyer as saying that "female judges are sometimes held to a different standard than their male counterparts." One of the attacks on Toal was that she used coarse language. The lawyer asserted that "I have never heard of a male judge being criticized for that."[110] In 1988 one newspaper quoted an anonymous legislator who opposed Toal because "[p]ure and simple, Jean Toal is an abrasive woman. . . . She is very intelligent. . . . [S]he fights for what she wants and believes in, and generally she gets it." The newspaper then editorialized in response, "it's odd that such a characterization is held up as an indictment of Mrs. Toal; such characteristics, when applied to a male legislator, generally are held in high esteem."[111] When the Ervin challenge first arose, the *State,* the major newspaper in South Carolina, opined that his candidacy was simply an attempt by the Republicans to flex their muscle.[112] Certainly prior sitting Supreme Court justices had been controversial.[113] However, it had been over one hundred years since a sitting justice had been challenged for reelection.[114]

When the first hearings were held on the qualification of the two candidates, Toal drew praise from the press, but soon it was announced that a second set of hearings would be held on Toal's "temperament."[115] Then a taxpayer group attacked Toal for being "liberal and elitist." The chief complaint was that Toal had been in the three-person majority in a controversial case.[116] The case was a challenge to a state environmental statute that allegedly resulted in a taking of private property without just compensation. Thereafter it was rumored that the Republican governor was opposed to her reelection because the court had ruled against his family in a large business dispute.[117] On January 16, 1996, the *State* newspaper labeled the second inquiry into Toal's qualifications "a witch hunt."[118] On the next day, the governor's father accused Toal of having stolen or erased the tape recordings of arguments in his case before the court.[119] Toal's reelection was in doubt. But some rallied to her side. Later, to the surprise of many conservatives, a right-to-life group endorsed her.[120]

When the second round of hearings began, three former chief justices testified, as well as a number of employees or former employees of the court.[121] Five individuals, including the clerk of court and a former court administrator, were quite critical of her language and her "abusive conduct." On the next day of the hearings, after a dozen former and current employees of the court defended Toal, she dramatically apologized to anyone she had "hurt or embarrassed."[122] While some still questioned whether a male justice would have been subject to such scrutiny, others concluded the process had been fair and appropriate.[123] In the end Toal was found qualified by the screening committee and her opponent withdrew, assuring her reelection.[124]

In a postelection interview Toal was "philosophical about the process. . . . She says the challenge was as much about politics—Republicans trying to unseat a Democrat—as about salty language and a tough approach to work." But she admitted, "It taught me some good lessons. I learned to be not so hard-charging. I came out of a very tough trial lawyer climate, and I need to learn to soften my approach."[125] Throughout this battle Toal always looked ahead and invariably gave credit for her success to others. One news article said she credited her husband, Bill, for his support in getting through tough times. The reporter noted that "her voice softens as she speaks of him," and she said Bill "has a gentle nature and an easy going personality."[126] With her resilience and her support network, Toal survived the toughest battle of her career.

But had the challenge been due to her sex, her personal demeanor, her religion, her judicial philosophy, her political affiliation, or simply a desire for closer scrutiny? Probably all these factors played a part. As her defenders noted, most of Toal's "abrasive and aggressive" traits were considered normal if not positive attributes of a male politician. Probably the bigger issue was the partisan political divide. Toal correctly identified the battle as being about party politics. But one cannot easily separate sex from the equation. When she assumed the bench, she said she would be a strict constructionist in her judicial philosophy. A newspaper's examination of the decisions for which she was attacked revealed that she and the court had strictly interpreted acts of the South Carolina legislature.[127] She certainly was no activist judge making new law. The fact that she was a female Democrat played into the misunderstanding of her. This is best illustrated by the surprise of many conservative Republican legislators when Toal was endorsed by the right-to-life organization. They were confounded, and some even moved to reconsider their opposition.[128] Associate editor Brad Warthen of the *State,* writing about the endorsement, offered the view that the "liberal" and "conservative" labels were absurd in many instances and that Toal could not be branded as a "liberal."[129] The battle over her reelection settled much about Toal's relationship with the legislature, and without question her ability in the end prevailed.

Chief Justice, South Carolina Supreme Court (2000–2015)

In February 1999 Chief Justice Ernest Finney announced he would retire in a year. As news of Finney's decision spread, Toal's ambition to become his successor as chief justice also became public.[130] The press immediately began to ask how tough the road would be for her. However, Republican leaders in the House and Senate were quick to praise the court's only female justice. Senator Glenn McConnell, who had chaired the screening committee in 1996, applauded her and said that her standing with the legislature was much improved.[131] Hardly a week later, the *State* newspaper endorsed Toal for chief justice.[132] After that point Toal seemed to have no critics. She drew endorsement after endorsement and quickly cleared the screening process, with no one to oppose her.[133]

On June 2, 1999, the South Carolina state legislature made history on two fronts as it elected Jean Toal chief justice of the South Carolina Supreme Court and Judge Kaye Hearn chief judge of the South Carolina Court of Appeals.[134] After being sworn in as the state's thirty-first chief justice, Toal noted that she was "the first woman, the first Roman Catholic, the first Richland County lawyer since 1876."[135] James Moore's eye was caught by the editorial in his local newspaper that seemed to capture the meaning of the moment and faxed it to Toal, Finney, and Hearn. The Greenwood newspaper praised retiring Chief Justice Finney, chief justice elect Toal and chief judge elect Hearn.[136] The editorial noted that some people might claim that the three judges had gotten their positions because of their race or sex. The editor stated firmly, "That would be wrong. . . . Finney, Toal, and Hearn made their reputations on the bench through ability, hard work, and courage, not on race, gender, social standing, or anything but their administration of the law."[137]

On the eve of Toal's swearing in, newspaper reporter John Monk's column was headlined "Toal teaches lessons in endurance."[138] In the piece Monk revealed that his early stories on Judge Rodney Peeples's ethical problems were leaked to him by an intermediary for then chief justice Julius "Bubba" Ness. Ness had been Peeples's mentor but had turned on the circuit judge, accusing him of disloyalty. If Peeples had not had these charges leveled against him, it seems highly unlikely that Toal would have been elected to the court in 1988. But the story was leaked, and Toal was elected. She was reelected in 1996 and then elected chief justice without opposition. Monk concluded that while Toal had been lucky against Peeples, the reality was that "when her time came, she was ready."[139]

In 2001 she was charged with leaving the scene of a minor automobile accident.[140] Toal pled guilty and admitted having had a drink before the accident. Shortly thereafter a newspaper headlined the story "A dent or a scratch?"[141] Obviously the incident was nothing more than a scratch on her record. Toal was reelected to a full term as chief justice on June 9, 2004, again without opposition. Her term expired on July 31, 2014.[142]

Conclusion

Jean Toal's journey to the Supreme Court came during a time of substantial progress for women in public life. By 1992 South Carolina ranked thirty-sixth in the nation in the number of women in public office. However, ten years later in 2002, the state had the lowest number of women holding public office among the fifty states.[143] In 2000 there were fifteen women in the South Carolina House of Representatives and two females in the Senate.[144] In the 2007–8 legislative session, there was one female senator and thirteen representatives.[145] On June 26, 2008, the *State* newspaper reported that the state was still last in the nation in the number of women in office.[146] In 2015 there was some improvement as there was one woman senator and twenty-two female house members.[147]

While the numbers of women in public office in South Carolina has declined, the numbers for African Americans show some steady progress. In 2000 there were thirty-one black legislators, and in 2008 there were thirty-four.[148] African Americans held eight state judgeships in 2001, and there were fourteen in 2015.[149] Less than 6 percent of the South Carolina bar is African American, but two of thirteen appellate judges are black, and twelve out of ninety-two circuit and family court judges were black as of May of 2015.[150] So at 13 percent, the percentage of Africans Americans on the bench exceeds the black bar membership percentage.[151]

The number of women in judgeships has also increased in recent years. Five out of thirteen members of the two appellate courts are women.[152] Eight out of forty-six circuit court judges are women.[153] Twenty of the fifty-two family court judges are women.[154] Two women serve on the United States District Court in South Carolina, and one of the three federal bankruptcy judges in the state is a woman. There has been a net gain of nineteen women judges since 2001.[155]

In 2004 Toal was nominated and ultimately awarded the prestigious Margaret Brent Women Lawyers of Achievement Award by the American Bar Association Commission on Women in the Profession. Citing Toal as their role model, virtually all the women judges in South Carolina joined in a letter supporting her nomination. These South Carolina women included a U.S. Circuit Court judge, two U.S. District Court judges, two South Carolina Court of Appeals judges, three circuit court judges, and thirteen family court judges.[156]

On March 23, 2000, when Jean Hoefer Toal was sworn in as the chief justice of the Supreme Court of South Carolina, a color photograph was taken on the steps of the Supreme Court building where the handwritten "IT'S A GIRL" sign had been displayed in 1988. In the photograph Toal is surrounded by a crowd of smiling women dressed in an array of colors, and the chief justice is in her black robe clutching a bouquet of roses, with her right fist thrust into the air.[157] This image must certainly indicate how Toal would like the moment to be remembered. Her words to a reporter after the ceremony also expressed the solidarity with other women Toal felt on that day. As she said, "It is an achievement by a lot of women, not just Jean Toal."[158]

Fittingly, senior United States district judge Matthew J. Perry said this about Toal: "Her accomplishments provide proof that women are fully capable of achieving everything that anyone else can accomplish. Her life demonstrates that discrimination against women does a disservice not only to women, but to the rest of the world who are deprived of the benefits that can be bestowed by women who are allowed to serve at their full potential."[159] While Toal's judicial record is still in the making, her legacy for women and minorities in the law is one of which she and the state can already be proud.

NOTES

1. Jeff Amberg, "Marking History," Columbia Record, January 29, 1988.

2. "Double first for S.C. Courts," Times & Democrat (Orangeburg, S.C.), January 28, 1988.

3. South Carolina Constitutional Convention, 1868, Proceedings of the Constitutional Convention of South Carolina, vol. 2 (New York: Arno Press, 1968), 838.

4. Ian W. Freeman, Court Examines the Application of the Necessaries Doctrine and the Preconditions of a Person's Liability for the Debts of a Spouse, 48 S.C. L. Rev. 53, 55 (1996).

5. W. Lewis Burke, Killing, Cheating, Legislating and Lying: A History of Voting Rights in South Carolina since the Civil War, 57 S.C. L. Rev. 859 (2006).

6. Walter Edgar, *South Carolina: A History* (Columbia: University of South Carolina Press, 1998), 471.

7. An Act to Confer upon Women the Vote in All Elections, Act No. 183, *Acts of the General Assembly of the State of South Carolina* (1921): 268.

8. Burke, *Killing, Cheating, Legislating and Lying*, 881.

9. An Act . . . Relating to Persons Exempt from Serving as Jurors by Including Their Female Electors, Act No. 184, *Acts of the General Assembly of the State of South* (1921): 269.

10. *State v. Mittle*, 120 S.C. 526, 113 S.E. 335 (1922).

11. U.S. 214 (1875).

12. Ruth Williams Cupp, *Portia Steps Up to the Bar*, 138 (Raleigh, N.C.: Ivy House, 2003).

13. *S.C. Code of Laws Ann.* § 14-7-850 (Lexis 1967).

14. *Biographical Directory of the South Carolina House of Representatives*, ed. Walter B. Edgar (Columbia: University of South Carolina Press: 1992), 475–76. John William Bolts of Georgetown was reelected to the South Carolina House of Representatives in 1900 and served until 1902.

15. *Brownfield v. South Carolina*, 189 U.S. 426 (1903), and *Franklin v. South Carolina*, 218 U.S. 161 (1910).

16. An Act to Provide for Women to Practice Law within the State of South Carolina, Act No. 441, *Acts and Joint Resolutions of the General Assembly of the State of South Carolina* (1917): 779, and Supreme Court of South Carolina, 1868 *Roll of Attorneys*.

17. W. Lewis Burke and Belinda Gergel, eds., *Matthew J. Perry: The Man, His Times and His Legacy* (Columbia: University of South Carolina Press, 2004), appendix 40–43. Also see James Lowell Underwood and W. Lewis Burke, *At Freedom's Door: African American Founding Fathers and Lawyers in Reconstruction South Carolina* (Columbia: University of South Carolina Press, 2000), 127–29.

18. Burke and Gergel, eds. *Matthew J. Perry*, 42, table 2.

19. David F. Kern "Way Clear for Finney to Take Seat on State Supreme Court," *State* (Columbia, S.C.), January 30, 1985. In fact Toal was the last candidate to withdraw from that 1985 race against Ernest A. Finney Jr.

20. Thirteenth U.S. Census, Richland Co., S.C. (1910); Fourteenth U.S. Census, Richland Co., S.C. (1920) and Fifteenth U.S. Census, Richland Co., S.C. (1930).

21. Rick Brundrett, "Jean Toal Sworn In as Chief Justice," *State* (Columbia, S.C.), March 24, 2000.

22. Editorial, "Toal Should Now Have Clear Sailing to Court," *State* (Columbia, S.C.), January 22, 1988.

23. Robert J. Moore, "Matthew J. Perry's Preparation," in *Matthew J. Perry*, ed. W. Lewis Burke and Belinda Gergel, 61.

24. Peter Lau, *Democracy Rising* (Lexington: University of Kentucky Press, 2006), 128.

25. *Duvall v. School Board*, Civil No. 1082 (E.D.S.C. 1944). Also see *Thompson v. Gibbes*, 60 F. Supp. 872 (E.D.S.C. 1945).

26. Ruth Williams Cupp, *Portia Steps Up to the Bar* (Raleigh, N.C.: Ivy House, 2003), 67.

27. *Ibid.*, 89–90.

28. *Ibid.*, 81.

29. *Ibid.*, 82.

30. *Ibid.*, 79, 82, 84.

31. 224 F.2d 752 (4th Cir. 1955). Followed in *Gayle v. Browder*, 142 F. Supp. 707 aff'd 352 US 903(1956).

32. 347 U.S. 483 (1954). *Briggs v. Elliott,* 98 F. Supp. 529 (E.D.S.C. 1951).

33. Jean Hoefer Toal Papers, vol. 1, Perry letter, December 10, 2003. The Toal Papers are the personal property of Chief Justice Toal but were graciously loaned to the authors. They will be referred to as the JHT Papers hereinafter.

34. Jean Hoefer Toal, "A Life Changed," *Matthew J. Perry,* ed. Burke and Gergel, 152.

35. 372 U.S. 229.

36. Toal, *Matthew J. Perry,* 153.

37. JHT Papers, col. 1, p. 1, short biography in her nomination package.

38. *Ibid.*

39. JHT Papers, vol. 1, p. 5 of short biography.

40. *Ibid.*

41. Jan Collins Stucker, "The Lady Is a Lawmaker," *State Magazine,* March 13, 1983.

42. I. S. Leevy Johnson, phone conversation with the author, June 3, 2008.

43. "The Longest," *Time,* June 28, 1968.

44. *Martindale-Hubbell Law Directory,* vol. 2 (Summit, N.J.: Martindale-Hubbell, 1957), 4021, and Alfonso A. Narvaez, "Clement Haynsworth Dies at 77; Lost Struggle for High Court Seat," *New York Times,* November 23, 1989.

45. Portia, 128. Also see *The Lawyer's List,* 65th ed. (New York: Law List Publishing, 1968), 920.

46. JHT Papers, book 1, narrative, p. 5.

47. "Toal Enjoys Busy Pace of the Court," *Shandon Times,* July 21, 1989.

48. Charlan Nemeth, Jeffrey Endicott, and Joel Wachtler, "From the 50's to the 70's: Women in Jury Deliberations," *Sociometry,* vol. 39, no. 4 (1976): 293–304.

49. Cupp, 154.

50. *Ibid.*

51. JHT Papers, book 1, biographical sketch, p. 7.

52. Stephanie Harvin, "Making History," *Charleston Post & Courier,* February 27, 2000.

53. Brooke Mulenex interview of Chief Justice Jean Toal, April 9, 2008, 2–5, South Carolina Women's Rights Collection, South Carolina Political Collections, University of South Carolina Library.

54. "Page Aspirant Gets Apology," *State* (Columbia, S.C.), April 2, 1971.

55. Mulenex interview, 3.

56. JHT Papers, Book 1, Biographical sketch, p. 7.

57. *Downey v. Peyton,* 452 F.2d 236 (4th Cir. 1971).

58. Fifth Judicial Circuit, General Sessions, 1980 Judge William Howell, presiding.

59. U.S. District Court District of South Carolina, C.A. No. 3-86-539-16, Judge Matthew J. Perry, presiding.

60. 476 U.S. 498, 106 S. Ct. 2039, 90 L. Ed. 2d 490 (1986); 740 F. 2d 305 (4th Cir. 1984); 718 F.2d 1291 (4th Cir. 1983).

61. 324 F. Supp. 1329 (D.S.C. 1971), 470 F. Supp. 866 (D.S.C.1972) aff'd and rev'd, 476 F.2d 225 (1973).

62. "St. Joseph Parishioner Chosen as Assoc. Justice," *Catholic Banner,* February 4, 1988.

63. See Jack Bass and Walter DeVries, *Transformation of Southern Politics* (Athens: University of Georgia Press, 1995) for a discussion of both the Southern Strategy as well as the emergence of new Democrats.

64. See 52 S.C. Legislative Manual 97, 98, and 100 (1971). Toal's classmate from law school, I. S. Leevy Johnson, was one of the three.

65. 54 S.C. Legislative Manual 91, 103, 123 and 125 (1973).

66. 413 U.S. 902 (1973).

67. "Toal Joins Washington Meet," *State* (Columbia, S.C.), February 14, 1974.

68. *Ibid.*

69. 56 S.C. Legislative Manual 67, 77, 78, 100, 103, and 106 (1975).

70. Edgar, 551. Also see Mary Jane Benston, "Counties Voting Past Important in Home Rule Decisions—Toal," *State* (Columbia, S.C.), October 29, 1975.

71. "Women Hit, Back Rights Amendment," *State* (Columbia, S.C.), May 18, 1972.

72. "ERA Opponents Kill Measure in House Vote," *State* (Columbia, S.C.), March 27, 1975.

73. "Toal Introduces ERA Resolution," *State* (Columbia, S.C.), March 2, 1977.

74. "ERA Dies in the House," April 29, 1982. Also see "ERA Makes a Fresh Start on Road to Ratification," *State* (Columbia, S.C.), July 15, 1982. The U.S. Congress had initially placed a seven-year time limit for ratification but did extend it until 1982.

75. Betsy Annese, "Pro," *State* (Columbia, S.C.), February 3, 1978, and Mulenex interview with Toal.

76. JHT Papers, book 1, p. 11.

77. "ERA needed, Toal Tells Girl Staters," *State* (Columbia, S.C.), June 11, 1976.

78. JHT Papers. See Letter of Judge Diane Schafer Goodstein to ABA Commission on Women in the Profession (December 9, 2003).

79. Cupp, 154.

80. Jan Collins Stucker, "The Lady Is a Lawmaker," *State Magazine,* March 13, 1983, 6.

81. *Ibid.*

82. David F. Kern, "Toal Thinks New Rules Will Prod House," *State* (Columbia, S.C.), December 19, 1982.

83. Stucker, 6.

84. Cupp, 153.

85. *Ibid.*

86 66 S.C. Legislative Manual 238 (1985).

87. *State* (Columbia, S.C.), December 24, 1984.

88. David F. Kern, "Way Clear for Finney to Take Seat on State Supreme Court," *State* (Columbia, S.C.), January 30, 1985.

89. John Monk, "Judicial Panelists Divided," *Charlotte Observer,* December 23, 1987.

90. Editorial, "Rep. Toal Logical Choice for Justice," *Sun News* (Myrtle Beach, S.C.), January 3, 1987 ([sic]; the year was really 1988).

91. Cindi Ross, "Peeples Tried to Silence Opponents," *State* (Columbia, S.C.), January 30, 1988.

92. *In the Matter of Peeples,* 297 S.C. 36 (1988).

93. *Ibid.*

94. Peter O'Boyle III, "Toal Steps Forward Today to Set Landmark Precedent," *State* (Columbia, S.C.), March 17, 1988.

95. *Ibid.*

96. Dawn Hinshaw, "Toal Dons New Robe for New Role," *State* (Columbia, S.C.), March 18, 1988.

97. Larry Crib, "She Plans to Be More Than Just the First," *Living in South Carolina,* March 1988, 5.

98. 301 S.C. 75, 390 S.E.2d 185 (1990).

99. 302 S.C. 13, 393 S.E.2d 184 (1990).

100. State v. Alexander, 303 S.C. 377, 401 S.E.2d 146 (1991).

101. Associated Press, "Panel Researches Toal, Ervin Backgrounds, "*Charleston Post and Courier,* January 4, 1996. Democratic representative Tim Rogers asserted that Ervin had admitted such encouragement in a telephone conversation. Ervin admitted they had talked but denied there was any organized effort to by Republicans to defeat Toal.

102. Editorial, "A Judge's Dilemma," *Independent Mail* (Anderson, S.C.), September 13, 1995.

103. Maureen Shurr, "Jean Toal Elected to Court," *Columbia Record,* January 27, 1988.

104. Al Dozier, "Peeples, Toal Set Sights on Ness' High Court Seat," *Greenville News,* August 23, 1987.

105. John Monk, "High Court Candidates Both Driven," *Charlotte Observer,* December 6, 1987.

106. Editorial, "Toal Has the Makings of a Good Court Justice," *Greenville Piedmont,* January 28, 1988.

107. Cindi Ross Scoppe and Lisa Greene, "Toal Stresses Conservative Credentials," *State* (Columbia, S.C.), December 13, 1995.

108. John Monk, "Judicial Panelist Divided," *Charlotte Observer,* December 24, 1987.

109. John Monk, "Judge's Lead Erodes Sharply in Legislature," *Charlotte Observer,* January 10, 1988.

110. Andrea Weigl, "Women Take Charge of Top State Courts," *Greenville News,* February 26, 2000.

111. Editorial, "Toal Has the Makings of a Good Court Justice," *Greenville Piedmont,* January 28, 1988.

112. Editorial, "Let's Keep Politics Out of Judicial Re-election Bids," *State* (Columbia, S.C.), September 10, 1995.

113. Editorial, *Columbia Record,* December 22, 1987, criticizing of Chief Justice Julius "Bubba" Ness.

114. Robert Tanner, "Judge Describes Pressure to Stay Out of Bench Race," *Sun Times* (Myrtle Beach, S.C.), December 12, 1995. Citing when sitting Justice Samuel McGowan was defeated by Lieutenant Governor Eugene Gary in 1893.

115. Cindi Ross Scoppe and Lisa Greene, "Toal Stresses Conservative Credentials," *State* (Columbia, S.C.), December 13, 1995. Also see editorial, "Expanding Influence," *Greenville News,* January 6, 1996.

116. Mark Johnson, "Justice Toal's Opinions Reflect 'Liberal, Elitist Contempt,'" *State* (Columbia, S.C.), January 11, 1996.

117. Sid Gaulden, "Toal Challenge May Be Result of '94 Ruling," *Charleston Post & Courier,* January 12, 1996.

118. Editorial, "Will Jean Toal's Hearing Become a Witch Hunt?" *State* (Columbia, S.C.), January 16, 1996.

119. Sid Gaulden, "Blank Tape Is Blamed on Toal," *Charleston Post & Courier,* January 17, 1996.

120. Brad Warthen, "Toal Endorsement Exposes Silliness of Political Labels," *State* (Columbia, S.C.), February 7, 1996.

121. Lisa Greene and Cindi Ross Scoppe, "Workers Pour Out Their Tales of Toal," *State* (Columbia, S.C.), January 24, 1996.

122. William Fox, "Justice Toal Apologizes to Detractors," *Greenville News,* January 25, 1996.

123. Robert Tanner, "Toal Victim of Double Standard?," *Charleston Post & Courier,* January 28, 1996, and editorial, "Toal Hearings Are Fair, but System Needs Changes," *State* (Columbia, S.C.), January 28, 1996.

124. Cindi Ross Scoppe and Lisa Greene, "Screening Panel's Report Lifts Toal," *State* (Columbia, S.C.), February 3, 1996, and Sid Gaulden, "Toal Challenge," *Charleston Post and Courier,* February 7, 1996.

125. Stephanie Harvin, "Making History, Jean Toal Poised to Become Chief Justice," *Charleston Post & Courier,* February 27, 2000.

126. *Ibid.*

127. Lisa Greene, "Critics See Liberal Slant in Some Rulings by Toal," *State* (Columbia, S.C.), January 17, 1996.

128. Cindi Ross Scoppe, "Toal's Opponent Steps Up Attacks," *State* (Columbia, S.C.), February 2, 1996.

129. Lisa Greene and Cindi Ross Scoppe, "Toal's Foe Quits Race," *State* (Columbia, S.C.), February 7, 1996.

130. Rick Brundrett and John Allard, "Finney, S.C. Judicial 'Giant' Plans to Step Down in 2000," and "Toal's Goal: Becoming 1st Female Chief Justice," *State* (Columbia, S.C.), February 24, 1999.

131. Bill Swindell, "Finney Set to Retire Next Year," *Charleston Post and Courier,* February 24, 1999.

132. Editorial, "Jean Toal Will Make an Excellent Chief Justice," *State* (Columbia, S.C.), March 4, 1999.

133. Rick Brundrett, "Toal Nominated to Lead State Supreme Court," *State* (Columbia, S.C.), May 13, 1999; Associated Press, "Toal Moves Closer to Top Court Post," *Greenville News,* May 5, 1999; editorial, "The Bell Toals," *Sun News* (Myrtle Beach, S.C.), April 4, 1999.

134. Associated Press, "Madame Chief Justice," *Item* (Sumter, S.C.), June 3, 1999.

135. Rick Brundrett, "Jean Toal Sworn In as Chief Justice," *State* (Columbia, S.C.), March 24, 2000.

136. JHT Papers, book 3. Fax transmission from Justice Moore to Finney, Toal, and Hearn (June 4, 1999).

137. Editorial, "Top Courts Get Top Women with History-Making Votes," *Index Journal* (Greenwood, S.C.), June 3, 1999.

138. *State* (Columbia, S.C.), March 22, 2000.

139. *Ibid.*

140. "Chief Justice Charged with Leaving Scene of Accident," *State* (Columbia, S.C.), May 19, 2001.

141. Clif LeBlanc and Rick Brundrett, "Toal's Car Accident: A Dent or a Scratch?," *State* (Columbia, S.C.), May 27, 2001.

142. *S.C. Bar Lawyers Desk Book,* 2007–8 ed., 434.

143. "The Status of Women in the States," Institute for Women's Policy Research, http://www.iwpr.org/states2002/tables02.pdf (accessed June 6, 2008).

144. Aaron Sheinin, "Toal Says Women Leaders Need to Be Developed," *State* (Columbia, S.C.), December 10, 2000.

145. 88 S.C. Legislative Manual 44, 84–141 (2007).

146. Roddie Burris, "S.C. Runoff: Senate a Boys Club Again," *State* (Columbia, S.C.), June 28, 2008.

147. See S.C. Legislative Manual, www.scstate.gov (January 13, 2015).

148. See 81 S.C. Legislative Manual (2000), and 88 S.C. Legislative Manual (2007).

149. Compare S.C. *Bar Lawyers Desk Book,* 2014–15 ed., with 2000–2001 ed.

150. S.C. *Bar Lawyers Desk Book,* 2014–15 ed.

151. S.C. Bar Membership Data as of June 2, 2008. (Data supplied by the bar to the authors. Information in authors' files.) Only 8,078 out of 12,777 members report their race. Just 5 percent report their race as black.

152. S.C. *Bar Lawyers Desk Book,* 2014–15 ed., 561–67.

153. *Ibid.,* 571–78.

154. *Ibid.,* 553–78. One of the women is a Filipino-American (475).

155. Aïda Rogers, "The Lady Is a Judge," *Sandlapper,* Summer 2001, 12, which noted that there seventeen women judges in the state. S.C. *Bar Lawyers Desk Book,* 2001–2 ed., reveals that there were nineteen including the two federal judges in 2001.

156. JHT Papers, Goodstein letter. This letter was written to support Toal's nomination and ultimate award of the prestigious Margaret Brent Women Lawyers of Achievement Award by the American Bar Association Commission on Women in the Profession in 2004. This letter was signed by three federal judges, two court of appeals judges, three circuit court judges, and thirteen family court judges.

157. Rick Brundrett, "Jean Toal Sworn In as Chief Justice," *State* (Columbia, S.C.), March 24, 2000.

158. Mark Pratt, "Chief Justice Toal Sworn In," *Greenville News,* March 24, 2000.

159. JHT Papers, Letter from Matthew J. Perry on behalf of Justice Toal for the Margaret Brent Award.

Jean Margaret Hoefer's family, March 1954. *Clock-wise from the upper left:* Jean Margaret Hoefer, Lilla Farrell Hoefer (mother) holding Christina Lindner Hoefer (sister), Lilla Farrell Hoefer (sister), Herbert Wellington Hoefer Jr. (brother), Herbert Wellington Hoefer (father), and Ann McCallum Hoefer (sister). Courtesy of the Herbert W. Hoefer Family Trust.

First Communion of Jean Margaret Hoefer at St. Joseph's Catholic Church, May 1951. Courtesy of Hunter Clarkson.

Jean with her mother, Lilla Farrell Hoefer, ready to host a tea at their Adger Road home, winter 1961. Courtesy of the Herbert W. Hoefer Family Trust.

Wedding photograph of Jean Hoefer Toal and William Thomas Toal at St. Joseph's Catholic Church, August 24, 1967. Courtesy of Toal Studio.

Baby Jean with her parents, Jean and Bill, spring 1973. Courtesy of the *State* newspaper.

Billboard for the first House District 75 campaign, summer, 1974. Courtesy of Toal Studio.

Lilla and her mother planting
in their garden, spring 1987.
Courtesy of the *State* newspaper.

The Belser law firm, March 1988: *Back row*: Warren C. Powell Jr., D. Cravens
Ravenel, Duncan Clinch Heyward Belser Jr., Duncan Clinch Heyward Belser,
Jerry Jay Bender, James L. Bruner, Jackson L. Barwick Jr., Charles E. Baker; *front
row*: Betty J. Gambrell Cobb and Jean Hoefer Toal. Courtesy of the Herbert W.
Hoefer Family Trust.

Representative Jean H. Toal and Representative Moffatt Burriss, to her right, are being sworn in as part of the Richland County delegation by Lois Shealy, clerk of the House, December 1984. Courtesy of the *State* newspaper.

Presenting the House Rules debate as leader of the Freshman Caucus, January 1975. Courtesy of the *State* newspaper.

"Mr. Speaker": Representative Jean Toal requesting to be recognized, spring 1982. Courtesy of the *State* newspaper.

Shandon Neighborhood Council hearing attended by Representative Jean Toal and South Kilbourne community leader Frankie Funchess, February, 1976. Courtesy of the *State* newspaper.

Campaign rally and pie-throwing contest in Emily Douglas Park, June 1976. Jay Bender is poised with pie in hand that was received by Representative Toal. Courtesy of the *State* newspaper.

Representative Jean Toal working on a House floor debate with Representative I. S. Leevy Johnson, May 1980. Courtesy of the *State* newspaper.

Representative Toal busy drafting amendments on the House floor, May 1983. Courtesy of the *State* newspaper.

Baby Lilla at her mother's desk on the House floor, 1983. Courtesy of the *State* newspaper.

Girl Scout Cookie Sales Day at the State House: Representative Jean Toal, Elizabeth Assey, Governor Richard W. Riley, Molly Bryan, and Representative Toal's daughter Jean, April 1984. Courtesy of the Herbert W. Hoefer Family Trust.

Serving on the 1987 State General Appropriations Conference Committee. *Left to right*: Representative Herbert Kirsh, Representative Jean Toal, Representative Robert N. McLellan (chairman of the House Ways and Means Committee), Senator Rembert C. Dennis (chairman of the Senate Finance Committee), Senator James M. Waddell Jr., and Senator John C. "Jack" Lindsay. Courtesy of the Herbert W. Hoefer Family Trust.

House strategy session with Speaker of the House Robert J. Sheheen, January 1987. Courtesy of the *State* newspaper.

On election day as an associate justice of the South Carolina Supreme Court, January 28, 1988. *Back:* Warren Powell (law partner), Inez Tenenbaum, Christina Myers (sister), Anne Cushman, Herbert W. Hoefer (father), Jay Bender (law partner), Townsend Myers (nephew). *Front:* Jean Toal (daughter), Bill Toal (husband), Lilla Toal (daughter), and Joan Assey. Courtesy of the *State* newspaper.

Jeepers! It's a Girl. A 1988 editorial cartoon. By Robert Ariail, the *State* newspaper.

Toal Road. A 1988 editorial cartoon. By Robert Ariail, the *State* newspaper.

You've Come a Long Way . . . Madam Chief Justice. A 2000 editorial cartoon.
By Roger Harvell, *Greenville News.*

You Don't Start Out as Chief Justice

EVERYONE HAS TO START somewhere. Where you end up is just part of the story. The story of Jean Hoefer Toal as chief justice of the Supreme Court of South Carolina is shaped by many influences, but this essay deals with Toal's years in the practice of law when she had to deal with the black-robed ministers of justice as an advocate—not a peer. Football coaches are fond of telling their overmatched teams, "They put their pants on one leg at a time, just like us." When Toal started practicing law, however, women lawyers didn't wear pants to court, so another aphorism would be more appropriate for use here. In fact when women first starting appearing as trial lawyers, the judges, all men, expected women to wear skirts to court.

It is often said of sailors that "if you have never run aground, you haven't sailed very far." Similarly a lawyer who says she or he has never lost a case hasn't tried many. Observing Toal in her own black robe—confident, commanding, prepared—a lawyer new to the practice might wonder if this woman was ever anxious about a case or frustrated by a judge when she found herself on the losing side of a case. The answer is, of course, yes.

In 1966 the South Carolina General Assembly enacted the Uniform Commercial Code (UCC), Act No. 1065 of the 1966 Acts and Joint Resolutions, now Title 36 of the Code of Laws of South Carolina (1976), to join other states seeking uniformity in many facets of commercial transactions, such as sales and banking. The portion of the UCC dealing with sales, Article 2, had no similar statutory antecedent in South Carolina.[1] Law school graduates entering the practice shortly after adoption of the UCC were thought to be at an advantage as they had studied the changing law in school while practitioners and judges were learning it on the fly. In fact some judges never got the hang of it.

Not long after the adoption of the UCC, Toal tried a case involving the sale and purchase of mining equipment before venerable Richland County judge Legare Bates. During a trial lawyers provide to the judge statements of law—called charges—they want to be given as instructions to the jury after they have presented all the evidence. Toal presented proposed charges concerning the UCC to Bates, who, stretching out his words, dismissed Toal's charges with a disdainful tone: "Mrs. Toal, we're not going to charge the . . . Uniform . . . Commercial . . . Code . . . , we're going to charge common sense." Obviously in such a situation all the power resides in the trial judge, often leaving a lawyer feeling helpless and frustrated at the inability to get the judge to see something that seems clear. Toal voiced her frustrations sputtering in disbelief in the sanctity of her law firm, "Common sense, we're talking about a controlling statute that should have been charged."

To use a jock metaphor, you can't win 'em all.

Not long after Toal was admitted to the bar and began her association with Haynsworth, Perry, Bryant, Marion, and Johnstone in Greenville, a sheriff's deputy delivered a bench warrant commanding her presence in court before circuit judge Julius B. "Bubba" Ness of Bamberg, who was holding court in Greenville. Closing her office door, Toal tried to inventory the actions that would result in her being summoned to court during her brief time in practice. Worried, Toal steeled herself for a terrible fate and walked out of her office. There, to her surprise, were other members of the firm gathered around Francis Marion, who was loudly and profanely questioning why every lawyer in the firm had been served a bench warrant from Bubba.

Entering the courthouse the Haynsworth lawyers discovered that they were not alone. It appeared that every lawyer in Greenville had been served with a similar warrant.

Not long before being assigned to hear cases in Greenville, Ness had lost a bruising and protracted contest in the General Assembly for a seat on the Supreme Court. The seat had gone to Bruce Littlejohn of Spartanburg, who had enjoyed the support of most of the lawyers in the upper part of the state.

Ness, who never forgot a slight, excoriated the Greenville lawyers for their support of Littlejohn. Ness said that as long as he was hearing cases in Greenville, he would require every lawyer whose name was affiliated with a case to be in court each day until that case was reached. Ordinarily lawyers are called to court when their cases are ready for trial, but Ness exacted his revenge by commanding that the lawyers who had supported his opponent to sit in the courtroom while other cases were being tried.

Ness announced that he had five friends in Greenville to whom this rule would not apply, and then stated their names. To her surprise Toal heard from the bench, "Mrs. Jean Hoefer Toal." It seems that Ness had called on Toal's father in Columbia to help him round up votes among Richland legislators who "Pete" Hoefer knew. Apparently Hoefer made some calls and perhaps corralled a vote or two for Ness, and Ness's less than subtle reward was to excuse his daughter from his revenge plot.

Returning to the Haynsworth offices, Marion announced that pleadings in all the firm's cases pending in circuit court would be amended to add Mrs. Toal as cocounsel. Thus the Haynsworth lawyers were henceforth excused from their political punishment.

The Haynsworth firm was nearly unique in South Carolina when Toal was hired in 1968 as it already had one woman lawyer, Jean Galloway, who focused her practice on trusts and estates and corporate matters—an "office" practice. But the presence of that one intelligent and skilled woman who preceded Toal did not translate into total acceptance of women lawyers within the firm. About six months after Toal was admitted to practice, women became eligible to serve on state court juries. However, because all the reasons allowing a juror to be excused envisioned prospective jurors as men, many juries ended up with more women than men sitting.

Toal was assisting Haynsworth colleague John McKay with the defense of a company that had manufactured a platform rocking chair that collapsed when the plaintiff sat in it. McKay did not want Toal to sit at counsel table with him at the start of the trial because trying cases was work for a man. The presiding judge, James Spruill, however, asked McKay if Toal was cocounsel. When McKay answered that she was, Spruill ordered her to sit at the table. The jury was all female. McKay tried the case in its entirety while Toal sat at the table. During his closing argument McKay suggested that the chair had collapsed because the plaintiff, a woman, was overweight. According to Toal, McKay had not seemed to notice that several of the jurors were themselves "much larger than runway models."

The jurors took little time in returning a very large verdict for the plaintiff. The forewoman of the jury then passed a note to the judge that asked, "Why wasn't the little lady lawyer allowed to speak to us?" Back at the firm a senior partner called Toal to his office to announce, "You're going to be in litigation. We need someone to speak to those women." And Toal became one of a very small number of women trying cases in South Carolina courts.

My Mama Didn't Raise No Fool

Joseph P. Willson was a senior United States district judge from Pennsylvania who in 1983 had been assigned to preside over a suit brought by the Catawba Indian Tribe against the State of South Carolina and other defendants after every South Carolina federal judge recused himself or herself.

The claim by the Catawbas was rooted in treaties the tribe made with the king of England in 1760 and 1763, under which the tribe had surrendered its aboriginal territory along the banks of what are now known as the Catawba and Wateree Rivers in the Carolina colonies, in exchange for a reservation of 144,000 acres which the Crown agreed to protect from European incursion.

In 1840 the State of South Carolina attempted to remove the tribe to western North Carolina but in the process failed to seek approval from Congress as required by the Nonintercourse Act, 1 Stat. 137 (1790).[2] This act requires the approval of Congress before the ownership of Indian lands may be transferred; however, without the approval of Congress, the State of South Carolina gave title to the reservation land to white settlers. In 1842 the state—rather than fulfill its commitments in the 1840 "treaty"— purchased 630 acres in the original reservation for a new reservation for the tribe.[3]

In 1975 Toal had been recruited by Don B. Miller, an attorney with the Native American Rights Fund, to be lead South Carolina counsel in asserting the claim for return of the tribal land and money damages. Toal and Miller and others representing the tribe sought to negotiate a settlement with the state, but when that process reached an impasse, suit was filed in the United States District Court.

The state and other defendants asserted that a 1959 Act of Congress, 25 U.S.C. §§ 931-38, terminated the trust relationship between the tribe and the federal government, and that as a consequence, the state's ten-year statute of limitations barred the tribe's claim by allowing each person or entity occupying the tribal land for ten years after the 1959 legislation to claim ownership of the land by adverse possession.[4]

The setting for Willson's introduction to Toal was the gloomy, cavernous federal courtroom in Rock Hill, built in the monument style favored by Depression-era W.P.A. architects.

Willson, as were most federal judges in 1983, was white and male, but also from a different era (a polite way to say he was old)—when he heard the Catawba case. Willson had been Dwight Eisenhower's campaign manager for western Pennsylvania in the 1952 presidential campaign and, as a result of the victory, was Eisenhower's third judicial nominee in 1953. When Willson went on the bench in 1953, there probably were not many women trial lawyers in Pennsylvania. There were none in South Carolina. It is likely that Willson had never met a lawyer like Toal—male or female— until he came to South Carolina.

The federal legislation relied on by the defendants had been introduced by Congressman Robert Hemphill of Chester, who, following John Kennedy's election, had been appointed a district judge. The land in dispute encompasses what is now the city of Rock Hill—and was Hemphill's congressional district.

Willson started the hearing on defendants' motion for summary judgment by walking into the courtroom from Hemphill's chambers and announcing that Hemphill was out of town that day. Simultaneous to that statement, Toal and others in the courtroom saw Hemphill emerge from his chambers and walk past the courtroom on his way out of the building, hardly invisible in his trademark red fedora. Obviously Hemphill was not out of town, and he and Willson had been together prior to the commencement of the proceeding. Whether or not the two discussed the legislation, without a doubt every person in the courtroom would have been justified in so believing, as it was Hemphill who had introduced the legislation. The statute of limitations argument, if adopted by the court, would have been fatal to the tribe's claim. Toal and Miller argued that the 1959 legislation had not altered the federal trust relationship with the tribe, and this trust relationship would have prevented the application of the state statute of limitations to the claim. Toal also insisted that Miller include a backup argument in case the federal court did not buy their contention that federal Indian law trumped state property law. Her backup argument was that under South Carolina's unusual approach to adverse possession, the Catawbas still had a legitimate state property claim to thousands of parcels within the original reservation lands granted to the tribe by the king of England.

Willson's view of the Hemphill legislation was consistent with Republican Indian policy during the Eisenhower administration, when the federal government acted to "terminate" the historical trust relationship that existed between the federal government and Indian tribes. From the bench Willson made it clear that he did not care for Indians, Indian law, or lawyers for Indians. Toal's response to Willson's indignation: "My mama didn't raise no fool. I see this train is on the track." Toal was correct on both counts.

Unsurprisingly Willson dismissed the tribe's claim, setting in motion appeals that ultimately reached the United States Supreme Court. The Court of Appeals for the Fourth Circuit reversed Willson in an appeal argued by Toal and Miller, holding that the 1959 legislation did not ratify the 1840 state treaty and make the statute of limitations applicable to the tribe's claim.[5] The United States Supreme Court reversed the court of appeals, ruling that the 1959 legislation caused the state statute of limitations to be applicable to the tribe's claim, and remanded the case to the court of appeals for a determination of which defendants could raise the statute of limitations defense.

South Carolina has a distinctive rule with respect to the application of statutes of limitation to land title disputes. In South Carolina title to land can pass by a rule of law (known as adverse possession) if the person wrongly in possession of the lands of another remains in possession continuously for ten years without interruption in the possession of the disputed land.[6] If there is an interruption, however, the separate periods of possession cannot be "tacked," or joined, to provide the ten years of adverse possession necessary for the title to pass to the adverse possessor. Clearly

Toal's mama didn't raise no fool as Toal formulated the argument on remand that led the court of appeals to conclude that the tribe's claim remained valid with respect to thousands of occupiers of the tribal lands, and that these occupiers would be required to prove ten years of uninterrupted possession of the tribal land following the 1959 legislation. Had Toal's argument not been available, the claim would have ended. But because of Toal's use of this distinctive feature of South Carolina law, the claim survived and settlement legislation was enacted by Congress and the South Carolina General Assembly to restore the trust relationship between the Catawba and the federal government; to grant the tribe sovereignty over internal affairs; and to provide funds for educational and economic programs for tribal members.

Toal in Action

If Toal were in the movies, she would be tough and combative Jimmy Cagney. If she were a boxer, she would be one of those Irish welterweights who jab repeatedly with precision to set up the knock-out punch. If Toal were a baseball player (and she may have been in another life) she would be an undersized second baseman with great glove and steady bat. To see Toal in a black robe on a high bench in the Supreme Court sanctuary is to miss most of the show—Toal on her feet in front of a crowd or a jury is energetic, focused, and convincing.

When Toal first met Catawba tribal members in 1975, it was on a warm spring day in a decrepit former school building on the tribe's reservation south of Rock Hill. There were no chairs. Windows had been broken out and not replaced. The roof had leaked so long the floor beneath had rotted through. Tribal members were crowded into a central room. Chief Gilbert Blue was presiding. Blue and Miller laid out the tribe's executive committee's vision for the land claim: to restore the federal relationship, obtain tribal sovereignty, expand the reservation, and obtain resources to ensure tribal survival. Not all members present shared that vision. Some called loudly and forcefully for cash payments to individuals in place of the more abstract and visionary goals of the executive committee.

In this setting Toal was introduced as the prospective local lawyer. She didn't know these people. They didn't know her. She didn't know much Indian law at that point, but she did know South Carolina, and South Carolina politics.

Without stating her premise in the starkest terms available, Toal introduced the notion that no white South Carolina politicians would support payments to Indians for something that had been done in 1840. Toal also suggested that if the members were divided about the objectives of the land claim, that division would enable the state and federal governments to avoid any redress. Toal didn't fully unite the tribal members, but her performance led to a vote by the tribe to engage her as local counsel to work along with Miller and the other lawyers from the Native American Rights Fund. In 1975 it would have been a safe bet that Indians represented by a young woman lawyer had no chance of success against the state and the thousands of occupants of the tribal lands. That bet would have been lost.

Toal in front of a jury was a lesson in effective advocacy. Toal was a debater in high school and college, and one suspects that she went to law school for the chance to make closing arguments.

Many trial lawyers are orators. Toal is a weaver, taking every piece of evidence and winding it into a tapestry pointing the jury to a verdict for her client. The exhibits were the warp, and the testimony was the woof of the fabric of her argument, each element supporting the other and each pointing to a favorable decision.

A *Perry Mason* Moment

Perhaps no case better illustrates Toal's intense preparation and effective technique than the criminal trial of *United States v. Adams, et al.* The government was prosecuting workers at the post exchange Baskin-Robbins ice cream shop on Fort Jackson in Columbia for theft. Hidden cameras had been installed in the ceiling above the cash register. Hundreds of hours of film showed the cash drawer opening, hands reaching into the drawer, and the drawer closing. Because of the limited range of the camera lenses, the film never showed the fully opened register drawer or the person at the register. As a result the government sought to identify the actions of individual defendants by the color of their skin and the jewelry worn on their hands. In one sequence on film, Toal's client appeared to fold a bill and remove it from the drawer.

At trial the prosecution witness testified on direct examination that the film showed an act of theft. Warren C. Powell Jr., Toal's law partner and cocounsel, recalls that on cross-examination, as the film rolled through the opening and closing of the drawer, Toal yelled, "Stop!" to the film technician and asked that the technician replay the film for the jury. She pointed out that as the drawer was opening, a coin slot was empty; but as the drawer was closing, the slot was full of coins, and the defendant had paper in her hand. The government witness had mistaken the folding of the wrapper from the coins that had been placed in the register as the pocketing of cash from the register. Toal had seen something that no one else had seen: an empty coin slot as the register opened and a full slot as the drawer closed. Toal's client was found not guilty thanks to what Powell calls "a real *Perry Mason* moment."

I'm Going across the Street and Changing the Law

In 1974 the South Carolina General Assembly enacted a law to give citizens access to public meetings and public records, the Freedom of Information Act. One of the first suits brought under the law was brought by Toal on behalf of Richland County school teachers who objected to the Richland County School District 1 Board of Trustees' practice of meeting behind closed doors to adopt an annual budget. The teachers also sought access to reference material provided to board members during the week prior to each meeting.

The suit, brought in the name of Ellen Cooper, president of the Richland County Education Association, asserted that citizens—including school teachers—had a right under the law to be present when board members debated the budget, and to inspect the reference material the board members had before them at the meeting. The case was tried before Joseph R. Moss, the retired chief justice of the Supreme Court of South Carolina, who stayed active in the judicial system by presiding over trials.

As Dr. Walter Edgar has explained in his excellent and comprehensive work *South Carolina, a History*, the political culture of South Carolina from the colonial period forward has been characterized by top-down decision making by elites with the expectation that the decisions would be accepted by the populace.

Moss was a product of this culture, having served in the General Assembly prior to becoming first a trial judge then a Supreme Court justice. At the trial of the case, Moss discounted the thrust of the Freedom of Information Act by stating that he did not believe the General Assembly of South Carolina had intended for citizens to have an opportunity to observe the budget discussions of a school board or to have access to board materials in advance of a decision. It was good enough if the citizens learned of the budget once it had been adopted.

The appeal to the Supreme Court of South Carolina was heard by five old, white men who were products of the same political culture as Judge Moss, and the justices, too, could not believe that the General Assembly intended for citizens to observe the process or have access to materials before a decision was announced by those who had made it out of public view.

The school board was represented by Francis P. Mood, who argued at the Supreme Court that advance access to board materials and observation of the budgeting process would stifle the flexibility needed by board members to reach consensus. The court agreed.

According to Mood's recollections, as the lawyers were leaving the courtroom Toal said to him, "Damn you, Mood, you came up with the only argument that would sustain your position, and they bought it." Mood also recalls that, intending to inquire about the lawyers going to lunch together, he asked Toal, "What are you going to do?" Toal replied, "I'm going across the street [to the General Assembly] and changing the law."

As Toal's later legislative record reveals, she became a driving force in amending the law to give citizens greater access to public business. The law in its current form, provides as a starting point that where public money is involved, an entity supported in whole or in part by public funds, whether it is a governmental entity or a private not-for-profit corporation, must meet in public and—subject to exemptions that must be established by the entity—make its records available for public inspection and copying.[7]

A Lesson in Candor

The only lawyer in South Carolina who cannot appear before Toal in court, her husband, William T. Toal, recalls a time when he was a professor at the University of South Carolina School of Law. With his faculty colleague Roy Stuckey, Bill recruited Jean to argue a constitutional case before a three-judge panel comprising federal judges. One of the judges sitting on that court was Clement Haynsworth, a highly regarded South Carolinian who had been Richard Nixon's first nominee for the United States Supreme Court (and rejected by the Senate because of, in the view of many, Nixon's own attacks on the judiciary). A second member of the panel was retired United States Supreme Court justice Tom Clark, sitting as a special judge. Bill and Roy briefed Jean on the facts of the case and the applicable law on the drive to court. During arguments Haynsworth asked Jean if a certain case was controlling, for example, "Mrs. Toal, isn't this case controlled by *Smith v. Jones?*" Jean paused. Roy and Bill gulped. Jean replied, "Your honor, I'm afraid I'm not familiar with *Smith v. Jones.*" Haynsworth leaned to his law clerk, and looking toward Jean again said, "I'm sorry Mrs. Toal. I meant *Doe v. Doe.*" Of course Jean had an answer for *Doe v. Doe.* Herein lies a lesson in candor: If you don't know something, say so.

Toal and Toal for the Defense

In years gone by, before the public defender system was as highly developed as it is in Richland County as of this writing, lawyers in private practice were assigned to represent criminal defendants. The assignments were made in alphabetical order from the roster of attorneys in the Richland County Bar Association, which accounts for the assignment of Jean Hoefer Toal and William Thomas Toal to represent one Larry Portee. Portee was on trial for murder during the commission of an armed robbery. The prosecution sought the death penalty, as Mr. Portee was accused of stabbing a motel desk clerk with the clerk's own knife during the attempted robbery. The fact that the clerk had been stabbed more than twenty-five times made a self-defense argument difficult.

The case was not going well, and it appeared that a conviction was inevitable. But, in law as in life, luck arrives. It seems that a brother of the defendant was attracted to a woman on the jury. So attracted, it seems, that the brother followed the juror home from court one day. The attraction was not reciprocal, and the juror reported the incident to the trial judge. As a mistrial was about to be declared, the prosecution offered, and the defendant—at the urging of Toal and Toal—accepted a manslaughter plea.

A Young Lady in the Senate

Victoria Eslinger was a student at the University of South Carolina School of Law when she applied for appointment as a page in the South Carolina Senate for the 1971 legislative session. Eslinger's application was endorsed by Richland County senator Walter J. Bristow Jr., but when Eslinger approached the clerk of the Senate, Lovick Thomas, about the appointment, he told her that she was not eligible for the position because she was female. Eslinger says that because she was a law student, she felt compelled to tell Thomas that she did not think that was right. Eslinger recalls that Thomas, who was at least a foot taller than Eslinger, leaned over, patted her on the head and said, "So, sue me."

Accepting the invitation, Eslinger filed suit in the United States District Court, where she was represented by Toal and others. Eslinger remembers she was happy to have a woman trial lawyer representing her. The case was initially assigned to Judge Robert Hemphill. More than thirty years after the suit was filed, Eslinger recalls that it was against "all the giants in South Carolina—the lieutenant governor, the president pro tempore of the Senate, the Chairman of the Judiciary Committee and the Chairman of the Finance Committee." Eslinger adds, "I don't know what they thought about this at the Belser firm (where Toal was an associate), but it took courage for Jean to have her name on that suit."

In their answer the defendants asserted that having women serve as pages would harm the reputation of the members of the Senate. Specifically the defendants averred that the public would infer immoral conduct on the part of the senators because the young women would be asked to run personal errands, including going to a member's hotel room or driving the member's car. At one argument on a motion by defendants, counsel for defendants asserted that having women pages would create the impression that the young women were available to senators for immoral conduct. When Toal tried to respond, Hemphill said something to the effect of, "Mrs. Toal, perhaps that is the opportunity your client seeks."

Eslinger recalls that Toal remained calm and replied, "Your honor, that is unfair to my client." Soon thereafter Columbia's morning newspaper, the *State*, published an editorial headlined, "Unbecoming to the Bench," in which it praised Hemphill for his forthrightness and his "candid asides and editorial comments from the bench" but said he had gone too far with his comments about an opportunity sought by Eslinger. While the editorial characterized the case as "relatively trivial" and brought by "over-zealous lawyers," it did end by saying: "This remark went beyond the bounds of propriety; it was improper, indiscreet, and insulting. The woman deserves a public apology."[8]

Toal, Eslinger, and the reporter—a woman—who had covered the hearing and reported Hemphill's remarks in the *State* received a summons by way of bench warrants, delivered by a United States marshal, commanding their immediate appearance before Hemphill. With all assembled Hemphill took the bench, claimed his remarks had been misheard or misconstrued, said that if he had offended anyone he regretted it, and announced that he was recusing himself from the case. Toal recalls Hemphill's robe flapping in his wake as he quickly exited the courtroom. Hemphill was replaced by Judge Robert Chapman.

Ultimately the Court of Appeals for the Fourth Circuit ruled that Eslinger had been the victim of illegal discrimination by the South Carolina Senate.

Eslinger (who received her law degree and who became an outstanding trial lawyer herself) credits Toal with being "a fabulous role model." She notes with admiration that Toal "never cowed nor kowtowed" to Hemphill.

Administrative Law Is Constitutional Law

Toal started her practice in Greenville, while her husband was law clerk for United States circuit judge Clement Haynsworth of Greenville. The Haynsworth firm then, as it is now, was one of the larger firms in the state and highly regarded, with a client roster including Daniel Construction Company, J. P. Stevens, Alice Mills, Hollingsworth on Wheels, real estate firms, and insurance companies. There Toal worked on a wide range of matters, including the initial public offering of stock in Daniel Construction Company, corporate tax matters, will contests in probate court, and, as previously discussed, becoming a trial lawyer "who could talk to those women" on juries.

Toal credits her short time in Greenville as invaluable in terms of the experience she gained and the people she met. Toal recounts that when the General Assembly threatened to eviscerate funding for the court system during her tenure as chief justice she was able to call on the business and industry leaders she had met during her Haynsworth days to rally business support for court funding. Because she was married to a clerk for a federal circuit court judge, Toal notes that she, along with the clerks, was added to the roster of lawyers eligible for assignment to represent indigent parties before the Fourth Circuit Court of Appeals. That appointment, Toal says, provided her an early opportunity to argue cases before the court of appeals—an opportunity she otherwise would not have had.

In 1970 Toal returned to Columbia and became an associate in the firm of Belser, Belser, and Baker. The late David Means, a longtime professor of property law at the University of South Carolina School of Law (and considered by many to be the oracle on South Carolina property law), described the Belser firm as one that got the hard cases—the easy ones going elsewhere.

Means also said of Charles Baker (the Baker in the firm name) that "he and Harry Lightsey were the two smartest students I ever had." Good company. Lightsey followed a successful law practice with a deanship of the University of South Carolina School of Law and the presidency of the College of Charleston.

At the firm, Baker and Heyward Belser mentored Toal in the law. Belser, who had served in the House of Representatives and had been chairman of the Judiciary Committee, also mentored Toal in politics and the operation of the General Assembly.

As Toal developed her practice, she moved away from insurance defense cases, which were a mainstay of the firm's practice, into administrative law, employment law, and criminal defense at the trial and appellate level. Toal also became involved in civil rights litigation beyond the *Eslinger* case discussed previously.

The practice area that sets Toal apart from other lawyers who had become judges before her was her focus on the administrative law practice. Two factors, in addition to her legal ability, account for this distinction. First, most judges elected by the General Assembly prior to Toal had come from smaller, plaintiff-oriented practices, and second, administrative law as an area of practice became more focused in the 1970s with the adoption of the state Administrative Procedures Act.[9]

One intense administrative law case involved competing applications by for-profit hospitals Humana and HCA for a Certificate of Need (CON) to construct a new hospital in Columbia. Toal represented Humana, and Francis Mood represented HCA. Aside from the competition between the two applicants, the major obstacle to obtaining the CON was an apparent bias by the South Carolina Department of Health and Environmental Control (DHEC) in favor of not-for-profit hospitals. The CON process was adopted by the General Assembly for the stated purpose of preventing "unnecessary duplication of facilities."

DHEC took the position that any for-profit hospital would result in an unnecessary duplication of facilities. DHEC denied the applications of both Humana and HCA, but a DHEC hearing officer, Ellison Smith IV, ruled that the denial was arbitrary and capricious because there was no established institutional standard by which "unnecessary duplication" could be determined by DHEC.

DHEC appealed to the court of common pleas, where former senator, then circuit judge Walter Bristow Jr. ruled in favor of Humana and HCA on constitutional grounds. Mood, whose career included service as interim dean of the University of South Carolina School of Law and interim president of the Citadel, said of the case, "I had as much fun lawyering that case as any I had in all my years of practice, having the chance to discuss and argue what the constitutional guarantee of due process of law meant in the context of agency action." He added, "Jean is one of my favorite people in the world."

Before Bristow's ruling could be reviewed by an appellate court, both Humana and HCA withdrew their applications.

An Unusual Path to the Supreme Court

It is distinction enough that Toal was the first woman named to the Supreme Court of South Carolina, but another distinction informed her work on the court perhaps more than her gender. Toal joined the Supreme Court without first having served as a trial judge, thereby making her practice experience more contemporary to her appointment and her judgments less influenced by "that's the way the courts have always done it."

Prior to Toal's election to the Supreme Court in 1988, the justices in recent times had been elevated to the court from the circuit court. These judges had practiced law during a time when pretrial discovery was less involved and regulated than in the years Toal was in practice before joining the bench, and their exposure to complex litigation came as a judge rather than a lawyer. Toal, on the other hand, had practiced such discovery-intensive law in medical malpractice cases and in a protracted personal injury case, where she represented a Marine veteran injured in an Amtrak derailment. This experience became relevant and valuable when Toal guided revisions to the rules of practice for lawyers in South Carolina courts. Further, because disputes over discovery—where litigants are required to disclose their evidence to the opponents—often become acrimonious, Toal's exposure to these disputes shaped her call for civility among lawyers.

Outsider on the Inside

Toal is Catholic in a state that, until recent Hispanic migration, had a population that was less than 5 percent Catholic. Toal, a white woman, participated in civil rights activities as a college student and was appointed to the South Carolina Human Affairs Commission by Governor John West in a state where race is an issue in almost all aspects of society. Toal was a philosophy major at a women's college, Agnes Scott, rather than a business or political science major at the Citadel, University of South Carolina, or Clemson like many male lawyers at the time. Toal was one of only four women in her law school class. Toal's husband practices in one of the first racially integrated law firms in the state, Johnson, Toal, and Battiste. Toal's parents belonged to a country club. She did not. Toal has smoked cigars in public on occasion and can swear on an equal footing with her brother Herb, who was a sailor. Toal smoked unfiltered Lucky Strike cigarettes long after most smokers had switched to filtered brands. These are not establishment credentials.

At the Haynsworth firm, Toal's nickname was "Coach" because the lawyers there did not know any other women who knew as much about sports as Toal. At baseball games Toal keeps a scorebook, noting not only the hits, the errors, and the runs, but tracking each ball and strike for each batter. Similar attention to detail shows up in her courtroom during oral argument when she might ask a lawyer, "Counsel, doesn't the material on page 47 of the record conflict with your argument now?" Toal was a friend and fan of legendary University of South Carolina basketball coach Frank McGuire and today mentors members of the USC women's basketball team—a coach on life matters. In earlier days Toal was an enthusiastic and dogged tennis player—often playing mixed doubles with other members of the legislature. Toal was never the most athletic or gifted player on the court, but she couldn't be outworked or out thought, just as in her law practice. As a result Toal was a success on the tennis court and in the law courts.

Toal has sharp elbows, high expectations, and a willingness to express displeasure with those who do not measure up to her standards. That Toal ended up as the chief justice on a Supreme Court that battled for years to be independent of legislative domination is a testament to her ability. That Toal is criticized for being an insider is a testament to impaired observation. That Toal is criticized for her actions or her decisions is fair game. Lawyers get to cuss judges for their decisions, and judges get to cuss their critics and then get on with business. As a lawyer, win, lose or draw, Toal did not hold grudges and was always able to get on with the business of the next case.

NOTES

1. South Carolina reporter's comments to §10.2-101, now §36-2-101.
2. See 25 U.S.C. §177 ("No purchase, grant, lease, or other conveyance of lands, or of any title or claim thereto, from any Indian nation or tribe of Indians, shall be of any validity in law or equity, unless the same be made by treaty or convention entered into pursuant to the Constitution.").
3. *South Carolina v. Catawba Indian Tribe*, 476 U.S. 498, 501 (1986).
4. S.C. Code Ann. §15-3-340 (1976).

5. *Catawba Indian Tribe of S.C. v. State of South Carolina,* 740 F.2d 305 (4th Cir. 1984).

6. For title to pass by adverse possession pursuant to S.C. Code Ann. §15-3-340, the adverse possession must have been continued by the same person for ten years, and the possession of one cannot be united or tacked to that of those under whom he claims. *Garrett v. Weinberg,* 48 S.C. 28, 26 S.E. 3 (1896).

7. S.C. Code Ann. §§30-4-10, *et seq.* (1976).

8. *State* (Columbia, S.C.), March 27, 1971, p. 12-A.

9. S.C. Code Ann. §§1-23-310 *et seq.*

M. ELIZABETH CRUM

Into the Twentieth Century
as a Lawyer Legislator

IN NOVEMBER 1974 Jean Hoefer Toal was elected as the first person to serve as a member from House District 75, the newly created single-member district, thus launching her legislative career. Prior to Toal's election, Matthew J. Perry Jr. brought a federal law suit titled *Stevenson v. West*, seeking an order requiring the South Carolina House of Representatives to implement the one-man, one-vote principle enunciated by the United States Supreme Court in *Reynolds v. Sims*.[1] Ultimately the Supreme Court ordered the House to reapportion itself into single-member districts.[2] This change from countywide election to single-member districts helped make the House a more diverse body, upset the status quo, and ultimately derailed the "good ole boy" system that had ruled the House for most of the twentieth century.

Toal took her seat the second Tuesday in January 1975. The freshman class had fifty-two new members. Toal organized[3] and was elected as chair of the first Freshman Caucus—the first woman to be elected chair of an incoming House class in South Carolina's history. From day one, Toal was neither stingy nor shy about sharing her views and knowledge of the law with her fellow House members, answering their questions even if they were on opposite sides of an issue. Speaker Rex Carter (D-Greenville)[4] promptly appointed her to the Judiciary Committee, a plum committee assignment for any House member, much less a freshman and a woman.

While serving in the House, Toal had many other firsts—she was the first female to serve on an annual appropriation (budget) conference committee,[5] the first woman to serve on the House Rules Committee (and its first female chair), and the first female Acting Speaker of the House. When Toal was elected as the chair of the Rules Committee, she became the first woman to serve in a House leadership role in the more than three-hundred-year history of the South Carolina House of Representatives.

Toal's election to the House coincided with multiple sweeping amendments to the South Carolina Constitution of 1895. In 1966 the General Assembly had established the Constitutional Revision Committee to propose amendments to the state constitution on an article-by-article basis. In 1969 the West Committee, as the Constitutional Revision Committee was known, issued its final report, recommending sweeping amendments to a number of articles in the state constitution.[6] In succeeding years the General Assembly adopted the amendments to the various articles and placed the proposed amendments on the general election ballots. In 1970 the voters approved Article I, Declaration of Rights; Article II, Right of Suffrage; Article IX, Corporations; Article XII, Functions of Government; and Article XV, Impeachment. The General Assembly ratified each of these amendments the following year. In 1972 the voters approved Article IV, the Executive Department; Article V, the Judicial Department; Article VI, Officers; Article VIII, Local Government; Article VIII-A, Alcoholic Liquor and Beverages; and Article XI, Public Education. The General Assembly likewise ratified each of these amendments the following year. In 1976 the voters approved Article X, Finance, Taxation, and Bonded Debt. The General Assembly ratified this amendment in 1977.

Toal took her seat in the House at the time the General Assembly was faced with drafting and enacting the implementing legislation for the sweeping amendments made to the state constitution. In helping to fashion various pieces of the implementing legislation, Toal undoubtedly changed South Carolina for the better through her intellect, work ethic, and dedication to improving the state. In her almost fourteen years of legislative service, she floor-led many pieces of complex legislation involving constitutional law, utilities regulation, criminal law, local government and judicial system restructuring, budgetary matters, banking and finance legislation, corporate law, tort claims, workers' compensation, freedom of information, and environmental law.

The House from 1975 to 1988

When Toal was sworn in, Carter served as Speaker of the House, and J. Clator Arrants (D-Kershaw) served as Speaker pro tempore. Speaker Carter had been elected in 1973, when Speaker Solomon Blatt (D-Barnwell) retired as presiding officer of the House. The new Speaker was intent on modernizing state government, and in particular the House of Representatives. Speaker Carter implemented and oversaw the hiring of professional research staff, beginning with the employment of Charles T. (Bud) Ferrillo as executive director of Research and Administration, and then the hiring of the directors of Research and Administration for the standing legislative committees. In 1973 Speaker Carter introduced electronic voting, thereby bringing the House into the information technology age. It was under his watch and championship that the House and Senate's Blatt and Gressette office buildings were constructed and occupied. Toal immediately recognized the atmosphere of change and the possibilities associated with technology. She became one of its biggest and most successful advocates. "As one state house observer noted, 'Even on one of her bad days, she's one of the best legislators here.'"[7]

The House operated through committees. There were six standing committees, whose members were appointed by the Speaker: the Judiciary Committee; the Ways and Means Committee; the Labor, Commerce, and Industry (LCI) Committee; the Education and Public Works (Education) Committee; the Medical, Military, Public, and Municipal Affairs (3M) Committee; and the Agriculture and Natural Resources (Natural Resources) Committee.[8] Those committees handled all the substantive legislation considered by the House.[9] The Judiciary and Ways and Means Committees comprised twenty-five members apiece; and the LCI, Education, 3M, and Natural Resources Committees each contained eighteen members.[10] In addition to the six standing committees that considered substantive legislation, there were four other standing committees—Rules, Interstate Cooperation, Invitations, and Legislative Ethics—that dealt with important House matters not constituting substantive legislation. In 1975, as it had been historically in South Carolina, all the Judiciary Committee members were lawyers, and each standing committee had at least one lawyer as a member.[11]

After the standing committees endorsed a particular version of substantive legislation, the House would vote on the legislation. However, when the House and Senate versions of legislation were different, the Speaker appointed three House members on a bill-by-bill basis to a Committee of Conference (conference committee consisting of three members from each body), whose duties were to negotiate with their Senate counterparts to resolve the legislative differences.

Judiciary Committee

Toal served on the Judiciary Committee throughout her tenure in the House. The committee consisted of five subcommittees: Constitutional Laws (Con Laws), Election Laws, Criminal Laws, General Laws, and Special Laws. Toal served on the Con Laws Subcommittee and served as its chair, where she helped draft and shepherd through numerous bills of significant importance to the state, such as the Judicial Adjustment Act discussed below.

Rules Committee

As a lawyer Toal knew the importance of mastering the Rules of the House (the House Rules).[12] Particularly as a freshman member, Toal understood that the way she and her fellow freshmen could have more of an impact on a system that was historically based on seniority was through a mastery of the House Rules. Her mastery of the Rules served her and her other colleagues in good stead whether she was fighting to pass, amend, delay, or defeat legislation.

Crazy Caucus.[13] While it was not a committee of the House, the Crazy Caucus played an important role in the passage of significant, progressive, and modernizing legislation while Toal was a member of the House. Formed in 1978, the nucleus of the Caucus included Jean Toal, Robert L. (Bob) McFadden (D-York), Robert Joseph Sheheen (D-Kershaw), Harriet H. Keyserling (D-Beaufort), Palmer Freeman (D-York), Thomas L. (Tommy) Hughston (D-Greenwood), John M. (Johnny) Rucker (D-Newberry), Virginia L. (Ginger) Crocker (D-Laurens), Malloy D. McEachin (D-Florence), and W. Paul Cantrell (D-Charleston).[14] McFadden was the chairman of the House Judiciary Committee and the senior member of the Crazy Caucus. Elected in 1961, he and Toal were the de facto leaders of the Crazy Caucus. The Crazy Caucus socialized with each other and their committee staffers in small, (mostly) quiet dinners, usually at a restaurant (without lobbyists) or at a member's or staffer's home. The caucus reviewed the events of the day and planned for the events to come.

The Crazy Caucus was a group of like-minded progressive thinkers attempting to bring South Carolina into the twentieth century by passing legislation providing ordinary citizens—be they male or female, black or white, young or old—with (1) equal access to governmental services; (2) a transparent government, from local government to state agencies, boards, and commissions; (3) protection of the environment; and (4) a judiciary accessible to all. Keyserling aptly described the Crazy Caucus: "They were bright, progressive, funny, and very energetic."[15]

Led by Toal's example, members of the Crazy Caucus were the first members of the House to embrace and use Speaker Carter's new research staff. Having been a law clerk and having used law clerks in her private practice, Toal understood the advantages of having staff gather research and dissect issues for her review, allowing her to maximize her available time on any given issue. Toal would ask her staff, me included,[16] to look at existing law and determine how a bill would impact it; research legislation in other states; draft opinions as to the constitutionality of proposed legislation, draft bills, and amendments; and develop position statements or gather material for her review. The other members of the Crazy Caucus also made extensive use of all the research staff, not just those assigned to the members' committees.

Toal's effective use of House professional staff was best illustrated in 1981, the first time she (and the first time a woman) was appointed to serve on the House conference committee for the annual appropriations bill. She went to Robert C. Toomey, director of research for the House Ways and Means Committee, and requested that he prepare a side-by-side comparison of the House and Senate versions of the appropriation bills. The conference committee, chaired by Senator Rembert B. Dennis (D-Berkeley),[17] met at Wampee Plantation, a conference center owned by Santee Cooper. During the conference committee meetings, Senator Dennis watched Toal continue to refer to her notes as they discussed the various disagreements between the House and Senate versions of the appropriations bill. Finally he asked Toal what she was referring to, and she explained that it was the comparison of the two bills that the House staff had prepared for her.

As the negotiations continued, Senator Dennis began asking to look at Toal's notes, and of course, she obliged. Later in the day, a large box was wheeled into the conference room and unpacked. Senator Dennis had ordered a copier, which was promptly installed so that all House members (and Senate staff) could have copies of Toal's notes comparing the bills. Such research is now commonplace at the General Assembly.

In addition to her many other skills, Toal was an excellent speed reader. The first time I wrote a legal memorandum for her, it was lengthy and dealt with several complicated issues. Toal took it and read it in two or three minutes, and I assumed she had just skimmed it. On the contrary, she then began to ask detailed questions about the memorandum.

Toal was always thoroughly prepared, no matter what the topic. She was known for her extraordinary work ethic, mastery of the House Rules, and knowledge of the law. Toal's persona, intelligence, and success demanded respect from friends and foes alike. That talent and toughness she had displayed from an early age served her well. When asked about her style, Toal simply said, "I did my homework on the issues and I know each of the other 123 members of the House. I know their names. I've had conversations with them. That's how you get legislation passed."[18]

As a House member, Toal used the skills she had developed as a lawyer. She was an excellent negotiator and knew the art of compromise. Toal understood that passing legislation was much more difficult than preventing its passage. She understood that it was better to get a law "on the books," even if it did not contain all the items she thought were necessary, and then work to amend the law in future legislative sessions.[19]

The Fat and Ugly Caucus

The genesis for the Crazy Caucus was the self-styled "Fat and Ugly Caucus." The Fat and Ugly chairman, George Gregory (D-Chesterfield), said that to look at the caucus, they had to be called the Fat and Uglies, leading to the caucus's name. The majority of progressive legislation was opposed and filibustered by the Fat and Uglies so the progressives formed their own caucus, "the Crazy Caucus." There were an estimated thirty members of the Fat and Uglies.[20] In her book *Against the Tide*, Keyserling wrote:

> How to describe the group as a whole? *Southern Magazine* summed it up in an October 1986 article about this unusual group of men (and an occasional woman): "What truly holds this eclectic team together is their unapologetic lust for power and influence. What sets them apart from other politicians is a relentless self-parody in the gratification of that lust." The article continued: "What with Democratic moderates [including the Crazy Caucus], the emerging Republican party, women and the new Black Caucus, state politics just wasn't the same. In 1978, they decided to form their own caucus, and the name was selected by Representative George Gregory, who said 'to look at us, you'd have to call us the Fat and Ugly Caucus.'"[21]

Generally, the Fat and Uglies tried to stop change, and the Crazy Caucus tried to implement change.

While the Crazy Caucus and the Fat and Uglies, with rare exception, were on opposite sides of issues, it was not uncommon for one of the Fat and Uglies to ask "Mrs. Toal"[22] to draft an amendment for him. In those days most amendments were handwritten and projected on screens on either side of the House with an overhead projector (new technology then). Members of the House recognized Toal's handwriting, as she was the author of many, many amendments. Initially members were confused when they would see an amendment in Toal's handwriting (but sponsored by another member), and then Toal would vote against the amendment she had "written." Members quickly learned that Toal would lend her expertise to make the House a more deliberative body, and they ceased to be surprised by her vote against an amendment she had drafted.

Legislation

Toal was instrumental in the passage of a number of substantive laws that significantly enhanced education, the environment, the way business was conducted in South Carolina, transparency in state and local government, the administration of government, and the administration of justice.

Article VIII and the Implementation of Home Rule

Prior to 1974 county legislative delegations ruled their own respective counties and school districts. Each county delegation, composed of the county's senator[23] and the county's pro rata share of the 124 House members, passed a "supply bill" (appropriating county revenues for the operations of the county or school district). County governments—including sheriffs, coroners, clerks of court, judges, masters-in-equity, and other county officers—were dependent on the county legislative delegation for funding to operate and carry out their official duties.[24] Unlike municipal governments, county governments did not have the authority to provide, for example, water, sewer, or fire services, resulting in the General Assembly creating a plethora of public service districts to provide these essential governmental services.[25]

Thus, historically, municipalities had more autonomy, taxing and eminent domain powers, and self-governing authority than did counties. However, in the 1940s a movement began in South Carolina for counties to be self-governing and not be "governed from Columbia"—by the General Assembly.[26] In 1948 the General Assembly passed the act that established the Charleston County Council, giving it all the authority that a county government was allowed to exercise at that time.[27] By 1975 there were eighteen county councils patterned after Charleston County.

In the 1972 general election, the statewide constitutional amendment adopting Article VIII (the Home Rule Article) was approved by the voters. Among other things, the Home Rule Article authorized the General Assembly to enact laws that: (1) enabled county government to establish home rule, and prohibited special legislation as to counties; (2) permitted the establishment, expansion, or merger of municipalities, and prohibited special legislation as to municipalities; and (3) allowed local governments to consolidate and jointly administer services such as fire, water, and/or police. On March 7, 1973, the General Assembly ratified the Home Rule Article, and it became effective. Section 7 of the Home Rule Article provided:

> The General Assembly shall provide by general law for the structure, organization, powers, duties, functions, and the responsibilities of counties, including the power to tax different areas at different rates of taxation related to the nature and level of government services provided. Alternate forms of government, not to exceed five, shall be established. No laws for a specific county shall be enacted and no county shall be exempted from the general laws or laws applicable to the selected alternative form of government.[28]

The overarching purpose of the Home Rule Article is encapsulated in section 17, which provides, "The provisions of this Constitution and all laws concerning local government shall be liberally construed in their favor. Powers, duties, and responsibilities granted local government subdivisions by this Constitution and by law shall include those fairly implied and not prohibited by this Constitution."[29]

Important for the passage of the general laws implementing the Home Rule Article, on June 25, 1974, the United States Supreme Court upheld the lower court's determination in *Stevenson* that the House had to reapportion into single-member districts. No longer would a county legislative delegation be composed solely of individuals elected at large from a single county. Many House members would have districts that crossed county lines, sometimes more than two counties. Having nonresident House members in a county delegation, or having a House member on more than one county delegation, could have created numerous challenges and left the county senator(s) with even greater powers. Of course it was also only a matter of time until the Senate would also be forced to reapportion into single-member districts.[30]

Knight v. Salisbury was the first case to test the reach of the Home Rule Article.[31] Section 7 of the article provides, in pertinent part: "No laws for a specific county shall be enacted and no county shall be exempted from the general laws or laws applicable to the selected alternative form of government."[32] After the General Assembly ratified the Home Rule Article, but before it enacted the article's implementing legislation, the General Assembly passed an act that established the Lower Dorchester Recreation District (a body politic), a special purpose district authorized to provide recreational services only in a portion of Dorchester County. At issue, given the adoption of the Home Rule Article, was the continued authority of the General Assembly to create special purpose districts in the several counties. The plaintiff contended that section 7 of the Home Rule Article abolished the General Assembly's power to create special purpose districts. The defendants argued the article: (1) was not self-enacting and not effective until general legislation establishing the functions of the counties was passed; and (2) did not strip the General Assembly of its inherent authority to carve out a district of the state to meet a public need.[33]

In determining the intent of the framers of the amendment, the South Carolina Supreme Court held: "It is clearly intended that home rule be given to the counties and that county government should function in the county seats rather than at the State Capitol. If the counties are to remain units of government, the power to function must exist at the county level. Quite obviously, the framers of Article VIII had this in mind."[34] The court held section 7 expressly curtailed the legislature's plenary powers vis-à-vis special laws for counties and prohibited the General Assembly from enacting any special purpose district for or within a county. The counties now had the authority and funding ability to provide for water and/or sewer services, recreation services, and services previously provided by special purpose districts.

Against this backdrop Toal came to the House. Her first major task was passage of the legislation implementing Home Rule. The fight for the passage of Home Rule was difficult and complex, as local decisions had always been made by the General Assembly.[35] Early in the 1975 session, the Constitutional Laws Subcommittee of the House Judiciary began to draft a Home Rule Bill. Toal was the leader of these drafting efforts. Hearings were held around the state and the subcommittee conducted many hours of drafting sessions, even conducted on weekends. The House had a bill ready to go when the Senate finally finished its floor deliberations.

The Senate initially filed Senate Bill 18 (S. 18), which ultimately became Act 283, the Home Rule Act of 1975, establishing the forms of government and delegation of powers of county councils.[36] The Senate sent S. 18 to the House on May 6, 1975, and the House referred the bill to the Judiciary Committee.[37] On the same day, Toal moved to recall the bill from the Judiciary Committee, which the House agreed to do.[38] On May 8, after the twenty-four-hour point objection was raised (under the House Rules, a bill in printed form has to be on the desks of the members for twenty-four hours), the House began debate on S. 18. Representatives Robert Kneece (D-Richland),[39] McFadden (D-York), Henry F. Floyd (D-Pickens), and Toal offered an amendment to the bill striking all the language after the enacting words and inserted a new bill in its place, which Jean and her subcommittee had spent months preparing (the House version of Home Rule).[40] The House further amended this version, ordered it to a third reading, and sent the bill back to the Senate.[41] On May 13, the House agreed to reconsider the amended bill and accepted an additional amendment proposed by the same four sponsors.[42] S. 18, as amended, was adopted on third reading and again returned to the Senate.

On May 15, 1975, the Senate sent its message to the House refusing to concur in the House's amendment to S. 18.[43] The Speaker appointed Cecil Collins (D-Aiken), McFadden (D-York), and Toal (D-Richland, then a freshman member) as the three House conferees on this all-important conference committee.[44] The Senate appointed Senators Walter Bristow (D-Richland), Horace Smith (D-Spartanburg), and Marshall B. Williams (D-Orangeburg, Senate Judiciary vice chairman).

On May 27 the House conferees gave the initial conference committee report to the House,[45] which the House considered on May 30.[46] Toal explained the report and moved to recommit the report to the conference committee, to which the House agreed.[47] On May 30, the House conferees gave the second conference committee report.[48] The House members debated the second report on the House floor on June 4 and recommitted it to the conference committee.[49] Collins, McFadden, and Toal gave a third conference committee report on June 6, and initially the House refused to give its conferees free conference powers.[50] However, later that day the House granted the conferees free conference powers.[51] On June 8 the conferees gave the Free Conference Report.[52] Finally, on June 10, 1975, the House adopted the Free Conference Report negotiated by McFadden, Collins, and Toal.[53] However, the Senate did not adopt the Free Conference Report, thus recommitting the Report to the Free Conference Committee.[54] On June 12 the House Conferees presented the second Free Conference Report,[55] which the House adopted[56] and in which the Senate concurred.[57] The Home Rule Act was signed by Governor James B. Edwards on June 23, 1975.

The Home Rule Act of 1975 authorized each of South Carolina's forty-six counties to adopt by referendum its chosen form of self-governance and method of election from five forms established in the act. The forms of government included: Council, Council-Supervisor, Council-Administrator, Council-Manager, and Board of Commissioners.[58] The county governments were given very broad powers, including but not limited to acquiring property; issuing bonds; executing contracts and the power of eminent domain; levying property and licensing taxes; and establishing agencies, departments, boards, and commissions necessary to carry out the functions of the county.[59] The act also authorized election of council members from single-member districts and required reapportionment.[60] This mandate to establish county local self-governance was a sea change for South Carolina. Legislative delegations in Columbia no longer managed the unincorporated areas of South Carolina.

Although municipalities had significant autonomy going back to colonial days, the Home Rule Act provided for the creation of new municipalities and established the minimum criteria for incorporation.[61] Three municipal forms of government were established: (1) Mayor-Council; (2) Council; and (3) Council-Manager.[62]

While the General Assembly has found creative ways—and some not so creative—to circumvent the prohibition against special legislation effecting local government, the Home Rule Act of 1975, as amended, still forms the backbone of local governance in South Carolina. Toal, as the chief floor leader of the bill in the House, was a major actor in achieving home rule for local government.

The Freedom of Information Act—Act No. 593 of 1978

In 1972 the General Assembly enacted South Carolina's first Freedom of Information Act, Act 1396, 1972 S.C. Acts 2585. The 1972 act was based on the premise that "it is vital in a democratic society that public business be performed in an open and public manner . . . so that citizens are advised of the performance of public officials and of the decisions that are reached in public activity and in the formation of public policy."[63] The 1972 act provided:

- Open meeting requirements applied only to meetings of the governing body of public agencies and not to subcommittees or ad hoc committees (public meeting was defined only as the meeting of the "governing body").

- Public records could be viewed and copied by the requesting party at available facilities during normal business hours, but there was no requirement that the public body provide copies of the requested records.
- Administrative briefings and committee reports could be made to governing bodies during executive sessions.
- A citizen could apply for injunctive relief at his or her own expense, and no criminal sanctions were provided for violation of the act.

Thus, the Freedom of Information Act of 1972 had limited applicability and limited enforcement authority.

Representatives William M. Campbell (D-Richland), Ralph K. Anderson (D-Florence), and Toal introduced House Bill 2727 (H. 2727) on March 23, 1977, which the House referred to the Judiciary Committee.[64] On April 21, 1977, the House recalled H. 2727 from the Judiciary Committee and placed the bill on its calendar.[65] On April 27, the House recommitted the bill to the Judiciary Committee, although the bill retained its place on the House calendar.[66] Throughout the remainder of the 1977 legislative session, there were a series of motions to adjourn debate (made most often by the three cosponsors),[67] and debate on the bill was continued to the next session on June 8, 1977.[68]

As a lawyer Toal learned firsthand the necessity of strengthening the state's freedom of information law so that the people's business could be conducted in an open and public manner. In *Cooper v. Bales,* Toal and her law partner Jay Bender represented a group of public school teachers challenging a Richland County School District's decision to withhold from the public the contents of its proposed annual budget and seeking to require the school board to make the district's proposed budget publically available prior to its adoption by the board.[69] The South Carolina Supreme Court found that the proposed budget was exempt from disclosure under the "administrative briefing" exemption of the 1972 FOIA Act and denied the citizens' request to see the school district's proposed budget prior to its adoption.[70]

On March 29, 1978, debate began in earnest over H. 2727. Toal was the floor leader of the bill, overseeing the drafting and adoption of several amendments to the bill.[71] On March 29 the House gave a second reading to the bill.[72] On March 30 the House conducted a third reading and sent the bill to the Senate.[73] On July 6, 1978, the Senate returned the bill with amendments. Toal explained the Senate amendments to the members of the House, and upon her motion, the House agreed to the Senate amendments.[74]

Act 593, the Freedom of Information Act (FOIA), made the executive branch of state and local government transparent. During the debate Toal stated that H. 2727 was based on Florida's "Sunshine Law," considered at the time to be one of the strongest freedom of information laws in the country.[75]

Act 593 repealed the 1972 act and implemented significant new transparency requirements and enforcement mechanisms. The major changes to the FOIA included:

- Abolishing the exemption allowing administrative briefings in executive session;
- Requiring twenty-four-hour notice of any meeting, including posting the agenda;
- Requiring public bodies to keep minutes of their meetings;
- Requiring a majority vote to go into executive session, which can be held only for specifically identified purposes such as hiring, compensation, or discipline of employees; discussions incident to contract negotiation; and security matters;
- Requiring a FOIA request to be responded to within fifteen calendar days, excluding Saturdays, Sundays, and legal holidays;
- Providing the right for the public to inspect or receive a copy of records, and for the agency copy at the lowest possible cost to the requestor;
- Delineating specific documents that are considered public, and those considered exempt from disclosure;
- Requiring that any action taken in executive session has to be ratified publically;[76]
- Forbidding state and local government from using "chance meetings, social meetings or electronic communications" to circumvent the spirit of the FOIA; and
- Providing that a citizen has a statutory right (standing) to bring suit to enforce the FOIA, and if successful, to recover costs and reasonable attorney's fees for being forced to bring such action.

During the debate on the bill, the *State* wrote an editorial applauding the House's adoption of the FOIA. The editorial stated that the FOIA dealt "with the most basic relationship between the people and their state and local governments—the peoples' right to know how their business is being performed."[77] Toal had an abiding belief that the people should know how their business is being conducted.

However, the 1978 FOIA did not contain all the provisions for which Toal had advocated. As reported in the *State*: "A lobbyist for the South Carolina Press Association said the measure does not go as far in some areas a newspaper publisher in South Carolina might have liked but added, 'I think the association respects the compromises that have been struck.'" The Press

Association lobbyist called it "a legitimate accommodation respecting the various interests."[78]

In 1987, addressing the shortcomings of the 1978 FOIA, Toal floor-led House Bill 2263 (H. 2263), which eventually became Act 118 of 1987. Act 118 added further clarification and teeth to the FOIA. Among other things Act 118 provided for the manner in which the FOIA should be construed: "[P]rovisions of this chapter must be construed so as to make it possible for citizens, or their representatives, to learn and report fully the activities of their public officials at a minimum cost or delay to the persons seeking access to public documents or meetings."[79] Clearly Toal understood that the legislative process was one of give-and-take, and that to pass legislation successfully, opposing sides had to compromise. If a piece of legislation was not ideal upon initial passage, Toal believed that it could be revisited later and amended.

The Coastal Tidelands and Wetlands Act—Act No. 123 of 1977

In 1972 Congress enacted the Coastal Zone Management Act (CZMA). At a federal level, the Office of Ocean and Coastal Resource Management (OCRM), a subdivision of the National Oceanographic and Atmospheric Administration (NOAA), administered the CZMA. In 1976 Toal and Campbell (Toal's House seat mate) introduced House Bill 2420 (H. 2420). Toal and Campbell were not only two of H. 2420's primary sponsors but also became champions and primary floor leaders for the bill. The House and Senate passed H. 2420 in hopes of taking advantage of the federal CZMA funding and of regaining state control over South Carolina's coastal zone.[80] However, it was vetoed by Governor Edwards, and the legislature sustained his veto, lacking the two-thirds vote to override it.

As with the FOIA, Toal's legal experience helped her understand the problems the state and private citizens had managing the coastal zone without comprehensive state legislation. Between the times Governor Edwards vetoed H. 2420 and the CZMA went into effect, a developer attempted to bulldoze sand dunes as part of its development in Georgetown County. A few of Toal's clients telephoned her, said they were standing in front of the bulldozers, and asked if there was anything she could do legally to help them stop the bulldozing of the dunes. She called Attorney General Daniel R. McLeod to enlist his assistance, because it was a misdemeanor under state law to destroy sea oats on public property, and the beach sand dunes were public property. Attorney General McLeod obtained a temporary restraining order (TRO) hearing with a circuit judge in Georgetown and told me and another assistant attorney general to go with Toal to the hearing to represent the state.[81] In order to get to Georgetown before the hearing, we had to find a state plane to fly us to the Georgetown airport. The only plane available was a very small plane from the Wildlife Department. The other assistant attorney general did not like to fly in small planes, so he told us he would take his chances driving rapidly to get to the hearing on time.

The plane was a small, single-engine propeller plane with room for the pilot and two passengers crammed in the back. We scrambled on board and told the pilot we needed to fly to the Georgetown airport for a court hearing. On the way Toal and I shouted over the engine noise to plan our presentation. After we had been flying awhile, we saw the ocean. To our shock we were about to land in Myrtle Beach, not Georgetown, and we could not convince the pilot otherwise. As the pilot made his approach, however, the Myrtle Beach Air Force Base tower came over the radio. Finally realizing his error, the pilot turned to us and asked how to get to Georgetown. We spotted United States Highway 17 South from the air and told him to follow it to the Georgetown airport. We thus made it to the courthouse in time, and the judge granted the TRO. The dunes were saved.[82] This adventure just reinforced Toal's resolve to get the Coastal Zone Management Act passed so that there were permitting requirements to protect the coastal zone.

In 1977 the Senate introduced Senate Bill 280 (S. 280) in another effort to protect the coastal tidelands and wetlands. When the Senate sent the bill to the House, Toal again was one of the floor leaders of the bill.[83] The CZMA set up a comprehensive statutory scheme aimed at regulating the coastal zone and taking control back from the federal government. As the General Assembly stated in its findings: "A variety of federal agencies presently operate land use controls and permit systems in the coastal zone. South Carolina can only regain control of the regulation of its critical areas by developing its own management program. The key to accomplishing this is to encourage the state and local governments to exercise their full authority over the lands and waters in the coastal zone."[84]

Act 123 defined the coastal zone and established the South Carolina Coastal Council and gave it broad powers. These included the ability to employ staff with the expertise to manage coastal zone development, the authority to develop a comprehensive coastal management program, and the power to enforce and administer the program in accordance with the rules and regulations promulgated pursuant to the act.[85] Beginning August 24, 1977, no one could utilize a critical area (as defined in the act) other than for its existing use without receiving a permit from the Coastal Council.[86] The passage of Act 123 allowed South Carolina to regain management control of her coastal zone from the federal government.

The Administrative Procedures Act—Act No. 176 of 1977

The adoption of the Administrative Procedures Act (APA)[87] implemented some of the most sweeping changes in the way state agencies operated and interacted with the entities and people they regulated. An article in the

South Carolina Law Review at the time described the adoption of the APA as "[a] notable occurrence in South Carolina administrative law."[88] The APA provided South Carolina with a uniform, transparent method of enacting regulations that provided for public input and comment, and with procedures to be followed in "contested cases," which are constitutionally or statutorily required hearings on state agency decisions that affect an individual's or entity's private rights under the South Carolina Constitution's administrative due process requirement.[89] A "contested case" is an executive branch hearing designed to provide parties administrative due process and is defined as a "proceeding including, but not restricted to[,] ratemaking, price fixing, and licensing, in which the legal rights, duties or privileges of a party are required by law to be determined by an agency after an opportunity for hearing."[90]

Sponsors Toal, Sheheen, McFadden, Floyd, and Paul D. Gelegotis (D-Charleston) introduced House Bill 2326 (H. 2326)[91] on January 27, 1977, and the House referred the bill to the Judiciary Committee.[92] The Judiciary Committee reported it out favorably on April 7, 1977.[93] Toal floor-led the APA bill.[94] The bill was given a second reading on April 19, 1977,[95] and given a third reading and sent to the Senate on April 20, 1977.[96] On Friday, June 3, the Senate returned the bill with amendments, in which the House concurred, and the General Assembly enrolled the bill for ratification.[97]

The APA brought unified and mostly standardized procedures to the administrative branch of government in terms of its regulatory functions, licensing/permitting and enforcement, and administrative hearings to review agency decisions. The APA established the *State Register,* the monthly publication by the Legislative Council, which provides notice of proposed agency rule making and public hearings, agency permitting actions—both proposed and approved—and other agency regulatory notices.[98] The *State Register* was required to be published at least once every thirty days.[99] The APA also required a legislative council to publish a Code of Regulations,[100] the first time that all the regulations promulgated by state agencies were collected and made readily available to the public and the legal professional alike.

Unlike most states at the time, in South Carolina under provisions of the new APA, the General Assembly reserved unto itself the right to approve or reject an agency regulatory promulgation. Once an agency had adopted a regulation, the proposed regulation was sent to the General Assembly.[101] If both branches adopted the proposed regulation by joint resolution within ninety days of the time it was introduced, or if no joint resolution was enacted within the time frame, the regulation became law.[102] If the regulation was disapproved by joint resolution, the regulation did not go into effect, and the agency had to start the process again.[103] The APA did not authorize the General Assembly to revise any proposed regulation, only to approve, disapprove, or allow the regulation to become law without action. This process prevented the agencies from adopting far reaching regulations with no public review process.

Equally important, and having a more far-reaching effect on the regulated community in South Carolina, the APA also implemented the 1970 amendment to Article I, section 22 of the state constitution (administrative due process) by establishing administrative contested case procedures and notice and hearing requirements. The APA established several new requirements.[104] Perhaps most important, the APA instituted a uniform hearing process, which gave parties aggrieved by a ruling of the agency the right to notice of a contested case hearing, the right to receive a statement of the matters asserted, the right to specified discovery, and the right to issue agency subpoenas for the production of documents and the like.[105] Similarly the APA gave all parties the right to respond, established a new requirement for the agency to create a record in cases of appeal, and specified the contents of that record.[106] Moreover any final decision or order had to be in writing and contain findings of fact (supported by a concise statement of the underlying facts) and conclusions of law.[107] The contested case procedures applied to the grant, denial, or renewal of a license and to enforcement actions against a licensee.[108] The APA also guaranteed the right of judicial review for any final administrative decision.[109]

Without doubt the APA has had an enormous impact on the operation of state government and the ability of all South Carolina citizens and regulated entities to have input into the regulation of government functions (for example, the environment, health care, insurance, and licensed professions). Toal's leadership during the debate on the APA helped make the regulatory process much more uniform and transparent to regulated industries and to the public.

The Education Finance Act—Act No. 163 of 1977

The Education Finance Act (EFA) had the support of a number of House members, including its primary sponsors Representative Nick A. Theodore (D-Greenville), chair of the Education Committee, and Toal. On February 2, 1977, the bill, H. 2385, was introduced and referred to the Education Committee.[110] On March 10 the Education Committee reported the bill out favorably, with amendments and with a minority unfavorable report.[111] Toal offered amendments from the floor, including one that required every public school district in South Carolina to publish its budget for the year, and provided that any district that did not would not receive state funding.[112] The Senate returned the bill with amendments on May 20,[113] and the House concurred.[114]

Implementation of Article V—The Judicial Department

Toal was also a leading figure in the implementation of Article V, as ratified in 1973, which restructured South Carolina's judicial branch of government.[115] Specifically, she floor-led six critical acts that unified the judicial system.[116]

One of these acts was Act 690, which began the lengthy process of unification.[117] As a freshman, Toal sponsored the Judiciary Committee's amendments to Act 690 prior to its passage and floor-led the bill in the House.[118] Once approved of by the General Assembly, Act 690 went into effect on July 1, 1977, and established a judicial system that included a Supreme Court, a circuit court, and such other courts as were provided by South Carolina's general laws.[119] Act 690 made significant changes to the existing probate court system,[120] added additional circuit judges to several of the circuits,[121] and amended the civil jurisdiction of the magistrate's court.[122] Likewise Act 690 created a family court in each of the state's sixteen judicial circuits.[123]

More important, the act abolished all single-county and multicounty courts—including any such existing family courts, juvenile courts, and domestic relations courts—and devolved the abolished courts' jurisdiction into the newly created statewide family court system.[124] Similarly, beginning July 1, 1979, Act 690 abolished county courts and other similar courts with jurisdiction inferior to the circuit courts, and authorized the Supreme Court to provide for the transition of jurisdiction to the circuit courts by rule or order.[125]

Finally, Act 690 implemented changes for court officials. For example the act mandated that the solicitors (prosecutors) in each of the judicial circuits must be full-time employees and authorized the solicitors in each circuit to hire assistant solicitors as necessary.[126] Further Act 690 established the "Judicial Qualifications Screening Committee," empowered to investigate all candidates for election and report to the General Assembly those that the committee found to be qualified to serve.

Toal was likewise heavily involved in three other critical acts that moved South Carolina toward its current unified judicial system. In 1979 Act 164, also known as the Judicial Adjustment Act, established the court of appeals. Prior to the Judicial Adjustment Act's passage, the Senate Judiciary Committee introduced Senate Bill 402 (S. 402) in 1978 as the comprehensive legislation intended to complete the implementation of Article V, including the establishment of the court of appeals.[127] After passage in the Senate, S. 402 was introduced in the House on April 17, 1979, and referred to the Judiciary Committee.[128]

The Judicial Adjustment Act established a court of appeals to hear appeals from circuit courts, with certain exceptions where appeal rested exclusively in the South Carolina Supreme Court's jurisdiction. It was created to relieve the substantial backlog in cases pending for hearing in the South Carolina Supreme Court. In its original form, the court of appeals was not a part of the unified judicial system. Five judges, elected by the General Assembly, made up the original court of appeals. Because there was no ban on their eligibility, four of the five judges elected were sitting members of the General Assembly.

In *State ex rel. Riley v. Martin,* the governor and attorney general challenged, among other things, the right of the General Assembly to create the court of appeals by legislation, based on the recent amendment to Article V of the state constitution.[129] The South Carolina Supreme Court determined that Article V did not prohibit the creation of the court of appeals, but required that the court be a part of the unified judicial system; have unified jurisdiction; and be created by general law.[130]

The governor and attorney general likewise challenged the provision of the act allowing sitting members of the General Assembly to run for seats on the court of appeals, in contravention of the general statutory prohibition on legislators being elected to a seat that they created.[131] The South Carolina Supreme Court held this provision to be a special law in contravention of the state constitution.[132] Thus, the South Carolina Supreme Court found the court of appeals, as an entity, was constitutional; however, as currently constituted, the court of appeals had only one judge out of five eligible for service.

Faced with the *Riley v. Martin* decision, the House and Senate formed a joint subcommittee of their Judiciary Committees to study the issue and make recommendations regarding the court of appeals.[133] Toal was a member of that subcommittee.

In 1983, in response to the *Riley v. Martin* decision, the Constitutional Laws Subcommittee of the Judiciary Committee proposed Acts 89 and 90, both authored in large part by Toal, and both promptly enacted by the General Assembly. These acts provided that the court of appeals would have six judges, headed by a chief judge, and would sit in panels of three. The court would be part of the unified judicial system, operating under the South Carolina Supreme Court. The court of appeals' jurisdiction extended to all appeals, except cases involving elections, murder, and public service rate setting. This intermediate appellate court continues to have a major impact on providing timely appellate review in South Carolina.

The Public Service Commission Merit Selection Act—Act No. 167 of 1979

The South Carolina Public Service Commission (PSC) is the state agency that regulates, among other things, investor-owned utilities. In the 1970s there was growing public unrest and outcry about the cozy relationship between lawyer legislators—who elected the members of the PSC—and employees and executives of the electric utility providers. Many lawyer legislators represented utilities before the PSC. Toal was the primary sponsor of House Bill 2321 (H. 2321), the bill eventually known as the PSC Merit Selection Act. H. 2321 aimed to reform the PSC. Compared to Home Rule, this bill was more contentious—even acrimonious[134]—but not more complex. The debate, including filibusters, lasted four weeks in the House.

H. 2321 pitted the Crazy Caucus against the Fat and Uglies. Unlike the Crazy Caucus, the Fat and Uglies were known for their fondness (some would say abuse) of accepting the fruits of lobbyists' largess. During the late-night filibusters on H. 2321, lobbyists set up bars in the House lobby and in committee offices, and the Fat and Uglies took advantage of the free liquor. There were myriad procedural votes (or test votes) to determine where the vote stood on the bill. Many of the votes were taken on the electronic board.[135] On more than one occasion, the Speaker announced the rule that a member could not assist another member in voting, thus requiring each member to push his own button to vote, and prohibiting legislators from voting on behalf of another member. As a result, at multiple points during the debate, inebriated members of the Fat and Uglies claimed either that they were physically unable to push their own voting buttons, or that they could not determine which way to vote on the issue.

Generally, during the test votes, there were rarely more than five or six votes difference.[136] At one point during the debate, I invited the members of the Crazy Caucus, who were understandably frustrated, to my house for dinner to cheer them up.[137] As Keyserling later wrote, many of the caucus members were weary of the constant fighting over a bill that would clearly help restore public faith in government, and several of them threatened not to run for office again.[138]

Fortunately the Crazy Caucus persevered, and they along with Governor Richard W. Riley, who had made reform of the PSC his top legislative priority,[139] were instrumental in the House's eventual adoption of the bill and the enactment of the Merit Selection Act. Its passage would have been doubtful but for Toal and Sheheen's knowledge and skillful application of the House Rules.

As enacted, the Merit Selection Act recognized that rate cases before the PSC had become increasingly complex and lengthy, with many legal, procedural, and evidentiary matters. The purpose of the act was "to improve the effectiveness of the commission, to strengthen the public's confidence that its interests are being properly monitored and protected and to insure equitable rates for utility services without endangering the financial stability of the suppliers of services."[140]

Previously the General Assembly elected the members of the PSC without screening of any sort, and there was no prohibition against the election of a sitting member of the General Assembly to the PSC. The act established a Merit Selection Committee, comprising three members who were appointed by the House, three members who were appointed by the Senate, and five members and a chairman who were appointed by the governor.[141] The Merit Selection Committee nominated two candidates for each PSC vacancy (it could nominate only one or up to three candidates, upon unanimous vote of the committee).[142] It was charged with screening applicants, based on their qualifications in such diverse fields as "business, government, accounting, law, engineering, statistics, consumer affairs and finance."[143] The General Assembly could elect one of the nominees selected by the Merit Selection Committee, or it could reject all nominees. If the General Assembly rejected all nominees, the merit selection nominating process would start anew.[144]

The Merit Selection Act also forbade members of the General Assembly (or any member of a legislator's law firm) from appearing before the PSC on behalf of a party to a rate-fixing proceeding.[145] With the passage of the Merit Selection Act, the "good ole boy" system suffered a blow.

The Constitutional 5 Percent Legislative Reserve Fund—
Article III, Section 36

In 1975 the General Assembly determined there was a need to establish a reserve fund in the "interest of stability and financial prudence" and thus established a process to create a reserve fund in an amount equal to 5 percent of the general fund revenue for the latest completed fiscal year. In 1978 Governor Edwards, Treasurer Grady Patterson, and the leadership of the General Assembly determined that the statutory provision should become a constitutional amendment, and S. 330 was introduced to add section 36 to Article III of the state constitution. Initially a small group of House members—Toal, Sheheen, Keyserling, Ferdinand (Nancy) Stevenson (D-Charleston), and Freeman—opposed the constitutional amendment, instead arguing that the existing statutory approach was sufficient and gave the state the flexibility it needed to meet future conditions.

The House debate took place in 1979. Toal, Sheheen, Keyserling, Freeman, Crocker, and Stevenson led the fight, with Toal, Sheheen, and Freeman carrying the load during the debates.[146] The group continued to gain supporters during the debate, but not enough to win the day.

After the debate session, Toal, Sheheen, Freeman, and Keyserling formed the South Carolina's Taxpayers' Coalition (the Taxpayers' Coalition) to try to defeat the amendment.[147] The board members were Sheheen (chair), Toal (vice chair), Freeman (secretary), and Keyserling. At a press conference announcing their opposition to the reserve fund amendment,

Toal argued that the financial rating agencies did not believe that a constitutional amendment establishing a reserve fund was necessary to maintain the state's highly coveted Triple A credit rating.[148] Calling the proposed amendment a "big slush fund," the Taxpayers' Coalition grew to include McFadden, Hughston, A. Victor Rawl (D-Charleston), Stevenson, Floyd, Robert Woods (D-Charleston, and chairman of the Black Caucus), and Senator Thomas E. Smith (D-Florence).[149] Led by Toal and Sheheen, the members of the Taxpayers' Coalition placed newspaper ads and met with civic organizations and reporters working in newspaper, radio, and television. In fall 1978, Educational Television (ETV) organized a debate on the proposed constitutional amendment. McFadden—the only member of House leadership that joined the Taxpayers' Coalition—debated the merits and demerits of the proposed amendment with Senator Dennis, chairman of the Senate Finance Committee. At one point during the debate, McFadden looked Dennis in the eye and said: "Senator, five won't jive!" The slogan for the Taxpayers' Coalition was born. Despite the efforts of the coalition, the proposed amendment won by about 4 percent, which at the time was the narrowest vote for adoption of a constitutional amendment in the state's history.[150]

On Thursday, February 15, 1979, the House took up House Bill 2322 (H. 2322), the bill to ratify the amendment adding Article III, section 36 to the state constitution. Toal and the Crazy Caucus again led the fight to defeat ratification of the amendment.[151] Several members of the Taxpayers' Coalition, including Toal, spoke against the bill. Numerous procedural motions and points of order were raised. Finally opponents of H. 2322 narrowly passed a motion to table the bill by a vote of fifty-three to fifty-two, a significant defeat for the House leadership. Therefore the House adjourned until 10:00 A.M. the next day, Friday, February 16.

After H. 2322 was tabled by a single vote, the House leadership announced that they would ask a particular member of the House who had voted on the prevailing side to move to reconsider the ratification bill the following day. Fridays were traditionally "local sessions" where local legislation or bills undergoing a third reading were "passed" with no members present. After adjournment Toal, Sheheen, Hughston, Keyserling, and Crocker went to lunch across the street from the State House at the Frog and Brassiere, a restaurant where the Crazy Caucus often met. As the staffer for the Judiciary Committee—the committee on which most of the Crazy Caucus served—I was with those members at lunch after adjournment. Given their mastery of the House Rules, Toal and Sheheen devised a plan—relying on *Mason's Manual*—where a small group of members who had opposed the reserve fund would attend the local session on Friday, and would convene and adjourn the House without allowing a motion to reconsider to be made, which would effectively kill the bill and defeat ratification of the constitutional amendment.[152]

At 10:00 A.M. Friday, nine members of the Crazy Caucus convened. Toal assumed the chair of the House and announced that because neither the Speaker nor the Speaker pro tempore were present, the House should organize and elect an acting Speaker. The nine members elected Sheheen by acclamation, and he took the chair and announced that the House should likewise elect a temporary chaplain. The nine then elected Keyserling as temporary chaplain—the first member of the Jewish faith so elected.

After the prayer and correction of the *House Journal*, Campbell moved that the House adjourn, which it did. Representative Jim Kinard (D-Richland)—who had come to make the motion to reconsider the vote to table H. 2322—never got the opportunity to do so because he filed his motion with the clerk after adjournment. Toal and Sheheen then called Speaker Carter to explain what the group had done—used the rules, including *Mason's*, to defeat the constitutional amendment. Friday, January 16, 1979, became known as "Black Friday." The next Tuesday, Speaker Carter ruled the nine-member session convened improperly under *Mason's Manual* because the House was operating under the House Rules for local Friday sessions. The House reconsidered the motion tabling H. 2322, and eventually the House and the Senate ratified the reserve fund amendment.

The Consumer Protection Code Revision Act—Act No. 385 of 1982

Act 385 provided sweeping overhauls to and protections for citizens in their commercial transactions, including limiting interest rates on consumer loans. The Senate originally proposed Senate Bill 798 (S. 798) and sent it to the House. In turn the House referred S. 798 to the LCI committee, which reported the bill out with amendments. On the floor the House further amended S. 798, with Toal sponsoring or explaining a number of the amendments.[153] The House adopted S. 798 as amended and sent the bill back to the Senate.[154] Initially the Senate refused to concur in the House amendments, and it and the House formed a conference committee. Ultimately the General Assembly adopted the amended House version of S. 798.

The act protected citizens in numerous ways. It set maximum interest rates on such entities as pawn shops, established strict procedures for obtaining default judgments, and gave additional powers to the Office of Consumer Affairs to promulgate regulations and police creditors.

The Education Improvement Act—Act No. 512 of 1984

When Governor Riley entered office in 1979, one of his major initiatives was to improve the quality of public education. By 1984 South Carolina had fallen to last in the country in per pupil education funding.[155] The

Education Improvement Act (EIA) sought to increase public school academic standards through increasing teacher training and salaries; improving school administration management and leadership skills incentive programs; increasing partnerships between schools, parents, and the business community; implementing student testing standards; creating special programs for at-risk four-year-olds, gifted children, and advanced-placement students; and providing funding for new school buildings. A penny sales tax funded the EIA. The General Assembly enacted the EIA as part of the general appropriations act of 1984.

Initially the Crazy Caucus was split on the EIA. While Toal and Sheheen championed improvement in public education, they supported a different funding mechanism than did Governor Riley and Keyserling, Crocker, Crosby E. Lewis (D-Fairfield), and John R. Tally (D-Cherokee). Eventually the two sides reached a compromise: the sales tax would be increased by a penny, and some of the revenue would be used to phase out the sales tax on food over three years.[156] The House initially passed the compromised bill but amended it the next day. Under the new amendments, the bill reinstated the food sales tax and instead offered a tax credit equal to the average annual cost of food for a family of four.[157] The EIA passed the House on March 27, 1984, with the strong help of Toal and Sheheen—the parliamentarians who could maneuver through the House Rules.

The Rules Committee

Toal was appointed to the Rules Committee in 1977. She became second vice chair in 1979, and vice chair in 1980. Since the end of her first session, Toal had worked to limit the length of time the House spent in session.[158] One of the major factors that extended the sessions was the House Rule regarding filibusters and the necessity of garnering sixty-eight votes to limit debate.[159] Starting in 1977 members of the Crazy Caucus began trying to limit filibusters in the House.[160]

A breakthrough in session reform occurred in 1979. Act 146[161] required the Budget and Control Board to make its budget report to the House Ways and Means Committee no later than the first Tuesday in January and required the General Assembly to adjourn not later than the first Thursday in June, unless extended by a concurrent resolution adopted by a two-thirds vote of both the House and the Senate.

On May 12, 1982, Toal was elected chair of the Rules Committee. Toal, with the help of fellow Crazy Caucus members, particularly Sheheen and Freeman, drafted a major overhaul to the House Rules. At the House's organizational session, December 7–9, 1982, Toal was the floor leader for House Bill 2079 (H. 2079), the House resolution to adopt the Rules for the 1983–84 session. After three days of debate, filled with points of order, the

House adopted its Rules for 1983–84. The Rules significantly streamlined the operations of the House. One of the major changes was amending Rule 8.4 to make it easier to limit debate.

Other Legislation

There were a number of other important legislative initiatives that Toal led or in which she actively participated. In 1976 she was one of the sponsors of the resolution to adopt the Equal Rights Amendment (ERA) to the United States Constitution. Once an amendment to the United States Constitution is proposed, there is a ten-year deadline for the states to ratify it. Over that ten-year period, Toal introduced a South Carolina resolution in each of the two-year legislative sessions until the deadline expired. Thus, even though the states ultimately did not ratify the ERA, Toal's advocacy for the amendment helped advance the cause of equal opportunity and access for women in the workplace in South Carolina.

Further, Toal was one of the primary sponsors and floor leader for reducing the "no fault" divorce separation period from three years to one year. She also played a significant role in the sweeping revisions to the South Carolina Children's Code, in establishing the Patient's Compensation Fund, and in expanding the jurisdiction of the South Carolina Human Affairs Commission and giving it enforcement authority. Finally, Toal was the sponsor of Act 5, 1981 S.C. Acts 5, which ratified the amendment to Article IV, section 3 of the state constitution to allow the governor to serve two terms in office.

Legislative Legacy

Toal made it a point of becoming personally acquainted with every member of the House and Senate, whether they agreed with her on positions or not. She had the ability to put the rancor and heat of debate aside and be friends after adjournment. It was the relationships she formed with her fellow legislators that enabled her to form coalitions or to find compromise to pass legislation. She understood the camaraderie necessary to govern.

Toal was elected at a crucial time in the state's history—as the electorate approved of and the General Assembly implemented sweeping amendments to the South Carolina Constitution of 1895. Toal will always be seen as an organizing and moving force in the House of Representatives. During her almost fourteen-year tenure in the House, she helped shape and pass much of the legislation that implemented the constitutional amendments concerning administrative due process, the Judicial Department, local government/Home Rule, and education reform. As a leader in the House of Representative, Toal helped orchestrate changes in South Carolina's three branches of government that will long endure.

NOTES

1. 337 U.S. 533 (1964).

2. *See Stevenson v. West*, 413 U.S. 902 (1973). The South Carolina Constitution required the House to reapportion itself every ten years beginning in 1901, with reapportionment based on each county as an election district and the election district receiving its pro rata share of the 124 House members. S.C. Const. art. III, § 3.

3. No one had ever tried to organize the freshman class before.

4. Carter served as Speaker of the House from 1973 until 1980, when he retired from the House. Upon his death in 2014, Toal, then serving as chief justice of the South Carolina Supreme Court, credited Speaker Carter with helping lead the modernization effort in South Carolina. Ron Barnett, *Rex Carter, Former House Speaker, Dies at 88, Greenville News*, June 10, 2014, 10:26 A.M., http://www.greenvilleonline.com/story/news/local/2014/06/09/rex-carter-former-house-speaker-dies/10244241/.

5. Toal was appointed by Speaker Ramon Schwartz to serve as a member of the House Committee of Conference for the General Appropriation bill on July 9, 1981. *House Journal South Carolina Regular Session* 1981, vol. 2, p. 3716.

6. Other articles of the state constitution were amended piecemeal.

7. W. Lewis Burke and Bakari T. Sellers, "The Rise of Women in the Legal Profession," in 3 *South Carolina Women: Their Lives and Times*, Marjorie Julian Spruill et al., eds. (Athens: University of Georgia Press, 2012), 409, 420.

8. The committee membership elected committee officers.

9. If adopted, substantive legislation has the effect of amending state laws and, if ratified, the state constitution.

10. The Speaker and Speaker pro tempore do not serve on standing committees.

11. In contrast, in 1988, when Toal was elected to the South Carolina Supreme Court, there were not enough lawyers in the General Assembly to fill the Judiciary Committee's membership and also have at least one lawyer on each standing committee.

12. The House Rules are based on *Mason's Manual of Legislative Procedure*, while the Senate Rules are based on *Jefferson's Manual*. Toal knew them both. *Mason's Manual* is a compilation of parliamentary rules, similar to *Robert's Rules of Order*. The National Conference of State Legislatures (NCSL) owns the copyright to *Mason's Manual*, which is used by seventy of the ninety-nine legislative chambers in the United States. *About State Legislatures*, Nat'l Conference of State Legislatures, http://www.ncsl.org/research/about-state-legislatures/masons-manual-for-legsilative-bodies.aspx (accessed January 27, 2015).

13. The "Fat and Ugly" Caucus, discussed below, was formed just prior to the Crazy Caucus. Most often the "Fat and Uglies" and the "Crazies" fought on opposite sides of legislation. The Crazy Caucus drove the Fat and Uglies crazy, and the Fat and Uglies drove the Crazy Caucus crazy—thus the name "Crazy Caucus."

14. Sheheen, Keyserling, Freeman, Hughston, and Rucker were elected in 1976 and seated in 1977. Crocker came in 1978, having been elected to fill an unexpired term. McEachin and Cantrell were elected in 1978 and seated in 1979.

15. Harriet Keyserling, *Against the Tide: One Woman's Political Struggle* (University of South Carolina Press ed., 1998), 72.

16. I served as director of research and staff counsel for the House Judiciary Committee from 1977 to 1981.

17. In those days all conference committees were chaired by senators.

18. Burke and Sellers, *supra* note 7, at 419.

19. The Freedom of Information Act, discussed in further detail below, is an excellent example of her "get what you can and then amend" philosophy.

20. Some of the members included John G. Felder (D-Calhoun), David O. Hawkins (D-Spartanburg), and John I. Rogers (D-Marlboro).

21. Keyserling, *supra* note 13, at 78.

22. During debate House members always referred to each other formally as "Mrs. Toal" or "Mr. McFadden" or "the Representative from Kershaw County."

23. At that time each county in South Carolina had only one senator, who wielded considerable power.

24. In the 1960s and 1970s, South Carolina was still a largely rural state without significant incorporated municipalities. Thus a large portion of South Carolina was governed in Columbia, through the legislative delegation's annual adoption of supply bills.

25. These services are now provided by the counties rather than by the General Assembly directly.

26. *See Knight v. Salisbury*, 262 S.C. 565, 571, 206 S.E.2d 875, 877 (1974).

27. *Id.*

28. S.C. Const. art. VIII, § 7.

29. S.C. Const. art. VIII, § 17.

30. Senate reapportionment with counties going to single member districts did not occur until 1984.

31. *Knight*, 262 S.C. at 565, 206 S.E.2d at 875.

32. S.C. Const. art. VIII, § 7.

33. *Knight*, 262 S.C. at 569–70, 206 S.E.2d at 876.

34. *Id.* at 571, 206 S.E.2d at 877.

35. Burke & Sellers, *supra* note 7, at 419.

36. *See* Act 283, 1975 S.C. Acts 692.

37. *House Journal South Carolina Regular Session* 1975, vol. 1, pp. 1613–14.

38. *Id.* at 1626.

39. Representative Kneece was then the chair of the Judiciary Committee.

40. *House Journal South Carolina Regular Session* 1975, vol. 1, p. 1751.

41. *Id.* at 1796, 1862.

42. *Id.* at 1876–77.

43. *Id.* at 2015.

44. *Id.* at 2016.

45. *House Journal South Carolina Regular Session* 1975, vol. 1, p. 2341.

46. *Id.* at 2563.

47. *Id.* at 2564.

48. *Id.* at 2568.

49. *Id.* at 2681.

50. A conference report agreeing to language in a bill can contain only language that is in the House or Senate versions last adopted by the respective bodies. In order to put any new language in a conference report, both bodies must vote to give their conferees free conference powers. It takes a two-thirds vote of each body for free conference.

51. *House Journal South Carolina Regular Session* 1975, vol. 1, p. 2864.

52. *Id.* at 2867.

53. *Id.* at 2918–19.

54. *Id.* at 3020–21.

55. *Id.* at 3043.

56. *House Journal South Carolina Regular Session* 1975, vol. 1, pp. 3090–91.

57. *Id.* at 3095.

58. Act 283, 1975 S.C. Acts 692, 695.

59. *Id.* at 695–96.

60. *Id.* at 702–3.

61. *Id.* at 717–18.

62. *Id.* at 721.

63. 1972 S.C. Acts 2585, 2585–86.

64. *House Journal South Carolina Regular Session* 1977, vol. 1, p. 1134.

65. *Id.* at 1688.

66. *Id.* at 1781.

67. Sometimes legislators choose to delay debate to reach compromises and/or garner votes.

68. *House Journal South Carolina Regular Session* 1977, vol. 1, p. 3074.

69. *Cooper v. Bales,* 268 S.C. 270, 272–73, 233 S.E.2d 306, 307 (1977).

70. *Id.* at 275, 233 S.E.2d at 308.

71. *See generally House Journal South Carolina Regular Session* 1978, vol. 2, pp. 1540–43, 1548–49, 3047.

72. *Id.* at 1549.

73. *Id.* at 1573–74.

74. *Id.* at 3047–48.

75. Editorial, *State* (Columbia, S.C.), April 3, 1977, at A17.

76. After additional amendment to the FOIA, no action can be taken in executive session.

77. *State* (Columbia, S.C.), April 9, 1978, at 20.

78. *State* (Columbia, S.C.), July 7, 1978, at 26.

79. 1987 S.C. Acts 301, 301.

80. Unless and until the General Assembly passed this legislation, the OCRM and the NOAA regulated South Carolina's coastal zone.

81. At the time I was a lawyer in the Special Litigation unit in the attorney general's office.

82. Given the adventure of getting to Georgetown, on the way to the airport to fly home, we politely suggested to the pilot that we fly to I-95, follow it to I-26, and follow I-26 home.

83. *House Journal South Carolina Regular Session* 1977, vol. 2, pp. 23–32.

84 1977 S.C. Acts 224, 224.

85. *Id.* at 229–33.

86. *Id.* at 236–38.

87. Act 176, 1977 S.C. Acts 391. Article I, section 22 of the South Carolina Constitution (constitutional amendment approved by the electors in the 1970 general election and ratified by the General Assembly in 1971) provides for administrative due process for any person whose private rights are affected by a judicial or quasi-judicial decision of an administrative agency.

88. John R. Steer, *Administrative Law,* 30 S.C. L. REV. 1, 1 (1979).

89. *See Stono River Envtl. Protection Ass'n v. S.C. Dep't of Health & Envtl. Control,* 305 S.C. 90, 406 S.E.2d 340 (1991); *see also* S.C. Const. art. I, § 22.

90. 1977 S.C. Acts 391, 400.

91. The APA was first enacted by Act 671, 1976 S.C. Acts 1758. Act 176 repealed and replaced it in its entirety.

92. *House Journal South Carolina Regular Session* 1977, vol. 1, p. 257.

93. *Id.* at 1384.

94. *Id.* at 1502, 1586–87.

95. *Id.* at 1587.

96. *Id.* at 1615–16.

97. *House Journal South Carolina Regular Session* 1977, vol. 2, p. 2959.

98. 1977 S.C. Acts 391, 392–93.

99. *Id.*

100. *Id.* at 395–96.

101. *Id.* at 396–97. The approval or disapproval process is the same today, except that the time frame for legislative action has been extended, and details on referral to committees and the like have also changed.

102. *Id.*

103. 1977 S.C. Acts at 396–97.

104. *See, e.g., id.* at 392–93.

105. *Id.* The court of common pleas enforced the agency subpoenas at the time.

106. *Id.*

107. *Id.* at 393.

108. 1977 S.C. Acts at 395.

109. *Id.*

110. *House Journal South Carolina Regular Session* 1977, vol. 1, pp. 323–24.

111. *Id.* at 865.

112. *Cooper v. Bales*, discussed above, was decided March 17, 1977.

113. *House Journal South Carolina Regular Session* 1977, vol. 1, p. 2432.

114. *Id.* at 2733.

115. *See* S.C. Const. art. V.

116. *See* Act 690, 1976 S.C. Acts 1859; Act 164, 1979 S.C. Acts 311, 338; Act 89, 1983 S.C. Acts 160; Act 90, 1983 S.C. Acts 167; Act 8, 1985 S.C. Acts 12; Act 9, 1985 S.C. Acts 13.

117. Prior to Act 690, the General Assembly controlled the terms of court, number of solicitors, and number of clerks of court.

118. *House Journal South Carolina Regular Session* 1976, vol. 2., p. 3229.

119. 1976 S.C. Acts 1859, 1860–61.

120. *Id.* at 1867–72. Specifically Act 690 established probate courts of uniform jurisdiction in the counties; authorized the respective probate judges to appoint associate probate judges; made the probate court a court of record; authorized the Supreme Court to issue rules to regulate probate practice; and established jurisdiction of the probate courts.

121. *Id.* at 1872–73.

122. *Id.* at 1861–67.

123. *Id.* at 1861–67.

124. 1976 S.C. Acts at 1873.

125. *Id.* at 1874.

126. *Id.* at 1879.

127. In addition to the West Commission, the legislature created the Judicial Reform Committee to make a comprehensive study of the judicial system. It amended the West Commission report to allow the General Assembly to create an intermediate appellate court.

128. *House Journal South Carolina Regular Session* 1979, vol. 1, pp. 1413–14.

129. *State ex rel. Riley v. Martin*, 274 S.C. 106, 109, 262 S.E.2d 404, 405 (1980) (per curiam).

130. *Id.* at 110, 111, 262 S.E.2d at 406.

131. *Id.* at 114, 262 S.E.2d at 408.

132. *Id.* at 116, 262 S.E.2d at 409; *see also* S.C. Const. art. III, § 34, subsec. 9.

133. Act 89, 1983 S.C. Acts 160.

134. At one point a member of the Fat and Uglies made such a derogatory remark about Toal that Senator Marion Gressette (D-Calhoun), president pro tempore of the Senate, walked across the lobby to the House to apologize to her.

135. As part of the modernization process, Speaker Carter installed an electronic voting board that he used to record members' votes.

136. *House Journal South Carolina Regular Session* 1979, vol. 2, pp. 2193–94.

137. Not only did I undertake research for the Crazy Caucus members, but I was also the unofficial organizer of events like dinners, birthday parties, and tennis matches.

138. Keyserling, *supra* note 13, at 199–200.

139. *State* (Columbia, S.C.), January 12, 1979, and January 18, 1979.

140. Act 167, 1979 S.C. Acts 351, 352.

141. *Id.* at 354–56.

142. *Id.*

143. *Id.* at 356.

144. *Id.* at 354–56.

145. 1979 S.C. Acts 351, 357.

146. *See generally House Journal South Carolina Regular Session* 1979, vol. 2.

147. This appears to be the first taxpayers' coalition formed in South Carolina to fight against a measure that could cause a rise in taxes, as the Taxpayers' Coalition contended it would.

148. Al Lanier, "The Second Front," *Sumter Daily Item,* September 11, 1979, at 1. In a nut shell, the Triple A credit rating allows the state to issue bonds at a lower interest rate.

149. Keyserling, *supra* note 13, at 213.

150. *Id.* at 214.

151. *House Journal South Carolina Regular Session* 1979, vol. 1, pp. 603–14.

152. In the absence of a quorum, the only action that can be taken is adjournment.

153. *House Journal South Carolina Regular Session* 1982, vol. 2, pp. 2883–928.

154. *Id.* at 2928.

155. Keyserling, *supra* note 13, at 220.

156. *House Journal South Carolina Regular Session* 1984, vol. 1, pp. 1404–24, 1484–92.

157. *Id.* at 1557–60.

158. In 1976 the session did not end until July 23; in 1978 it ended on July 25; and in 1979 it ended August 16. In 1980 the session ended August 28.

159. *Rules of the House,* Rule 8.6 (1978).

160. Keyserling, *supra* note 13, at 194.

161. Act 146, 1979 S.C. Acts 253.

1988 South Carolina Supreme Court with Chief Justice Ernest A. Finney Jr.,
Justice David W. Harwell, Justice George T. Gregory, Justice A. Lee Chandler,
and Justice Jean H. Toal. Courtesy of the South Carolina Supreme Court.

Jean Hoefer Toal installed as chief
justice, March 23, 2000. Madam
Chief Justice received roses on the
Supreme Court steps. Courtesy of
the *State* newspaper.

South Carolina Supreme Court, 2000–2008. Justice E. C. Burnett III, Justice James E. Moore, Chief Justice Jean H. Toal, Justice John H. Waller, and Justice Costa M. Pleicones. Courtesy of the South Carolina Supreme Court.

South Carolina Supreme Court members, 2009–15. *Front row*: Justice Costa M. Pleicones, Chief Justice Jean H. Toal, Justice Donald W. Beatty; *back row*: Justice John W. Kittredge and Justice Kaye G. Hearn. Courtesy of the South Carolina Supreme Court.

The chief justice at her computer verifying her credentials in the Attorney Information System (AIS). In October 2011 she was the first South Carolina attorney to enter her information into this in-house system. Courtesy of Keith McGraw, University of South Carolina.

The Conference of Chief Justices in Charleston, 2005, hosted by Chief Justice Jean Toal. Courtesy of the South Carolina Supreme Court.

At presentation of "A Short History of Charleston" by Robert N. Rosen (*far left*), as part of the Law and Literature Program for the July 2005 Conference of Chief Justices held in Charleston, S.C.; also in attendance are attorney, now U.S. District Court judge Richard M. Gergel, U.S. District Court judge Matthew J. Perry Jr., U.S. District Court chief judge Joseph F. Anderson Jr., chief justice of the South Carolina Supreme Court Jean H. Toal, and retired chief judge of the South Carolina Court of Appeals Alexander (Alex) M. Sanders Jr. Courtesy of Mary Germack, South Carolina Bar.

Chief Justice Jean Toal being greeted by lawmakers after presenting the annual State of the Judiciary in which she lauded South Carolina as a national model for use of the Internet for handling court records, March 2011. Courtesy of the *State* newspaper.

U.S. Supreme Court justice Sandra Day O'Connor and South Carolina chief justice Jean H. Toal. Chief Justice Jean H. Toal received the first national iCivics Award from Justice Sandra Day O'Connor, United States Supreme Court, in June 2011. This iCivics application teaches middle and high school civics curriculum using computer technology. Courtesy of Gary Coleman.

Moot Court of the "Chiefs," 2006. *Left to right:* Chief Judge Joseph F. Anderson Jr., of the U.S. District Court for the District of South Carolina; Chief Judge William F. Wilkins Jr., Court of Appeals for the Fourth Circuit; Chief Justice of the United States John G. Roberts; Chief Justice Jean H. Toal, South Carolina Supreme Court; and Chief Judge Kaye G. Hearn, South Carolina Court of Appeals. Courtesy of Keith McGraw, University of South Carolina

Chief Justice Toal valets Justice Stephen Breyer, United States Supreme Court, for his conversation with Justice Antonin Scalia, United States Supreme Court, at the South Carolina Bar Association Annual Dinner, 2012. Courtesy of Keith McGraw, University of South Carolina.

Chief Justice Toal presenting the 2012 Bissell Award to Victoria Eslinger. *Left to right:* Cynthia Hall Ouzts (2012 Bissell Award Committee chair), U.S. District Court judge J. Michelle Childs, Victoria Eslinger, and Chief Justice Jean Toal, October 2012. Courtesy of Captured by Kate Photography.

Jean and Bill playing golf at St. Andrews Old Course and finishing up at the Swilcan Burn Bridge, 2012. Courtesy of James Assey Jr.

Toal family portrait, Isle of Palms, South Carolina, summer 2014. *Left to right*: Ruth Margaret Mandsager, Lilla Toal Mandsager, John Robert Mandsager, Jean Hoefer Toal, William Thomas Toal, Patrick Jacob Eisen, Peter Reuben Eisen, and Jean Toal Eisen. Courtesy of Bette Walker Photography.

Jean and Bill, Isle of Palms, South Carolina, 2014. Courtesy of Bette Walker Photography.

A New Associate Justice

First Meeting

I FIRST MET JEAN Hoefer Toal when she was still an attorney at the Belser, Baker, Barwick, Ravenel, Toal, and Bender law firm in Columbia, South Carolina. I worked at the firm as a law clerk while I was in law school. Most of my clerking assignments came from other lawyers in the firm including Cravens Ravenel, Charlie Baker, Jay Bender, and Warren Powell. Jean Toal had the reputation of being both very organized and quite busy, both as a lawyer and as a public official. Because Toal was busy as a leader in the state House of Representatives, I had little interaction with her at that particular time. Moreover at that time she was a candidate for a seat on the state Supreme Court. What I did see of her confirmed what others said about her—that she was a dynamo going back and forth from the firm to the legislature and from various courtrooms. One day, when it became apparent she would indeed be elected to the Supreme Court, she called me into her office there at the firm and asked me if I would have an interest, after law school, in becoming one of her law clerks on the court. Of course I immediately said yes, knowing the benefits of a clerkship in general, and expecting, from what I knew of her, that a clerkship for her would be especially interesting and rewarding. And I was exactly right.

A New Justice—and New Approaches

From her earliest days on the Supreme Court in 1988, Justice Toal emphasized preparation and excellence, just as she had as a lawyer and legislator. Not only was the election of the first woman to serve on the court a major change for the court, the election of the particular person—Jean Hoefer Toal—changed the court. At the time I started as a law clerk for her in 1989, the practice on the Supreme Court was that, prior to oral argument, a justice would be assigned to write the opinion for the court for each case. The general practice at the time Justice Toal ascended to the court was that *only* the assigned justice would have his clerks prepare a "bench memo" regarding that particular case. In the bench memo, the law clerk would summarize the briefings of the parties and make a recommendation and provide an analysis independent of the parties' arguments to the justice. The bench memo was not shared with the other justices and their law clerks. Justice Toal changed this practice. She required her clerks to prepare a bench memo on each and every case coming before the South Carolina Supreme Court. She wanted to be fully prepared, including receiving preparation from her law clerks, for *every* case, not just for those cases she was assigned to write. Additionally, and what is very important, she persuaded the other justices to allow their clerks to circulate the bench memo prepared for their assigned case to all other justices and their clerks. Now the bench memo process has been standardized, and the justices and their staff have access to the bench memos for every case. Although the bench memo generally recommends an outcome, all points of view on the issues raised by the appeal are presented. The bench memo has encouraged much stronger participation by the court in oral argument.

This approach has also been adopted by the court of appeals.

Justice Toal also adopted a structure to her opinions. In her opinions, she would first set forth a factual background or "facts" section, followed by a "law/analysis" section, wherein she would set forth her analysis, for the court, in a particular opinion. While this seems somewhat simple and obvious, this was not the practice of many appellate jurists when Justice Toal first assumed a seat on the court. Rather opinions were written many times as straight prose, with no structure aside from the sentence and paragraph. See, for example, *Hamm v. South Carolina Pub. Serv. Comm'n.*[1] Thus lawyers would be required to read opinions and try to ascertain where in the opinion the court transitioned merely from reciting the factual background into incorporating evidence into legal conclusions and holdings. The structure adopted by Justice Toal for her opinions eliminated this difficulty for the bench and bar. See, for example, *State v. Wilson.*[2] It is rare in modern times to see appellate court opinions in South Carolina, whether emanating from the Supreme Court or court of appeals, where this clear structure is not employed.

Justice Toal's approach impacted the oral arguments made to the court. Many judges have different views of the role and importance of oral argument. As a lawyer I have moderated several seminar panels of appellate judges throughout the United States. On these panels I have heard many appellate judges, both federal and state, report that the oral argument by counsel plays a small and even insignificant role in the ultimate decision of an appeal. Justice Toal never believed this. In fact when I have heard her speak on the topic of oral argument, she frequently cites "The Argument of an Appeal" by John W. Davis, in which the author states: "Or supposing fishes had the gift of speech, who would listen to a fisherman's weary discourse on flycasting, the shape and color of the fly, the size of the tackle, the length of the line, the merit of different rod makers and all the other tiresome stuff that fishermen talk about, if the fish himself could be induced to give his views on the most effective methods of approach."[3] After quoting the above, Justice Toal then proceeds to say that she will advise the audience on oral argument as "one of the fishes."[4] As a result of this belief in the importance of oral argument, Justice Toal is rigorously prepared and engages advocates in a conversation that she believes will assist the court in reaching the proper decision in each matter before the court.

Further, as an outstanding appellate and trial advocate as an attorney, when Justice Toal assumed her seat on the bench, she demonstrated that oral advocacy before the court would never again be merely a presentation to the court by an attorney. Instead it would be a vital exchange between the advocate and the court, probing the strengths and weaknesses of the points that each side attempted to present. Today an oral argument advocate should expect to receive questions from every member of the court sitting on the panel. While I can understand a judge ascribing to the belief that oral argument is not useful in the era when oral argument was nothing more than an oral presentation of the lawyer's brief, I agree with Justice Toal that the spirited questioning and exchange that occurs in today's oral argument is of vital importance. Without question Justice Toal has played a major role in creating today's oral advocacy environment for South Carolina appellate courts.

Another important contribution by Justice Toal is her ability to keep an open mind about a matter. When I was a young law clerk, I remember distinctly a matter in which I was assigned to write a draft affirmance opinion for Justice Toal to review regarding a trial court's decision. The Supreme Court had been unanimous in its vote with respect to the matter in conference after oral argument, and the members of the court desired to affirm. I received my assignment in earnest, but my subsequent independent research led me not once, not twice, but three times to authorities that compelled me to believe that the proper result would be to reverse the trial court decision. After sheepishly showing Justice Toal these new authorities (which supported the underlying arguments for reversal, but which were not cited by the parties), Justice Toal said words to the effect of, "I can see you don't really want to write this opinion as you were asked to do, as an affirmance. Well then, write it up as a reversal and bring it to me along with the new authorities you have found for me to consider." Justice Toal subsequently reviewed the draft and the new opinions, and at the next opportunity discussed the new authorities with the other members of the court. Ultimately the court decided to reverse the trial court. I do not chalk this up as a piece of personal persuasion by me as a young attorney. Instead I attribute this result to the ability of Justice Toal, despite being a justice on South Carolina's highest court, to maintain an open mind and to reconsider her initial conclusions in the face of the information presented, whether the ideas came from a senior colleague or a junior law clerk. Finding the "right" answer rather than "being right" in a strongly held opinion is one of Justice Toal's great strengths.

Significant Case Law

Justice Toal authored numerous important opinions as an associate Supreme Court justice. These opinions touched on diverse areas of the law, ranging from death penalty matters to consumer protection. One of these significant decisions was *Kennedy v. Columbia Lumber & Mfg. Co.,*[5] in which the court expressly noted it was in "the vanguard" of consumer protection for residential home buyers among the state courts. In *Kennedy,* a material supplier, Columbia Lumber, took title by deed to a newly constructed home when the builder could not afford to pay the supplier. Columbia Lumber did not participate in any manner in the construction of the home. Subsequently Columbia Lumber sold the home to John Kennedy. Five years later Kennedy noticed a crack in the brick veneer at the rear of the house. Two years after that, Kennedy hired an engineer, who opined that the crack was caused by a defective foundation. Kennedy then brought suit against Columbia Lumber for breach of the implied warranty of habitability.

The court, in an opinion authored by Justice Toal, held that: (1) Columbia Lumber was not liable under an implied warranty of habitability theory as Columbia Lumber sold the home in its capacity as a lender attempting to recoup losses; (2) Kennedy could bring suit against the builder on an implied warranty of service theory despite a lack of privity between Kennedy and the builder; and (3) a cause of action for negligence is available to a new home purchaser when a builder violates a legal duty—such as failing to adhere to building codes, deviating from the industry standard, or constructing a house the builder knows or should know poses a risk of serious physical harm—no matter the type of resulting damage. One significant aspect of the opinion was the creation of an exception carved out of the "economic loss rule," which would allow home purchasers to bring an action in tort for negligent construction. The traditional "economic loss rule" is that where a product defect results in damage only to the product itself, the purchaser's remedy lies in contract, and not tort. By opening these actions up to tort remedies in the case of a violation of a legal duty as set forth above (as long as that duty was not solely a contractual one), the court allowed consumers to seek damages (such as punitive damages) not available when an action is brought under contract law.

Another significant case authored by Justice Toal as a new associate justice was *State v. Bell.*[6] *Bell* was a death penalty case involving the infamous serial killer Larry Gene Bell, who kidnapped and murdered two young women, seventeen-year-old Sharon "Shari" Faye Smith and nine-year-old Debra May Helmick. For twenty-eight days, while the largest manhunt in South Carolina history took place, Bell tormented the Smith family—particularly Shari's sister Dawn Smith—by repeatedly calling the Smith household to discuss the kidnapping and to assure the family Shari was still alive. In one of the more demented phone calls, Bell described how he allowed Shari to choose the method he would use to kill her. Bell then went on to describe, in detail, how he killed Shari: suffocating her by wrapping duct tape around her head. Eventually Bell gave Dawn precise directions to the locations of both bodies. The authorities determined both women were killed by suffocation.

Bell was tried separately for each murder and received the death penalty in both instances. During his trials, Bell often blurted out bizarre comments and engaged in nonstop theatrics. His antics reached such a high level in his first trial that the judge removed Bell from the courtroom after Bell stated he would not sit quietly through the remainder of the trial.

The opinion for Bell's appeal from his second trial, for the murder of Debra May Helmick, was authored by Justice Toal. Bell appealed on several grounds: (1) that improper jurors were qualified; (2) that tapes of Bell's phone calls were improperly admitted into evidence; (3) that Bell was prejudiced by having to elect to utilize his statutory waiting period between the guilt and sentencing phase of a death penalty case in the presence of the jury; (4) that the solicitor's closing argument was improper; and (5) that the trial judge's jury instructions were improper.

Justice Toal, writing for the court, concluded that all of Bell's arguments were without merit and affirmed his conviction and death sentence. The court held that even though several of the jurors were aware of Bell's previous conviction for murder, they nonetheless were properly qualified, as all stated they could set aside any preconceived notions and fairly try the case on its merits. The court held that the tapes of phone calls between Bell and Dawn Smith were properly admitted as evidence of a common scheme or plan, and that Bell was not prejudiced by electing to utilize the statutory period in front of the jury because the judge explained the waiting period was statutorily mandated. The court also found that the solicitor's closing arguments did not improperly challenge the jurors to find in favor of sentencing Bell to death. Finally the court held that the trial judge's instructions, viewed as a whole, were proper and did not prejudice Bell.

Bell chose to be executed by the electric chair instead of lethal injection and was executed on October 4, 1996. The impact of this decision is clear:

it upheld the ultimate punishment imposed by a jury on one of the most heinous murderers in South Carolina history.

In *State v. Major*,[7] Justice Toal's opinion for the court overruled an opinion that was only three years old—*State v. Ball*.[8] *Major* involved the arrest of Jimmy Major for the sale of crack cocaine to undercover police officers in Olanta, South Carolina. At trial Major testified on direct examination that he did not sell drugs to the undercover officers on the date in question and that he did not sell drugs at all. On cross-examination Major further contended that he did not use nor did he ever possess cocaine. The solicitor then introduced Major's prior conviction for simple possession of cocaine as a crime of moral turpitude in order to impeach Major and affect his credibility with the jury.

The South Carolina Supreme Court held that the admission of this evidence was proper because the crime of simple possession of cocaine is a crime of moral turpitude. This overruled the *Ball* decision, which explicitly held that simple possession of cocaine was not a crime of moral turpitude. Justice Toal had not been on the court when *Ball* was decided. The overruling of *Ball* was not without sound reasoning. In the 1980s crack cocaine had become the scourge of the nation, and the primary focus of the "war on drugs." The United States was soon to join the hunt for Pablo Escobar—the most infamous drug kingpin in the world. As Justice Toal noted in the Major opinion, "cocaine has torn apart the very fabric of our nation." Hence a split court, with Justice Toal writing for the majority, overruled the *Ball* case (also a split opinion), thus providing law enforcement with a lasting and important new tool in the ongoing fight against drugs and the damage drugs do to the people and communities of the United States.

Justice Toal's concurrence in another death penalty case—*State v. Torrence*[9]—is significant because the court used it to abolish the doctrine of *in favorem vitae* review for capital defendants in South Carolina.[10]

The doctrine of *in favorem vitae*—meaning literally "in favor of life," had existed in South Carolina for almost two hundred years before *Torrence* ended South Carolina's adherence to it. The *in favorem vitae* doctrine required the Supreme Court to review the entire record for legal error and to consider arguments on appeal for reversal of death penalty convictions even when the arguments on appeal were never made to the trial court. The doctrine thus stood as an exception to the ordinary rules regarding error preservation (or when an appellate court should consider arguments on appeal). The court found this doctrine to be outdated, from a time when capital punishment was much more frequent and safeguards such as postconviction relief (PCR) were not available to capital defendants. Justice Toal also wrote for the court that the doctrine was subject to misuse. Trial lawyers for death penalty defendants could essentially "sandbag" and knowingly allow errors to be made at trial and fail to mention them there, when they could be corrected, instead waiting to bring the arguments up for the first time on appeal. Hence Justice Toal played an important role in the elimination of this long-standing but outdated doctrine. Michael Torrence was executed by lethal injection in 1996.

Aice v. State[11] is another noteworthy early criminal opinion authored by Justice Toal, this time concerning postconviction relief. Michael Aice was convicted of two murders in a drive-by shooting that occurred on the evening of July 5, 1980, in Columbia, South Carolina. Aice filed his first application for PCR in 1983, which was denied. Aice next attempted to obtain habeas corpus relief in federal court but was unsuccessful. He then filed a subsequent, successive application for PCR raising several grounds for relief, alleging the ineffectiveness of his first PCR counsel.

Justice Toal, writing for the majority of the court, held that a successive PCR application is not allowed on grounds that the first PCR counsel was ineffective. The court noted that the South Carolina statute governing PCR allows for successive PCR applications only if there is a sufficient reason to grant one and held that claiming ineffective counsel was not a sufficient reason. Justice Toal noted for the court that allowing a successive PCR application on those grounds could allow the case to continue almost in perpetuity. Thus, the *Aice* opinion helped clarify PCR rules in South Carolina and provided that criminal cases would have a definite end once a convicted defendant exhausted his or her statutory right to seek postconviction relief.

Justice Toal's next important opinion involved facts that have unfortunately repeated in various tragic forms and that have made national news in other states. *State v. Wilson*[12] involved a school shooting in Greenwood, South Carolina. On September 26, 1988, Jamie Wilson drove to Oakland Elementary School in Greenwood with a .22 caliber, nine-shot revolver loaded with destructive hollow-point ammunition. Wilson entered the school and made his way to the cafeteria. It was lunch time, and the room was full of children and adults. Wilson opened fire, selecting his victims at random. Once Wilson had fired all nine rounds he left the cafeteria and entered a restroom where he reloaded his firearm. Wilson then proceeded to a third-grade classroom, where he again fired all nine rounds from his revolver. He then climbed out a window to make his escape. A teacher confronted Wilson before he could leave the school grounds and ordered Wilson to remain still with his hands up. Wilson complied and was arrested when the police arrived. Two little girls, both aged eight, were killed in the shooting.

Wilson was charged with two counts of murder, nine counts of assault and battery with intent to kill, and one count of illegally carrying a firearm. He pled guilty but mentally ill (GBMI) to the charges, which becomes a mitigating factor by law to be considered by the court when deciding whether to impose the death sentence. Wilson elected to have the sentencing phase tried by the judge without a jury. While the judge—the Honorable James Moore, who would later join Justice Toal on the South Carolina Supreme Court—did take into account the mitigating factor that Wilson pled GBMI, along with three other mitigating factors, he sentenced Wilson to death for each of the two murders.

Wilson argued that the General Assembly never contemplated a defendant who pled GBMI being sentenced to death, but Justice Toal, writing for the court, held the General Assembly intended that GBMI defendants be sentenced to death in appropriate cases. The trial judge concluded that the heinous nature of this crime made the death sentence appropriate in this instance even though Wilson pled GBMI. The court further held that a death sentence for Wilson did not violate the prohibition on cruel or unusual punishment, nor was it a disproportionate or excessive sentence.

Perhaps more important, the court in *Wilson* rejected the adoption of the "irresistible impulse" test for insanity. Wilson argued that when a defendant was acting under an "irresistible impulse" or compulsion, it would be cruel and unusual to execute him for his crimes. The court noted that South Carolina adhered to the older "*M'Naghten* test" for insanity, which is whether the defendant knew his acts were morally or legally wrong. Justice Toal, writing for the court, examined the systems of all fifty states and analyzed those that had adopted the "irresistible impulse" test for insanity. She noted the various problems with that test and declined to read it as constitutionally required by the cruel and unusual punishment prohibition of the federal or state constitutions. Noting that culpability related to knowing that what one was doing was wrong, and that the death penalty fulfilled the punishment goal of "retribution" under the facts, the court declined to overturn the trial judge's death sentence decree. Jamie Wilson remains on death row as of this writing.

In *Lucas v. S.C. Coastal Council*,[13] the court considered whether a state statute limiting construction in certain beach and dune areas effected a regulatory taking of such properties. Justice Toal, writing for the majority, concluded that the state's regulation of a valuable public resource—namely the beach and dune areas of South Carolina's shores—to prevent erosion and destruction of that resource was not a regulatory taking of property for which compensation was required. The United States Supreme Court subsequently granted certiorari and in its opinion conceded that it had previously eschewed any "set formula" or bright line test for what constituted a compensable regulatory taking.[14] Nevertheless the court stated there were "good reasons for our frequently expressed belief that when the owner of real property has been called on to sacrifice all economically beneficial

uses in the name of the common good, that is, to leave his property economically idle, he has suffered a taking."[15] The court concluded that construction on oceanfront property was not a "noxious" use or a nuisance
(either of which may be proscribed without effecting a taking), and thus
the state statute prohibiting all economically beneficial uses of the land
was an impermissible, compensable taking.

Justice Toal penned a noteworthy opinion shaping the interpretation
and application of the Unfair Trade Practices Act (UTPA) in *Ward v. Dick
Dyer & Associates, Inc.*[16] In *Ward* the Supreme Court considered whether
buyers could bring an unfair trade practice claim against a car dealership
for its alleged failure to disclose to the buyers that the car they purchased
had been previously involved in an accident. In finding the buyers could
bring an action against the car dealership despite its regulation by a South
Carolina regulatory agency, the court held the UTPA's "regulated activity"
exemption does not exempt every act or transaction that is in any way regulated by the state or federal government (which would be nearly every act
or transaction imaginable) but rather "is intended to exclude those actions
or transactions which are *allowed or authorized* by regulatory agencies or
other statutes."[17]

In another opinion authored by Justice Toal, the court set important new
precedent (and overruled prior case law) regarding the subject matter jurisdiction of the state's trial courts.[18] Before *Dove v. Gold Kist, Inc.*, the court's
precedent had held that the only court with subject matter jurisdiction to
hear an appeal from the Workers' Compensation Commission was the circuit court of the county where the accident occurred or where the employer
has his principle place of business. In overruling this prior case law, Justice
Toal's opinion emphasized the important distinction between subject matter
jurisdiction and venue, noting that these "terms are not synonymous."[19] The
opinion stated, "There is but one Circuit Court in South Carolina, with uniform subject matter jurisdiction 'throughout the State.'"[20]

Justice Toal, for the court, again molded the interpretation and application of the UTPA in *Daisy Outdoor Advertising Co. v. Abbott.*[21] In *Daisy* a
dispute arose between competition outdoor advertisers when one of them
erected billboards so as to block the view of the other's billboards. In determining whether the plaintiff had stated a cause of action under the UTPA,
the question was whether the defendant's actions had an adverse effect on
the public interest (rather than being merely a private dispute not affecting
the public). The court clarified that the potential for repetition of the
unfair or deceptive conduct was itself sufficient to satisfy the requisite
element of public impact and "expressly reject[ed] any rigid, bright line test
that delineates in minute detail exactly what a plaintiff must show to satisfy the potential for repetition/public impact prong of the UTPA test."[22]

In *Soil Remediation Co. v. Nu-Way Environmental, Inc.*[23] Justice Toal, writing for the court, held that the statutory requirements regarding notice of a contractual arbitration agreement were clear and must be applied according to their literal meaning. The notice provision in the *Soil Remediation* contract did not meet the statutory requirement because, although it was laser-printed and written in all capital letters on the first page of the contract, the statute required notice provisions to be typed in *underlined* capital letters, or rubber-stamped prominently, on the first page of the contract. Applying this statutory requirement strictly and literally, the court held that no variation on the arbitration notice was acceptable.

Justice Toal returned to the topic of arbitration in *Zabinski v. Bright Acres Associates,*[24] holding that the Federal Arbitration Act (FAA) controlled arbitrability of a dispute over distribution of partnership assets, despite the inclusion of a provision in the arbitration agreement stating that South Carolina law governed and despite the fact that the arbitration agreement was not enforceable under state law. She noted that while parties are free to enter into a contract requiring arbitration under state law rather than the FAA, the FAA will preempt any state law that completely invalidates the parties' agreement to arbitrate.[25]

In *Hodges v. Rainey,*[26] then governor Hodges brought an action in the original jurisdiction of the Supreme Court seeking to clarify his statutory authority to remove executive branch officials. Specifically Hodges had, by executive order, removed Rainey from the Board of Trustees of the South Carolina Public Service Commission (Santee Cooper). Rainey refused to relinquish his office, arguing that the statute granting the governor the power to remove state officers from their positions did not apply to him. Justice Toal, writing for the majority, concluded that Hodges had the authority to remove Rainey from his position. This conclusion was grounded in large part on the fact that the statutory grant of the removal power specifically limited that power in regard to certain agencies and departments but did not include Santee Cooper on that list.[27] The court also rejected Rainey's argument that the statute authorizing the governor to remove officials at his discretion conflicted with Santee Cooper's enabling legislation, which allowed for the removal of board members only for cause. The court ruled that the two statutes could be read in harmony with one another.[28] In addition the court concluded that Santee Cooper's directors have many indicia of public office holders (e.g., appointed by the governor, commissioned, and their duties defined by law) and that Santee Cooper is considered a state agency under statutory law, and thus Santee Cooper was a "state agency" for purposes of the governor's removal power.[29]

In *Kiriakides v. Atlas Food Systems & Services, Inc.,*[30] the court established an analytical framework for determining when majority shareholders in a closely held corporation have acted oppressively within the meaning of the statute authorizing judicial dissolution of a corporation. *Kiriakides* involved a family-owned close corporation, where the oldest brother, Alex, was the majority shareholder. His siblings John and Louise, the plaintiffs in the case, owned minority shares of the corporation. John and Louise brought a lawsuit against Alex and the corporation seeking, among other things, judicial dissolution for shareholder oppression. In establishing the proper considerations for finding oppression, Justice Toal, writing for the majority, observed that "the terms 'oppressive' and 'unfairly prejudicial' are elastic terms whose meaning varies with the circumstances presented in a particular case."[31] She also noted this was a fact-sensitive review and should therefore be determined through a "case-by-case analysis, supplemented by various factors which may be indicative of oppressive behavior."[32] Although the court declined to set out specific factors in *Kiriakides*, it observed several commonly considered ones including: "eliminating minority shareholders from directorate and excluding them from employment[,] . . . failure to enforce contracts for the benefit of the corporation[, and] withholding information from minority shareholders."[33]

As a new justice, Jean Toal was also not afraid to pen a dissent where she felt the circumstances warranted it. Her dissent in *Wise v. Broadway* is illustrative.[34] *Wise* involved a car accident where one motorist ran into the back of another when the car slowed to turn into a gas station. The defendant was guilty of following a car too closely, a violation of South Carolina traffic law. The majority sided with the plaintiff and held that a violation of a statute is evidence of recklessness that allows the issue of punitive damages to be submitted to a jury.

Justice Toal dissented, reasoning that normally, a jury may consider negligence per se, along with other factors, to determine whether someone acted willfully or negligently. But when the evidence permits only one reasonable inference—as the evidence in the case before the court did— willfulness becomes a question of law for the judge, and not a question of fact for the jury. Furthermore punitive damages must be proven by the higher standard of clear and convincing evidence. In Justice Toal's view, the mere violation of a statute, without more, was insufficient to prove punitive damages by clear and convincing evidence.

Similarly Justice Toal penned a vigorous dissent in *Johnson v. Collins Entertainment Co.*[35] In *Johnson* plaintiffs sought injunctive relief and damages from the owners and operators of video poker machines, arguing in part that these machines were being operated in violation of the state constitution's prohibition on lotteries. After the suit was removed to the federal district court, the district court certified two questions to the South Carolina Supreme Court, namely (1) what factors and standards should be

used to determine whether a particular activity is a prohibited lottery, and
(2) whether particular machines constitute prohibited lotteries. The majority ruled that because video poker machines did not involve a drawing,
tickets, or other indicium of entitlement to a prize, those machines were
not lotteries, and thus the particular type of machines at issue were not
prohibited lotteries. Justice Burnett disagreed in a lengthy dissent relying
on a different definition of lotteries. Justice Toal agreed with the dissent
but nonetheless wrote a separate dissent to note that the federal district
court was not bound by majority's opinion that the machines at issue were
permissible. She noted in conclusion that despite the divisive nature of the
issue of video poker—both in the public discourse and in the court's ruling—her "profound disagreement with my brothers in the majority is
matched by my enduring respect for their sincerity and integrity."[36]

Summation

As the brief summary of these few cases demonstrates, Chief Justice Toal
authored many significant opinions in her first years on the court as an
associate justice. The decisions ranged from death penalty cases replete
with shocking and disturbing facts to those involving home defects and car
wrecks. Regardless, Justice Toal's early opinions created lasting impacts on
South Carolina's criminal and civil justice systems and laws. Being the
first female justice on the Supreme Court did not cause Justice Toal to be
tentative in her work for the court. Rather she took on complex cases and
staked out concurring and dissenting positions from the start in what
would be a lengthy and illustrious judicial career.

NOTES

1. 291 S.C. 119, 352 S.E.2d 426 (1987).
2. 306 S.C. 498, 413 S.E.2d 19 (1992).
3. 3 J. App. Prac. & Process 745 (2001) (reprint of 1940 ABA Journal article).
4. She attributes the metaphor of an appellate judge as "one of the fishes" to Justice
Robert H. Jackson, "Advocacy before the Supreme Court," 37 ABAJ 801 (1951).
5. 299 S.C. 335, 384 S.E.2d 730 (1989).
6. 302 S.C. 18, 393 S.E.2d 364 (1990).
7. 301 S.C. 181, 391 S.E.2d 235 (1990).
8. 292 S.C. 71, 354 S.E.2d 906 (1987).
9. 305 S.C. 45, 406 S.E.2d 315 (1991).
10. Michael Torrence lured Charlie Bush to the Torrence household, where Michael
robbed Bush and then strangled him with a dog leash. Michael then went to Bush's
motel room where he stabbed Dennis Lollis nineteen times. Michael Torrence was
convicted of armed robbery, burglary, and the murders of Charlie Bush and Dennis
Lollis. Michael received a life sentence for the murder of Charlie Bush and a sentence
of death for the murder of Dennis Lollis.
11. 305 S.C. 448, 409 S.E.2d 392 (1991).
12. 306 S.C. 498, 413 S.E.2d 19 (1992).

13. 304 S.C. 376, 404 S.E.2d 895 (1991), reversed by *Lucas v. S.C. Coastal Council*, 505 U.S. 1003 (1992).

14. 505 U.S. at 1015.

15. *Id.* at 1019.

16. 304 S.C. 152, 403 S.E.2d 310 (1991).

17. 304 S.C. at 155, 403 S.E.2d at 312 (emphasis added).

18. *See Dove v. Gold Kist, Inc.*; 314 S.C. 235, 442 S.E.2d 598 (1994).

19. 314 S.C. at 237, 442 S.E.2d at 600 (citations omitted).

20. *Id.* at 238, 442 S.E.2d at 600 (citations omitted) (emphasis in original).

21. 322 S.C. 489, 473 S.E.2d 47 (1996).

22. 322 S.C. at 497, 473 S.E.2d at 51.

23. 323 S.C. 454, 476 S.E.2d 149 (1996).

24. 346 S.C. 580, 553 S.E.2d 110 (2001).

25. 346 S.C. at 592, 553 S.E.2d at 116.

26. 341 S.C. 79, 533 S.E.2d 578 (2000).

27. *See Hodges*, 341 S.C. at 87, 533 S.E.2d at 582 ("The fact that the Santee Cooper Board of Directors was not included in the list of exclusions implies that the General Assembly intended for section 1-3-240 (B) [i.e., the broad removal power] to apply to the Board.").

28. *Id.* at 88–89, 533 S.E.2d at 582–83.

29. *Id.* at 90–92, 533 S.E.2d at 583–84.

30. 343 S.C. 587, 541 S.E.2d 257 (2001).

31. 343 at 602, 541 S.E.2d at 266.

32. *Id.* at 603, 541 S.E.2d at 266.

33. *Id.* at 605 n. 28, 541 S.E.2d at 267 n. 28.

34. 315 S.C. 273, 433 S.E.2d 857 (1993).

35. 333 S.C. 96, 120–24, 508 S.E.2d 575, 588–90 (1998).

36. *Id.* 333 S.C. at 123, 508 S.E.2d at 589 (Toal, J. dissenting).

JUDGE RICHARD MARK GERGEL

An Unrelenting Judicial Warrior in South Carolina's Video Poker Wars

FOR THOSE UNFAMILIAR WITH South Carolina's brief and traumatic experience with essentially unregulated gambling in the 1990s, it may be difficult to fathom the level of widespread social costs or the intense battles that developed in the political and judicial arenas as efforts were made to reign in and abolish the video poker industry. As a litigator on behalf of addicted gamblers who sought to ban the industry, I battled this extremely well-funded and skillfully represented industry, which found no legal issue too small or insignificant to litigate until "the last dog barked." Video poker–related lawsuits filled court dockets, and judges adjudicating these cases were under intense pressure. In these video poker wars, no state court judge was more stalwart in upholding the rule of law or insightful in understanding the insidious nature of this industry than Jean Hoefer Toal.[1]

Dating from the earliest days of the colony, gambling had been prohibited in South Carolina, and there appeared in modern South Carolina history no real public interest in allowing casino gambling or other traditional games of chance to operate in the state.[2] Despite clear legal prohibitions under state law to any form of gambling, there had long been illicit gambling payoffs with pin ball machines and unauthorized high-stakes card games that were periodically the subject of criminal prosecutions.

With the development of personal computers in the 1980s, law enforcement in South Carolina began locating and seizing illegal video gambling devices that sought to replicate slot machines and traditional card games such as stud poker and black jack. These new gambling devices, which came to be known popularly as "video poker," soon developed a well-earned reputation of producing a high degree of compulsive gambling and addiction. *Time* magazine dubbed the machines the "crack cocaine" of gambling.[3] With the compulsive use of the machines by many of the players, the video poker machines proved to be wildly profitable, and many owners of the devices began actively (but quietly) pursuing methods to make the activity lawful in South Carolina.

During the tail end of the 1986 state budget bill process, the chairman of the Senate Finance Committee, Jack Lindsay, slipped into the voluminous bill changes in state gambling laws that exempted "coin operated non-payout machines with a free play feature" from the previous strict ban of all gambling devices in South Carolina.[4] U.S. district judge Joseph Anderson would later describe the Lindsay Amendment as a "little noticed, highly technical and slightly ambiguous amendment" that fundamentally altered gambling law in South Carolina.[5]

Soon thereafter, various owners of video poker machines began asserting that their gambling devices were lawful so long as any payoffs from the machines were paid by humans rather than the machines themselves. The issue came to a head before the South Carolina Supreme Court in 1991 when a grocery store operator by the name of Terry Blackmon challenged his arrest for operating a gambling house because of the presence of video poker devices on his premises. A reluctant South Carolina Supreme Court, noting the recent statutory changes, held in *State v. Blackmon*[6] that the defendant could not be prosecuted because his nonpayout gambling device was now lawful in South Carolina. The court noted that the General Assembly was aware that cash payouts were being made based on winnings on these machines and had refused to amend or repeal the law.[7] Associate Justice Toal, who had been elected to the court three years earlier and was its most junior member, joined in the unanimous opinion in *Blackmon*.

The *Blackmon* decision removed the threat of criminal prosecution for possession of video gambling devices, and over the ensuing months unregulated video gambling suddenly appeared across South Carolina. It seemed that every convenience store and bar in the state now had poker machines, and it became common to see gamblers sitting in front of machines for hours staring glassy-eyed into the video screens. For the first time, reports of widespread gambling addiction surfaced, and a number of Gambling Anonymous chapters were formed in the state.

The first of many gambling addiction–related cases came before the South Carolina Supreme Court in 1993 in *Berkebile v. Outen*.[8] In *Berkebile*, a gambler sought to recover her losses from playing video poker using an old state statute, dating from 1712, that allowed unsuccessful gamblers to recover damages for any losses incurred.[9] The gambling operator claimed that because the gambling activity in question was now lawful, it would make no sense to allow an unsuccessful gambler to recover video poker losses through a lawsuit. Justice Toal, writing for an unanimous court, rejected that defense and noted that the statute in question did not differentiate between legal and illegal gambling. Justice Toal observed that any changes in the law narrowing its provisions should be done by the General Assembly and not the court.[10] The *Berkebile* decision reflected the ambiguous legal status of video gambling in South Carolina and made clear to the industry that Associate Justice Toal was not particularly sympathetic or impressed with their legal arguments. Owners of gambling devices were now reaping massive profits, and they turned some of their newfound wealth into efforts to persuade the General Assembly to change the state's gambling laws to explicitly authorize their activities. The General Assembly proved reluctant to make South Carolina wide open to the gambling industry, but many legislators recognized that the present unregulated status of the industry was also unsustainable. Neither the pro- nor antigambling advocates had the political strength to have their way with the legislature, and efforts were made to reach some middle ground. This middle ground was accomplished in what became known as the Video Game Machine Act (VGMA), a 1993 statute that authorized the gambling machines but limited the amount that could be won to $125.00 in any twenty-four-hour period.[11] The VGMA further required that the devices be allowed only in locations that earned a "substantial portion" of their gross revenue from nongambling sources and allowed counties to vote to allow or deny video gambling. The VGMA reflected an intent to authorize low-stakes gambling in established businesses as a form of entertainment in those communities that voted to authorize it.

The VGMA represented to the gambling industry only a partial victory. On one hand, the legal status of the gambling devices was no longer in question, and local merchants and bar owners possessing the machines needed not fear criminal prosecution. On the other hand, the $125.00 payout limit was unacceptable because no one would wager thousands of dollars simply to win $125.00. As Professors Bridwell and Quinn observed in their definitive article on the history of the South Carolina video gambling industry, the gambling operators resolved simply to ignore the $125.00 limit and boldly advertised on the face of their machines jackpots of $10,000 and higher.[12] This willful disregard for the payout limits adopted in the VGMA would ultimately prove to be the industry's undoing.

Shortly after the adoption of the VGMA, the gambling industry began waging a legal war against a number of the provisions in the act that they had previously accepted to obtain adoption of the law. First, they persuaded United States district judge Ross Anderson in *Reyelt v. South Carolina Tax Commission*[13] in November 1993 to declare as unconstitutionally vague the provision of the VGMA that limited gambling devices to locations that derived a substantial portion of their revenue from nongambling sources. This decision led to the widespread creation of video gambling casinos that had clearly not been contemplated under the VGMA. Second, the industry successfully challenged, in *Martin v. Condon*,[14] the provision that allowed counties to vote up or down on video gambling, persuading a divided South Carolina Supreme Court that this amounted to unlawful local legislation. Justice Toal dissented, asserting that South Carolina had a long history of local regulation of alcohol and gambling.[15] The *Martin* decision overturned video gambling bans in twelve counties, and video gambling now extended to every community in the state regardless of local preference. With their successes in the General Assembly and in the courts, and their willingness to flagrantly disregard the $125.00 payout limit, the poker operators saw their business explode across the state. By 1999 South Carolina had more than seven thousand retail gambling locations and thirty-six thousand video gambling devices, second only to Nevada. The industry's revenue in 1999 was more than $3 billion, and its reported profits were $835 million.[16] The social costs associated with this massive increase in gambling activity were great: reports of parents gambling away their children's college accounts, employees embezzling funds from employers to feed their gambling habits, and Gambling Anonymous chapters overflowing with new members. One young mother, who was an addicted gambler, was reported to have allowed her infant child to die in an overheated automobile on a hot summer day while she played video poker in an air-conditioned facility. As an article in *Harper's Magazine* reported in August 1999, South Carolina's experience with video gambling "is a tale of how, in almost no time at all, a bunch of gas-station owners, juke box operators and barkeeps used lawsuits, strong-arm lobbying, dead-of-the-night legislation, and just plain deception to transform a small time illegal gambling business into a multi-billion dollar legal one."[17]

In June 1997 a lawsuit was brought in the Richland County Court of Common Pleas, *Johnson v. Collins Entertainment Company, Inc.*, on behalf of a class of addicted gamblers and their family members. The suit alleged that the state's major video gambling operators were willfully violating the $125.00 daily payout limit and unlawfully inducing persons to gamble with promises of payouts of tens of thousands of dollars. Claims were made under the state's Unfair Trade Practices Act (UTPA) and the federal Racketeer Influenced and Corrupt Organizations Act (RICO). The plaintiffs also asserted that video gambling constituted a lottery prohibited by the South Carolina Constitution. The plaintiffs requested legal and equitable relief, including an injunction prohibiting device operators from offering or paying cash amounts greater than $125.00. The plaintiffs included the father of the child who had died in the overheated vehicle while his mother played video poker. I was part of the legal team that brought these claims.

Shortly after filing our claims in state court, the defendants removed the case to federal court because the plaintiffs had asserted a federal statutory claim under RICO. This move was reportedly made because the gambling industry lawyers feared Justice Toal and her apparently growing influence over her colleagues on the South Carolina Supreme Court on matters related to video gambling. The case was assigned to United States district judge Joseph Anderson, who had been appointed to the federal bench in the District of South Carolina in 1986 at age thirty-six, making him, at the time, one of the youngest federal judges in America. Judge Anderson had graduated number one in his class in high school, college, and law school. Serving with a lifetime appointment, Judge Anderson was not the slightest bit intimidated by the video gambling industry, its lawyers, or its powerful political allies. One of my cocounsel later observed that the poker industry's removal of the case to federal court to avoid Justice Toal and the subsequent assignment of the case to Judge Anderson was like going from the frying pan into the fire.

Although the plaintiffs in *Johnson* requested that Judge Anderson initially address a motion for preliminary injunction regarding the widespread practice of offering and paying jackpots of greater than $125.00, he thought that the threshold question was whether video gambling constituted a lottery prohibited by the South Carolina Constitution. He certified the lottery question to the South Carolina Supreme Court, forcing the video poker lawyers to again contend with Justice Toal and face the potential of instant death if the outcome was not favorable. In what was certainly a near-death experience for the poker industry, the South Carolina Supreme Court, in a three-to-two vote, ruled on November 19, 1998, that video gambling was not a lottery under the South Carolina Constitution.[18] Justice Toal and Justice Burnett dissented. In her dissent Justice Toal stated that she "profoundly disagree[d]" with the majority decision and urged Judge Anderson to disregard the majority view and find independently that the gambling devices under question were lotteries prohibited by the South Carolina Constitution.[19]

The *Johnson* case returned to Judge Anderson's court, and he then turned his attention to the $125.00 payout issue. After the submission and review of voluminous discovery in the case and eight hours of oral argument, Judge Anderson issued an order on April 28, 1999, granting the plaintiffs summary judgment on the unlawful payout issue. Judge Anderson found the violations of law by the gambling industry "flagrant, common and pervasive" and entered a permanent injunction enjoining all payouts greater than $125.00 per day or offering on the face of any machine a payout amount greater than $125.00.[20] He also made it clear that violations of his order could result in sanctions for contempt.

The Anderson injunction sent the video gambling industry reeling, as their business dramatically decreased with the firm enforcement of the $125.00 payout limits. One person observed that it was like trying to sell beer without any alcohol. Again the pro- and antigambling forces did not seem to have enough political strength to pass legislation, but now the status quo (defined by Judge Anderson's injunction) was unsustainable to the gambling industry. Recognizing that they had a strong hand, particularly after the federal litigation disclosed widespread legal violations by the poker industry, the antigambling forces pushed to permanently ban video gambling. Progambling forces sought a binding public referendum, which the antigambling forces rejected because it was likely unlawful under South Carolina law. Finally, desperate to escape the stranglehold of Judge Anderson's injunction, the gambling industry agreed to a bill that banned video poker effective July 1, 2000, allowed for a referendum on the issue in November 1999 that, if passed, would allow video poker to continue after June 30, 2000, and allow an increase in payouts to $500 per hand, and provided a severability clause that made clear that, if the referendum was unlawful, the industry would be banned on July 1, 2000.[21]

Shortly after the General Assembly adopted the video poker legislation in June 1999, the South Carolina Supreme Court addressed an appeal of a dismissal of an addicted gambler's state court lawsuit, which raised some of the same UTPA and RICO issues that had been addressed by Judge Anderson in *Johnson*. In an opinion authored by Justice Moore and joined by all five justices, the South Carolina Supreme Court in *Gentry v. Yonce*[22] firmly and unequivocally endorsed Judge Anderson's interpretation of state law regarding the $125.00 payout limit and found the plaintiff had asserted potentially legally valid claims under the UTPA and RICO. This unanimous decision was an ominous sign for the poker industry lawyers because no longer was Justice Toal a dissenter; she was now part of a firm and likely unmovable majority.[23]

Confronted with a difficult legal environment in the state and federal courts, the poker industry turned its attention to the November 1999 referendum as essentially its only means of survival. But public sentiment was moving in the wrong direction for the industry. In August 1999 the state Chamber of Commerce joined a coalition of civic, business, and religious groups supporting a permanent ban on video poker, and a September 1999 poll showed that nearly 80 percent of the voters with an opinion on the subject opposed the video gambling industry.[24] Leaders of the state's Baptist, Methodist, and AME churches publicly endorsed a ban on video gambling, and daily newspapers, particularly the *State*, regularly editorialized against the industry.

In the face of this meltdown of public support for the video gambling industry, a lawsuit was filed by a video poker operator in Greenville County seeking to enjoin the November referendum. The South Carolina Supreme Court took original jurisdiction over the case and scheduled immediate oral argument. The case raised the issues of whether a public referendum was lawful under South Carolina law, and, if not, was the video poker industry effectively banned on July 1, 2000? During oral argument Justice Toal vigorously questioned the video gambling industry's lawyer in the case, making it clear she believed that the June 30, 2000, ban on video poker was severable from the provision providing for a public referendum. On October 14, 1999, two days after hearing oral argument, an unanimous South Carolina Supreme Court held in *Joytime Distributors and Amusement Co., Inc. v. State*[25] that the scheduled referendum was an unlawful delegation of legislative authority and was severable from the portion of the act banning video gambling after June 30, 2000. In sum the *Joytime* decision was an announcement that video gambling would die in South Carolina on June 30, 2000.

The morning after *Joytime* was issued the *State* newspaper called the decision "poetic justice" for an industry that had "slithered into South Carolina through surreptitious legislation" and now faced extinction as a result of a lawsuit brought by a video poker operator.[26] An editorial cartoon by Robert Ariail in the *State* depicted the video poker industry, drawn as a Mafia hoodlum, laying on the ground fatally shot and a car full of South Carolina Supreme Court justices driving by, one with a gun. The trigger person was depicted as Justice Toal and the cartoon was titled "Drive by Ruling."

But the drama was not over regarding video gambling in South Carolina. On June 30, 2000, state circuit judge Gerald Smoak issued an ex parte order enjoining the statute one day before the effective date of the ban and filed it in the Jasper County courthouse. The South Carolina Supreme Court learned of the circuit court order late in the afternoon of June 30, and now Chief Justice Toal presided over a telephone hearing from her kitchen table later that evening. On the motion of the attorney general, the trial judge's order was vacated by a handwritten order prepared by the chief justice with the oral assent of two other justices participating in the emergency hearing. Then, escorted to the Supreme Court building by Robert Stewart, the chief of the South Carolina Law Enforcement Division (SLED), Chief Justice Toal filed the handwritten order shortly before midnight on June 30, 2000.

The following morning SLED agents crossed the state enforcing the ban on video gambling. Agents walked into a Jasper County convenience store on the morning of July 1, 2000, and observed several operating video gambling devices. They advised the owner that video gambling was now illegal in South Carolina and that she needed to unplug her machines. The owner then handed the agents a copy of Judge Smoak's order enjoining the enforcement of the video gambling ban. The SLED agents handed the owner a copy of Chief Justice Toal's handwritten order vacating Smoak's order. The perplexed owner said that the handwritten document did not "look like no order to me" and refused to unplug her machines. The agents then called for backup and hauled the machines away. The curtain had closed on video gambling in South Carolina.

NOTES

1. Jean Hoefer Toal was elected an associate justice of the South Carolina Supreme Court on March 17, 1988, and was elected chief justice on March 23, 2000.

2. For a definitive history of gambling in South Carolina, see R. Randall Bridwell and Frank I. Quinn, "From Mad Joy to Misfortune: The Merger of Law and Politics in the World of Gambling," 72 Miss. L.J. 565 (Winter 2002); *Johnson v. Collins Entm't Co., Inc.,* 88 F. Supp. 2d 499, 502 (D.S.C. 1999), *vacated by* 199 F.3d 710 (4th Cir. 1999).

3. Viveca Novak, "They Call It Video Crack," *Time,* June 1, 1998.

4. The budget proviso was codified at S.C. Code Ann. § 12-21-2710 (Supp. 1998).

5. *Johnson,* 88 F. Supp. 2d at 502.

6. 403 S.E.2d 660 (S.C. 1991).

7. *Id.* at 274 n. 2.

8. 426 S.E.2d 760 (S.C. 1993).

9. S.C. Code Ann. § 32-1-10 (Supp. 1990).

10. *Berkebile,* 426 S.E.2d at 763.

11. S.C. Code Ann. § 12-21-2804 (A) (Supp. 1998).

12. Bridwell, *supra* note 2, at 580–81.

13. No. 6: 93-1491 (D.S.C. November 15, 1993).

14. 478 S.E.2d 272 (S.C. 1996).

15. *Id.* at 275.

16. Bridwell, *supra* note 2, at 583.

17. David Plotz, "Busted Flush," *Harper's Magazine,* August 1999.

18. *Johnson v. Collins Entm't Co., Inc.,* 508 S.E.2d 575 (S.C. 1998).

19. *Id.* at 588–90.

20. *Johnson v. Collins Entm't Co., Inc.,* 88 F. Supp. 2d 499, 518–19, 523–25 (D.S.C. 1999), *vacated by* 199 F.3d 710 (4th Cir. 1999).

21. Act 125, 1999 S.C. Acts; Bridwell, *supra* note 2, at 597–98.

22. 522 S.E.2d 137 (S.C. 1999).

23. The Fourth Circuit reversed Judge Anderson's decision in *Johnson,* finding that he should have abstained from interpreting state law questions relating to gambling. *Johnson v. Collins Entm't Co., Inc.,* 199 F.3d 710 (4th Cir. 1999). An effort to reverse the panel's decision *en banc* failed with a four-to-four tie and South Carolina's three judges on the Fourth Circuit all abstaining from the decision. Judge Motz wrote a vigorous dissent to the denial of *en banc* review, finding that it was mystifying to her how the defendants could remove the case to federal court and then assert abstention claims. 204 F.3d 573, 577–80 (4th Cir. 2000). Judge Anderson subsequently certified the state law questions to the South Carolina Supreme Court, which agreed with all his state law interpretations in a decision authored by Chief Justice Toal. The chief justice also stated in the order that Judge Anderson had been correct in his earlier decision not to certify these issues to the South Carolina Supreme Court, which was a clear rejoinder to the decision by the Fourth Circuit. *Johnson v. Collins Entm't Co., Inc.,* 564 S.E.2d 653 (S.C. 2002).

24. *State* (Columbia, S.C.), August 21, 1999, *State* (Columbia, S.C.), September 26, 1999.

25. 528 S.E.2d 647 (S.C. 1999).

26. *State* (Columbia, S.C.), October 15, 1999.

ROBERT L. FELIX

Toal on Torts (1987–2014)

The life of the law has not been logic: it has been experience. The felt necessities of the time, the prevalent moral and political theories, intuitions of public policy, avowed or unconscious, even the prejudices which judges share with their fellow-men, have had a good deal more to do than the syllogism in determining the rules by which men should be governed.

Oliver Wendell Holmes Jr., *The Common Law* (1881)

THE PURPOSE OF THIS essay is to consider several areas of tort or tort-related law in which the opinions of Justice Jean Hoefer Toal have had an impact on the exposition and development of this area of law.[1] Her opinions in other areas are of course an appropriate subject for comment, but to one who has followed Tort Law for some time, these invite particular attention.

Tort law focuses on civil cases that determine responsibility for personal injury and property damage inflicted by one person on another. The boundaries of tort law may narrow or expand over time and may overlap with other areas such as contract or property law. Torts may also involve multistate situations that require choice between the law of one state or another before the controversy can be resolved.

The areas of tort and tort-related law that this article will examine are improved real estate, the economic loss rule, defamation, and the public duty rule.

Improved Real Estate

South Carolina has a well-developed body of case law on the development of liability for injury or damage caused by defective construction in improved real estate, particularly residential construction. Issues regarding the liability of the various parties involved in home construction are the subject of well-reasoned opinions.[2]

Justice Toal's opinion for the court in *Kennedy v. Columbia Lumber &
Manufacturing Company, Inc.*[3] addresses two important aspects of liability
for defective home construction. The first concerns which persons in the
chain of design, material supply, building, financing, marketing, sale are
liable for injury or damage caused by defective construction. The second
concerns whether and on what basis the economic loss rule, which is
addressed in detail later, precludes an award in tort damages for pure economic loss. The two issues are interrelated.

Kennedy involved a homeowner's action for breach of implied warranty
of habitability against a lumber supplier from whom he bought his house.
After discovering a crack in the brick veneer at the back of the house,
caused by a defective foundation, the homeowner brought suit. The supplier had taken title to the house after the builder was unable to pay the
supplier and sold the house for an amount insufficient to satisfy the debt
owed. The court held that the supplier could not be held liable under an
implied warranty of habitability theory because the supplier sold the house
only in its capacity as lender attempting to recoup its loss. Justice Toal first
noted that the *Kennedy* case fell between two earlier cases involving
whether lenders in the pattern of development, construction, and sale of
residential housing could be held liable to the immediate or subsequent
purchaser for defective building. None of the possibilities for lender liability were found in this case, and therefore the supplier could not be found
responsible. "Columbia Lumber became a seller only by virtue of the fact
that it took a deed in lieu of foreclosure [on its mechanic's lien on the property for the outstanding debt]."[4]

Noting that *Kennedy* is the "latest in a series of cases we have concerning theories of liability in residential housing," Justice Toal examined a
recent decision by the court of appeals on comparable facts, *Carolina
Winds Owners' Association v. Joe Harden Builder,*[5] which held that because
the builder was not the seller, he was not liable in warranty and that the
economic loss rule prevented the imposition of tort liability on the builder
if the damage suffered is only to the product itself. *Carolina Winds* also
held that tort liability lies only for damage to other property or for personal
injury. Speaking for the court, Justice Toal stated: "To the extent herein
indicated, we express our disapproval and rejection of that opinion."[6] She
observed that the law involving the purchase of a new house had been in
"a state of flux since the early nineteenth century." Conceding that the
opinion of the court of appeals "appears to be a seamless web of proper
legal analysis," Justice Toal noted that the opinion reached a result that is
repugnant to the South Carolina policy of protecting the new home buyer.[7]
The choice is between the builder of defective housing and the innocent new
home purchaser. The *Kennedy* opinion brings South Carolina law forward

"to keep pace with the changing mechanics of ordinary new home purchase."[8] In the course of this organic development, the facts of *Carolina Winds* "present yet one more scenario which is not properly disposed of by our present set of rules governing new home sales."[9] Once more, "we respond by expanding our rules to provide the innocent buyer with protection."[10] The court distinguished between the implied warranty of habitability, which springs from the sale of the house, and the implied warranty of workmanlike construction, which springs from the undertaking of the builder. On this aspect of the case, the court concluded that "a purchaser may sue a builder on his implied warranty of service, despite the purchaser's lack of contractual privity. Any contrary implication by the court of appeals in *Carolina Winds* is rejected."[11]

The Economic Loss Rule

Tort law typically focuses on whether monetary awards should be made for bodily injury or property damage inflicted by another. Dollar awards are a way of shifting the loss inflicted from the victim to the wrongdoer. By contrast contract law is primarily concerned with claims of lost profit or other monetary advantage expected or agreed on in commercial or private arrangements. The sale of goods and services is the major focus of contract law. Thus viewed, the economic loss rule polices a boundary area between tort and contract. Pure economic damages—for example, damages only to a product itself, not to other property or to a person—are not available in tort but must be sought in contract.[12] The dimensions of the doctrine are explained by Justice Toal in *Kennedy v. Columbia Lumber & Manufacturing Company*,[13] in crafting an exception to the rule in cases involving home construction.

As to liability in tort, and the denial in *Carolina Winds* of plaintiff's tort claim by applying the economic loss rule, the court allowed that the rule "exists to assist in determining whether tort or contract theories are applicable to a given case."[14] However, the court found that "this legal framework generates difficulties . . . because the framework's focus is on consequence, not action. . . . The framework we adopt focuses on activity, not consequence."[15]

As noted earlier, although the *Kennedy* case involved suit by a new home purchaser against a lender, of greater interest is the question of the liability of the builder. The builder did not sell the home, and damages suffered were economic in nature.[16] The damage claimed in *Kennedy* was for the cost of repair. In analyzing the claim, Justice Toal held that the builder could be held responsible in negligence and breach of implied warranty of service in spite of the absence of contractual relation between the parties. The cause of action in negligence for economic loss would be available to the new home purchaser when the builder had violated some legal duty no matter what damage resulted, although the economic loss rule would apply where duties were created solely by contract.

The exception to the economic loss rule recognized in *Kennedy* was followed by the extension to other buildings in *Colleton Preparatory Academy, Inc. v. Hooker International, Inc.,*[17] a decision in which Justice Toal did not participate. This extension, however, was short-lived. In *Sapp v. Ford Motor Co.,*[18] the court, in its opinion by Justice Toal, expressly overruled *Colleton,* to the extent that it expanded the narrow exception to the economic loss rule established by *Kennedy* for residential buildings.[19] *Sapp* involved claims for economic loss from fire caused by a malfunctioning cruise control switch, in trucks manufactured by the defendant. Only the trucks were damaged. The court refused to extend *Kennedy* to this situation:

> The *Kennedy* opinion did not signal a watershed moment in products liability law in South Carolina, nor did it alter the application of the economic loss rule in products liability cases. . . .
>
> At the time of our decision in *Kennedy,* we had no intention of the exception extending beyond residential real estate construction and into commercial real estate construction. . . . Much less did we intend the exception to the economic loss rule to be applied well beyond the scope of real estate construction in an ordinary products liability claim."[20]

Defamation

The law of defamation in modern times is based on the common law as limited by United States Supreme Court decisions interpreting the First Amendment to the United States Constitution,[21] as made applicable to the states via the Fourteenth Amendment.[22]

The effect has been to enlarge the scope of permissible error in the reporting of facts about individuals in matters of public interest, particularly as reported in the media. Given occasional guidelines by United States Supreme Court decisions, the task of setting the boundaries of permissible error in particular cases has fallen to state courts.

In South Carolina a basic source for the law of defamation is Justice Toal's concurring opinion in *Holtzscheiter v. Thompson Newspapers, Inc.* (*Holtzscheiter II*),[23] which followed an earlier decision by the court (*Holtzscheiter I*). The case involved a newspaper report about a murder, which quoted the victim's physician as saying "there was simply no family support to encourage [the victim] to complete her education."[24] The victim's mother sued the newspaper for libel on the theory that the account falsely imputed to the family a disinterest in the victim's welfare. The trial court, persuaded that the account could only have indicated a lack of financial resources available for the victim's education, granted a directed verdict to the newspaper. The decision was appealed and, after several instances of review, reached the South Carolina Supreme Court a second time.[25] The court, by a vote of three to two, reversed the decision for the plaintiff in the second trial and sent the case back for another trial.[26] Justice Toal's concurring opinion appears in the second appearance of the *Holtzscheiter* case in the court.

However, to fully appreciate the usefulness of Justice Toal's guideline concurrence in *Holtzscheiter II*, attention should be given to her dissenting opinion in the court's first decision in the case. *Holtzscheiter I* was also a three-to-two decision. Justice Toal starts out boldly: "The majority does not address, nor did the parties here, the potential impact of the decisions of the United States Supreme Court on this case. Furthermore, the majority does not, in my opinion accurately interpret South Carolina case law."[27] What follows is a carefully crafted survey of "a series of pronouncements in which a deeply divided Supreme Court struggled with the proper parameters of state defamation law in light of first amendment rights."[28] The first cases in the series addressed media publications about matters of public interest involving a public officer[29] and a public figure.[30] These cases established the rule that "a public figure plaintiff suing for defamation must prove, by clear and convincing evidence that the defamatory falsehood was made with knowledge of its falsity or with reckless disregard for the truth."[31]

The murdered girl's mother in *Holtzscheiter* was not characterized by either party as a public figure. Convinced by the record that she was not, Justice Toal turned to Supreme Court cases dealing with private figures. In *Gertz v. Robert Welch, Inc.*,[32] a private figure sued a magazine publisher over a matter of public concern. The court held that "so long as they do not impose liability without fault, the States may define for themselves the appropriate standard of liability for a publisher or broadcaster of defamatory falsehood injurious to a private individual."[33] (Justice Toal returned to this issue in her concurring opinion in *Holtzscheiter II*.) At further distance from the main thrust of the Supreme Court's cases protecting First Amendment rights to freedom of speech and the press is *Dun & Bradstreet, Inc. v. Greenmoss Builders, Inc.*[34] Justice Toal succinctly tracked the several opinions in *Dun & Bradstreet* that held that false statements in a specific credit report did not involve matters of public concern that would require a showing of actual malice for the recovery of presumed and punitive damages.[35] Of particular interest to Justice Toal is the relevance of the status of the defendant.

> [A]pparently for the first time, the Court intimated that it was of some import that the defendant in *Gertz* was a media defendant. Four dissenters protested mightily, pointing out that the language of *Gertz* did not indicate such limitations. Justice Brennan went so far to note, in

dissenting, that six members of the Court at that point in time (the four dissenters and two members concurring in the judgment) did not agree with Powell's view that whether the defendant was a media member was relevant.[36]

Seizing on the point that *Dun & Bradstreet* involved a private figure plaintiff suing a nonmedia defendant over speech of only private concern, Justice Toal pointed out that in *Holtzscheiter,* "we are faced with a private figure plaintiff suing a media defendant over a matter of, in my view, private concern. The United States Supreme Court has not yet addressed such a scenario."[37]

Not long after *Dun & Bradstreet,* the U.S. Supreme Court decided *Philadelphia Newspapers, Inc. v. Hepps,*[38] in which the majority opinion, faced with a case like *Gertz*—the plaintiff was a private figure and the newspaper articles were of public concern—extends the logic of the *New York Times* rule about public figures involved in matters of public concern: "We believe the common laws rule on falsity—that the defendant must bear the burden of proving the truth—must similarly fall here to a constitutional requirement that the plaintiff bear the burden of showing falsity before recovering damages."[39] The conclusion seems obvious enough. About a case like *Dun & Bradstreet,* however, the court is less categorical about the inroads of its decisions on state defamation laws: "When the speech is of exclusively private concern and the plaintiff is a private figure, as in *Dun & Bradstreet,* the constitutional requirements do not necessarily force any changes in at least some of the features of the common-law landscape."[40] No mention is made of the significance of whether the defendant is a member of the media. For Justice Toal, as apparently so far for the court, the significance of the distinction remains to be decided. Thus, *Dun & Bradstreet* and *Holtzscheiter* are indistinguishable . . . perhaps. Justice Toal hedges her bets: "The United States Supreme Court has not yet addressed such a scenario. We might do well to assume that the rules anticipated in *Dun & Bradstreet* apply, and that Justice Brennan's view that a media/nonmedia distinction is irrelevant would prevail, although this prediction on my part of future Supreme Court action is just that, a prediction."[41]

The matter, then, is to be governed by state law, which Justice Toal next addressed and would deal definitively with in her concurring opinion in *Holtzscheiter II.*

In *Holtzscheiter II* Justice Toal agreed with the result reached by the plurality opinion and with its account of the constitutional issues implicated by defamation actions in media cases. Although Justice Toal agreed with the plurality's partial steps to modernize South Carolina's defamation law, she would go further: "Because a coherent, consistent, and constitutional approach is lacking in South Carolina defamation law, I would advocate and propose here, the adoption of a new theoretical framework for analyzing defamation issues."[42] What follows is a guideline that presents a systematic analysis of the subject against a backdrop in which certain areas are "mind-numbingly incoherent."[43] She noted that the reason for past confusion was two-fold and that the time had come to render the matter coherent: "Given the uncertainty existing in South Carolina defamation law, due to the lack of an analytical model and the failure to generally take account of the Supreme Court's recent opinions, this case presents an opportune time for this Court to look afresh at how defamation issues should be resolved."[44] The opinion tracks the elements of common law defamation, noting that pertinent points where constitutional adjustments must be taken into account in cases involving the media. "Under the common law, a defamatory communication was presumed to be false. . . . However, truth could be asserted as an affirmative defense. . . . The Supreme Court's holding in *Philadelphia Newspapers, Inc.* has modified the common law rule: '[A]t least where a newspaper publishes speech of public concern, a private figure plaintiff cannot recover damages without showing that the statements at issue are false.'"[45]

Although the common law recognized privileged occasions for defamatory statements,[46] as to which actual malice in the common law sense—ill will or the intention to injure reputation—much of defamation at common law was actionable without proof of fault.[47] As she brought her survey of constitutional limits on state defamation that impose some proof of wrong doing to bear on the case at hand, Justice Toal noted that "[t]he degree of fault a plaintiff must establish depends on his status as a public or private figure."[48] In such cases the Supreme Court has held that "'so long as they do not impose liability without fault, the States may define for themselves the appropriate standard of liability for a publisher or broadcaster of defamatory falsehood injurious to a private individual.'"[49]

Relying on the view of a large majority of states where negligence is the standard for private plaintiffs—a question not yet explicitly addressed by the South Carolina Supreme Court—Justice Toal agreed that "this is the appropriate standard of liability to be met by private figures."[50] As to punitive damages, Justice Toal found that the adoption of an actual malice standard "is consistent with our standard in other types of punitive damages cases."[51]

Justice Toal concluded her survey and analysis of defamation law with characteristic vigor as she examined what must seem to lay readers—as well as many, if not most, lawyers—the arcana of defamation law. "The greatest confusion in South Carolina defamation law, as evidenced by the present case, surrounds the issues of actionability and special damages. This stems from the fact that South Carolina has deviated from the majority rule by adopting the concept of libel per quod. . . . Only by completely rejecting this deviant formulation and by rejoining the mainstream of defamation law can any clarity be brought to the law in our state."[52]

Put simply, at issue are two related questions: (1) Is the statement defamatory without proof of additional facts? (2) Is the statement actionable without proof of actual injury? The mischief to be avoided is to confuse or conflate the questions when dealing with libel.[53] The "libel per quod" rule Justice Toal inveighed against does just that: where proof of defamatory meaning depends on facts outside the statement about the plaintiff, "specific" (usually monetary) damages must be established; "general" (assumed or implied) damages will not suffice. Justice Toal urged a return to the common law rule that all libel—whether defamatory on its face (libel per se) or by reason of particular circumstances (libel per quod) is actionable without proof of special damages.[54]

It remained only to apply Justice Toal's analysis to the facts of this case. Of particular interest is her conclusion that the statement complained of in *Holtzscheiter* was a matter of private concern.[55] Thus plaintiff needed not prove the statement false, but the truth of the statement could be raised by the newspaper as an affirmative defense.

Justice Toal's task in writing a long concurring opinion was not to stake out a different position to support the disposition of the case, but collegially to amplify and complete its own analysis. "In sum, the principal reason why I do not join the majority is not because of defects in the Chief Justice's opinion. He has admirably attempted to resolve the dispute by clarifying the current state of the law. Rather, I am firmly convinced that the present status of our defamation jurisprudence is so convoluted, so helplessly and irretrievably confused, that nothing short of a fresh start can bring any sanity, and predictability, to this very important area of the law."[56]

The Public Duty Rule

Duty, breach, proximate cause, damages—these necessary elements of a cause of action in tort are drummed into the heads of law students from the first days of law school. The source of an established duty must be found in decided law, and a newly minted duty must be introduced on the basis of principle and public policy. The "public duty rule" recognizes that most statutes are intended to regulate public matters. As a general rule such statutes do not ordinarily provide for a remedy when a claim of damage caused by a violation of a statute is the basis of a civil claim. In other words, they establish only a duty to the public; there is no duty in tort granted to individuals. To determine whether a duty can be based on a particular statute to identify a cause of action, the court has adopted a six-factor test to identify exceptions to the prevailing rule—the public duty rule—that a civil cause of action is not to be implied from a statute that is silent on the question.[57] Exceptionally, however, the court may recognize a special duty owed to individuals rather than only a public duty owed to the public at large. Speaking for the court in *Jensen v. Anderson County Department of Social Services*,[58] Justice Toal spelled out the six-factor test for identifying whether a specific duty exists.

> The six factors for determining whether such a special duty exists are:
> (1) an essential purpose of the statute is to protect against a particular kind of harm;
> (2) the statute, either directly or indirectly, imposes on a specific public officer a duty to guard against or not cause that harm;
> (3) the class of persons the statute intends to protect is identifiable before the fact;
> (4) the plaintiff is a person within the protected class;
> (5) the public officer knows or has reason to know the likelihood of harm to members of the class if he fails to do his duty; and
> (6) the officer is given sufficient authority to act in the circumstances or he undertakes to act in the exercise of his office.[59]

The *Jensen* case involved the death of a child as a result of abuse by his mother's boyfriend. The local office of Department of Social Services (DSS) had received a report of abuse from the child's teacher, but the assigned caseworker, after initial investigation, did not gather other information for the file or locate the family. The caseworker and her supervisor closed the file, concluding that the report was unfounded. Soon afterward the boyfriend beat the child to death.

Justice Toal held that negligence in failing to properly investigate a report of child abuse may give rise to a private cause of action under the South Carolina Child Protection Act.[60] The special duty test aids in the determination of legislative intent—regarding a matter about which the legislature has not expressed its intent. The opinion finds that the purpose of the child abuse statutes is to provide protection for children from being abused, by mandating investigation and intervention to remove endangered children when abuse has been reported. When abuse was reported in this case, a relationship was established between the children and DSS.

Even so the finding of a special duty does not by itself establish liability. "[I]t must still be determined whether the alleged negligent conduct occurred during the performance of a ministerial or discretionary duty."[61] Therefore the case was remanded for further proceedings to determine if the file in the case was closed because the investigation was incomplete and there were not enough facts on which to make an informed decision. If so, there would not be immunity from liability.

Justice Toal's opinion is a concise but thorough exposition of the special duty exception regarding official exercise of discretion in the exercise of ministerial duties. More particularly Justice Toal noted that "other jurisdictions are split on the issue whether the negligence of a social worker in failing to investigate report of child abuse may give rise to a private cause of action. While no other state has utilized an identical analysis, several other jurisdictions have reached the same result."[62] However innovative the analysis in the *Jensen* case, Justice Toal acknowledged that "subsequent cases controlled by the South Carolina Tort Claims Act, enacted after this suit, may require a slightly different analysis."[63]

In a later case, involving a claim to recover damages arising from abuse by the patient of a psychiatrist for failure to report to authorities or warn future victims of the patient's predilection for child molestation, Justice Toal joined in a decision holding that the case is distinguishable from the *Jensen* case because no special duty existed between the victim and the defendant psychiatrist, who was not a public official.[64]

Justice Toal's next examination of the special exception to the public duty rule involved the South Carolina Freedom of Information Act (FOIA). The *Jensen* case was invoked in *Bellamy v. Brown*,[65] which involved a claim that the South Carolina Freedom of Information Act[66] creates a cause of action for breach of a special duty of confidentiality. In *Bellamy*, a former county employee, removed from her job, sued her former governmental employer for violation of FOIA after board members were contacted by a local newspaper reporter, to whom they may have revealed personal information. The court held that FOIA is exclusively a disclosure statute designed to protect the public from secret government activity. Therefore the exemptions from disclosure[67] do not create a duty not to disclose records and cannot be used to enforce the confidentiality of records. "No legislative intent to create a duty of confidentiality can be found in the language of the Act. We hold therefore that no special duty of confidentiality is established by the FOIA."[68] Justice Toal relied in part on a comparable decision of the United States Supreme Court in *Chrysler Corp. v. Brown*[69] and stated: "We find the Supreme Court's analysis of the essential purpose of the federal FOIA applicable by analogy to the South Carolina FOIA."[70]

Tanner v. Florence County, another case decided in 1991,[71] found that a special duty existed in a landowner's negligence action against a county for failing to provide him with required notice of a delinquent tax sale of both his property and his mobile home. The redemption period had expired, and a tax title for the mobile home had been issued to a third party. Again writing for a unanimous court, Justice Toal first noted the procedural difference between immunity under the Tort Claims Act and the public duty doctrine.

Immunity is an affirmative defense which must be pleaded and can be waived. One who pleads immunity conditionally admits the plaintiff's case, but asserts immunity as a bar to liability. In contrast, the public duty rule is a negative defense which denies an element of the plaintiff's cause of action—the existence of a duty of care to the individual plaintiff. The burden is on the plaintiff to show a duty of care was owed to him.[72]

Building on the *Jensen* case and other precedents, Justice Toal observed that "[i]n general we have been reluctant to find special duties statutorily imposed."[73] By contrast, the statute in this case is different from those involved in previous cases. "All requirements of law leading up to tax sales are intended for the protection of the tax payer against surprise or the sacrifice of his property and are regarded as mandatory and are strictly enforced."[74] Although the statutory notice provision creates a special duty, in order to succeed plaintiff must prove that he has provided the county with his correct address and that the county has failed to use that address.[75]

Not every case involving injury or damage caused by the action or inaction of government employees implicates the public duty rule. In *Trousdell v. Cannon,*[76] a highway patrolman brought a tort action in negligence against a county sheriff's department. The patrolman had been chasing a speeding vehicle when he was rear-ended by a deputy sheriff after coming to a complete stop. Justice Toal's opinion for the court held that the public duty rule was not in issue because the tort claim was based on the common law duty of reasonable care, not on a statutory duty. The case was governed by the Tort Claims Act. As it turned out, the county sheriff was not immune from liability, because the case fell within the specific exception to the act's waiver of governmental immunity.[77] In so holding, Justice Toal's opinion rejects application of the fireman's rule, which "bar[s] an emergency professional, such as a firefighter, police officer, or public safety officer, who is injured as a result of performing his or her duties, from recovering tort based damages from the party whose negligence caused the injury-causing event."[78] The court thus rejected a defense to a claim in this case based on a common law claim made available under the Tort Claims Act's waiver of governmental immunity. As the opinion summarizes, "[g]enerally, the public duty rule is invoked in cases where the duty is created by statute and would not otherwise exist."[79]

Another example of Justice Toal's treatment of the intersection of statutory duty and exception to the public duty rule is the case of *Vaughan v. Town of Lyman.*[80] Plaintiff pedestrian claimed that the failure of the town to maintain its sidewalks caused her to trip and fall on the sidewalk and suffer injuries. The court found that the statute in question[81] did not create a special duty to plaintiff according to the six-factor test. As Justice Toal explained, "[t]he public duty rule is a rule of statutory construction which aids the court in determining whether the legislature intended to create a private cause of action for a statute's breach."[82] At one time a waiver statute—to avoid governmental immunity—did create a private right of action against a municipality for breach of duty. Today, however, the statutory basis for liability is no longer observed. "Instead, liability is now imposed through the waiver provisions of the Tort Claims Act."[83] The proper course for plaintiff then is to make out a common law cause of action in tort.

The last case to be examined for treatment of the public duty rule is *Platt v. CSX Transportation, Inc.,*[84] which involved a fatal collision between an automobile and a train at a railroad crossing. Writing again for the court, Justice Toal neatly explained a crucial distinction in the case: "When the duty is created by statute, we refer to this as a 'special duty,' whereas when the duty is founded on the common law, we refer to this as a legal duty arising from special 'circumstances.'"[85] Unfortunately for plaintiff the defendant of interest for present purposes, the South Carolina Department of Transportation, did not owe a special duty to plaintiff that derived from its statutory duty regarding the crossing, and plaintiff failed effectively to preserve a common law tort claim.[86]

The foregoing opinions present a thorough and coherent exposition of the public duty rule in a number of varied settings that give practical illustration of the court's determination of unexpressed legislative intent regarding whether a special exception to the rule exists. However, the waiver of governmental immunity in the Tort Claims Act, even with the exemptions preserved from waiver, has done much to deflect reliance on finding exceptions to the public duty rule.

Conclusion

This modest survey concludes with the observation that Justice Toal's opinions have enhanced the coherence and responsiveness to changing realities of South Carolina tort law. This accomplishment has been characterized by command of doctrine, clarity of analysis, and vigorous, but circumspect, expression.

Even within a single area, selection from a large number of significant opinions must seem arbitrary. However, those chosen for review, as do those set aside for another day, respect the tradition of the common law, mindful of precedent but attentive to changing needs. They reflect the realistic and practical views signaled more than a hundred years ago by Oliver Wendell Holmes. Pretty good company.

NOTES
1. Jean Hoefer Toal became a justice of the South Carolina Supreme Court on January 27, 1988, and chief justice on June 2, 1999. The opinions considered for this article date from her first appointment through the end of 2014. Jean Hoefer Toal and other notables of the class of 1968, including her husband, William Thomas Toal, were students in my conflicts of laws class when I first joined the faculty of the University of South Carolina School of Law. Since then I have followed her career as a friend and admiring critic.

2. For discussion of improved realty in the context of products liability, see F. Patrick Hubbard and Robert L. Felix, *The South Carolina Law of Torts*, 4th ed. (Columbia: South Carolina Bar, 2011), 308–18.

3. 299 S.C. 335, 384 S.E.2d 730 (1989).

4. *Id.* at 339, 384 S.E.2d at 733.

5. 297 S.C. 74, 374 S.E.2d 897 (Ct. App. 1988). The opinion for the court of appeals in *Carolina Winds* is by the late Judge Randall Bell, whose efforts to set (or reset) the boundaries between tort and contract might be the subject of another article. For a time Judge Bell taught contracts at the School of Law.

6. 299 S.C. at 341, 384 S.E.2d at 734.

7. *Id.*

8. *Id.*

9. *Id.* at 343, 384 S.E.2d at 735.

10. *Id.* at 344, 384 S.E.2d at 735.

11. *Id.* at 345, 384 S.E.2d at 736.

12. This is the view adopted in the *Restatement (Third) of Torts: Products Liability* (Philadelphia: American Law Institute, 1997). Section 21 provides:
§ 21. Definition of "Harm to Persons or Property": Recovery for Economic Loss

For purposes of this Restatement, harm to persons or property includes economic loss if caused by harm to:

(a) the plaintiff's person; or
(b) the person of another when harm to the other interferes with an interest of the plaintiff protected by tort law; or
(c) the plaintiff's property other than the defective product itself.

But houses are different, aren't they?

13. *Kennedy*, 299 S.C. at 345, 384 S.E.2d at 737. For discussion of *Kennedy* and the economic loss rule, see Hubbard and Felix, *supra* note 2, at 53–60, 358–60.

14. *Kennedy*, 299 S.C. at 345, 384 S.E.2d at 737.

15. *Id.* at 345, 384 S.E.2d at 736.

16. Recall that in this case, the builder was financially judgment proof.

17. 397 S.C. 81, 666 S.E.2d 247 (2008). In *Colleton* a private school brought a tort action in federal court against the manufacturer of fire retardant after determining that wood trusses treated with the retardant were in danger of falling and needed to be replaced for safety reasons.

18. 386 S.C. 143, 687 S.E.2d 47 (2009).

19. *Id.* at 145, 687 S.E.2d at 48.

20. *Id.* at 149–50, 687 S.E.2d at 50–51. Justice Toal also refers approvingly to several federal court decisions interpreting *Kennedy* in a similarly limited way in products liability cases.

21. "Congress shall make no law respecting an establishment of religion, or prohibiting the free exercise thereof; or abridging the freedom of speech, or of the press; or of the right of the people peaceably to assemble and to petition the Government for the redress of grievances." U.S. Const. amend I.

22. *See generally* Hubbard and Felix, *supra* note 2, at 513–65. For discussion of the interpretation of the First Amendment via the Fourteenth Amendment as binding upon the states, see *id*. at 514–15, 535–54.

23. *Holtzscheiter v. Thompson Newspapers, Inc.* (*Holtzscheiter II*), 332 S.C. 502, 506 S.E.2d 497 (1998).

24. *Id*. at 507, 506 S.E.2d at 500.

25. In the first decision, *Holtzscheiter v. Thompson Newspaper, Inc.* (*Holtzscheiter I*), 306 S.C. 297, 411 S.E.2d 664 (1991), the court reversed the trial court decision and remanded for further proceedings. In the subsequent retrial the jury awarded the mother $500,000 in actual damages and $1.5 million in punitive damages (reduced to $500,000 by the trial judge).

26. The plurality opinion by Chief Justice Finney held that plaintiff adequately resisted a directed verdict for the newspaper by offering evidence of its negligent failure to follow professional practices, but that the issue of punitive damages should not have gone to the jury because there was no clear and convincing evidence that the newspaper acted with "constitutional actual malice—that the newspaper either knew the statement was false or had serious reservations about its truthfulness." 332 S.C. at 515, 506 S.E.2d at 504. Additionally the opinion held that the parties were denied a fair trial because of the confusion generated by the court's decision in its first *Holtzscheiter* opinion. *Id*.

27. 306 S.C. at 303, 411 S.E.2d at 667.

28. *Id*. at 304, 411 S.E. 2d at 667.

29. *N.Y. Times, Co. v. Sullivan*, 376 U.S. 254 (1964) (civil rights demonstration, city commissioner).

30. *Curtis Publ'g, Co. v. Butts*, 388 U.S. 130 (1967) (college football; state university football coach).

31. 306 S.C. at 304, 411 S.E.2d at 667.

32. 418 U.S. 323 (1974).

33. *Id*. at 346.

34. 472 U.S. 749 (1985).

35. Two justices joined Justice Powell's opinion, and two more concurred in the judgment; four justices dissented regarding what kind of speech constituted a matter of public concern.

36. 306 S.C. at 306, 411 S.E.2d at 668–69.

37. *Id*. at 306, at 411 S.E.2d at 669.

38. 475 U.S. 767 (1986).

39. *Id*. at 776.

40. *Id*. at 775.

41. 306 S.C. at 307, 441 S.E.2d at 669.

42. 332 S.C. at 516, 506 S.E.2d at 505.

43. *Id*.

44. *Id*. at 517, 506 S.E.2d at 505.

45. *Philadelphia Newspapers, Inc. v. Hepps*, 475 U.S. 767, 768–69.

46. *Holtscheiter II*, 332 S.C. 508.

47. For discussion of common law privileges, see Hubbard and Felix, *supra* note 2, at 555–65.

48. *Id*. at 520–22.

49. 332 S.C. at 520, 506 S.E.2d at 507.

50. *Id.* at 523, 506 S.E.2d at 508 (quoting *Gertz,* 418 U.S. at 347).

51. *Id.* at 523, 506 S.E.2d at 509. In a later case in which Justice Toal concurred, the court stated that: "In order to prove defamation, the plaintiff must show (1) a false and defamatory statement was made; (2) the unprivileged publication was made to a third party; (3) the publisher was at fault; and (4) either actionability of the statement irrespective of special harm or the existence of special harm caused by the publication. *Holtzscheiter II,* 332 S.C. at 506, 506 S.E.2d at 518 (Toal, J., concurring)." *Erickson v. Jones St. Publishers, L.L.C.,* 368 S.C. 444, 465, 629 S.E.2d 653, 664 (2006).

52. 332 S.C. at 525, 506 S.E.2d at 509.

53. *Id.*

54. To be actionable without proof of actual damages, slander (nonmedia spoken deflamation) must fall into certain categories: imputation of unchastity, criminal offense, loathsome disease, or business incompetence or misconduct.

55. In so arguing Justice Toal advocated adoption of *Restatement (Second) of Torts* § 569, which provides: "One who falsely publishes matter defamatory of another in such a manner as to make the publication libel is subject to liability to the other although no special harm results from the publication."

56. The statement "solely relates to a matter of private concern: family support of an individual." 332 S.C. at 532, 506 S.E.2d at 513.

57. *Id.* at 534, 506 S.E.2d at 514.

58. For discussion of the public duty rule, see Hubbard and Felix, *supra* note 2, at 110–12, 118–21.

59. 304 S.C. 195, 403 S.E.2d 615 (1991).

60. *Id.* at 200, 403 S.E.2d at 617 (citing *Rayfield v. South Carolina Dep't of Corrections,* 297 S.C. 95, 374 S.E.2d 910 (Ct. App. 1988), *cert. denied* 298 S.C. 204, 379 S.E.2d 133 (1989)). As Justice Toal noted, the rule was first adopted in *Parker v. Brown,* 195 S.C. 35, 10 S.E.2d 625 (1940).

61. S.C. Code Ann. §§ 20-7-650, 20-7-736 (1985).

62. 304 S.C. at 203, 403 S.E.2d at 619.

63. *Id.* at 203 n.3, 403 S.E.2d at 619 n.3.

64. *Id.* at 201 n.2, 403 S.E.2d 618 n.2. The Tort Claims Act provides that government units "are liable for their torts in the same manner and to the same extent as a private individual under like circumstances, subject to the limitations upon liability and damages, and exemptions from liability and damages, contained herein." S.C. Code Ann. § 15-78-40 (1986).

65. *Doe v. Marion,* 373 S.C. 390, 645 S.E.2d 245 (2007). At issue were provisions of the same statute involved in *Jensen,* which required a physician to report information giving reason to believe that a child's health or welfare may be or has been adversely affected by abuse or neglect. *See* S.C. Code Ann. § 20-7-510. The court found the statute was aimed primarily at DSS.

66. 305 S.C. 291, 408 S.E.2d 219 (1991).

67. S.C. Code Ann. § 30-4-10-110 (1991).

68. *See id.* §§ 30-4-40 and -70.

69. 305 S.C. at 295, 408 S.E.2d at 221.

70. 441 U.S. 281 (1975).

71. 305 S.C. at 295, 408 S.E.2d at 221.

72. 336 S.C. 552, 521 S.E.2d 153 (1991).

73. *Id.* at 561, 521 S.E.2d at 157.

74. *Id.* at 562, 521 S.E.2d at 158 (citing a number of cases, including *Jensen*).

75. *Id.* at 563, 521 S.E.2d at 158–59.

76. S.C. Code Ann. § 12-51-40 (1977).

77. 351 S.C. 636, 572 S.E.2d 264 (2002).

78. *See* S.C. Code Ann. § 15-78-60 (1986).

79. 351 S.C. at 639, 572 S.E.2d at 265.

80. *Id.* at 641, 572 S.E.2d at 267.

81. 370 S.C. 436, 635 S.E.2d 631 (2006).

82. S.C. Code Ann. § 5-27-120 (1976).

83. 370 S.C. at 442, 635 S.E.2d at 634.

84. *Id.* at 442, 635 S.E.2d at 635; *see* S.C. Code Ann. § 15-78-10 *et seq.* (2005).

85. 388 S.C. 441, 697 S.E.2d 575 (2010).

86. *Id.* at 445, 697 S.E.2d at 577.

87. The trial court did not rule on the common law claim, and plaintiff failed to file a motion to alter and amend the judgment in order to preserve the issue on appeal. *Id.* at 446, 697 S.E.2d at 577.

JESSICA CHILDERS HARRINGTON
AND W. LEWIS BURKE JR.

Abbeville County School District v. State

Changing South Carolina

Today, education is perhaps the most important function of state and local governments. Compulsory school attendance laws and the great expenditures for education both demonstrate our recognition of the importance of education to our democratic society. It is required in the performance of our most basic public responsibilities, even service in the armed forces. It is the very foundation of good citizenship. Today it is a principal instrument in awakening the child to cultural values, in preparing him for later professional training, and in helping him to adjust normally to his environment. In these days, it is doubtful that any child may reasonably be expected to succeed in life if he is denied the opportunity of an education. Such an opportunity, where the state has undertaken to provide it, is a right which must be made available to all on equal terms.[1]

Abbeville County School District v. State is a South Carolina education decision many years in the making. This opening quotation from *Brown v. Board of Education* foreshadows how significant this case could be for South Carolina education. Chief Justice Toal authored the long-awaited opinion. The plaintiffs in the case were eight South Carolina school districts, including Allendale County, Dillon County District 2, Florence County District 4, Hampton County District 2, Jasper County, Lee County, Marion County District 7, and Orangeburg County District 3.[2] To date the case has reached the South Carolina Supreme Court twice. The first time the South Carolina Supreme Court heard the case (referred to as *Abbeville I*), it determined that South Carolina's constitution required the state to provide a "minimally adequate education" to students.[3]

Abbeville I began in 1993 with a lawsuit filed by nearly half of the state's ninety-one school districts (the plaintiff districts).[4] The suit challenged the

State's public education funding system. The primary issue that arose in *Abbeville I* was whether Article XI, section 3 of the South Carolina constitution (the education clause) contained a qualitative education standard.[5] The education clause states, "The General Assembly shall provide for the maintenance and support of a system of free public schools open to all children in the state and shall establish, organize and support such other public institutions of learning as may be desirable."[6] Despite allegations that the funding system violated both the state and federal constitutions, the trial court dismissed the suit.[7] In 1999 the South Carolina Supreme Court in a four-to-one decision, in which Associate Justice Jean Toal joined, upheld the plaintiff districts' claims.[8] In its remand to the trial court, the Supreme Court defined "minimally adequate education" as:

1. The ability to read, write, and speak the English language, and knowledge of mathematics and physical science;
2. A fundamental knowledge of economic, social, and political systems, and of history and governmental processes; and
3. Academic and vocational skills.[9]

The Supreme Court's decision was met with optimism. As one newspaper reported, "Educators in poorer South Carolina school districts saw new life breathed into their battle for more education dollars Thursday when the state Supreme Court refused to dismiss their case."[10]   On remand the sole issue in the case was whether "the students in the Plaintiff Districts [are] being provided the opportunity to acquire a minimally adequate education in adequate and safe facilities as defined by the South Carolina Supreme Court?"[11] Carl Epps, one of the attorneys for the plaintiff districts, observed that "if the U.S. Supreme Court justices from the 1950's *Brown* era walked into some of the South Carolina rural schools, they would wonder if their decision had any effect."[12] The plaintiff districts focused the inquiry on "inputs" and "outputs." Inputs were the resources the legislature provided to the school districts, and outputs were the results achieved by students and school districts as a result of these inputs.[13] During the 101-day trial, the court heard from 112 witnesses, producing a transcript of over twenty-three thousand pages.[14] The plaintiff districts offered testimony about the myriad difficulties they faced in attempting to educate their resident children. These difficulties included a devastating teacher turnover rate, a proliferation of uncertified teachers, crumbling facilities, a lack of equipment, overcrowding, a growing number of ESL students, the crushing poverty with which many of the students grew up, inadequate bus transportation, and poor graduation rates.[15]

The state argued that it was providing adequate inputs and that "some students chose to take advantage of the opportunity, while others did not."[16]

Bobby Stepp, an attorney for the state, observed that "there are no silver bullets. This is a very complicated, multi-faceted issue. You can't legislate better student performance."[17] The trial court held that legislative inputs were sufficient to provide a minimally adequate education, except in the area of early childhood education intervention programs. The trial court reasoned that children form most of their cognitive abilities before reaching age six, and children born into poverty may miss the opportunity to develop those abilities early in life; thus the trial court found that the legislature should fund early childhood education to overcome the poverty barrier so students could achieve greater academic success.[18]

Both sides appealed the ruling to the South Carolina Supreme Court, and the court squarely faced the issue of whether South Carolina was meeting the minimally adequate standard in the plaintiff districts.[19] The court heard oral arguments in June 2008 and again in September 2012. When the court issued its decision on November 12, 2014, Chief Justice Toal was the only member of the court who had participated in the original case and heard all the oral arguments. Fittingly, Chief Justice Toal authored the court's opinion in *Abbeville II*.

Before the court could determine if the state provided the children in the plaintiff school districts with a minimally adequate education, the court had to make a threshold decision: whether it was appropriate for the court to settle this controversy.[20] The dissent argued that "minimally adequate education" was an ambiguous phrase, and the resulting issue was a "non-justiciable political question."[21] Chief Justice Toal and the majority viewed the issue differently. The court determined that it had the authority to interpret the state constitution. It quoted *Marbury v. Madison,* in which Chief Justice Marshall stated, "[I]t is emphatically the province and duty of the judicial department to say what the law is."[22] The court acknowledged the policy implications of the case but determined that this case was about interpreting the law, which was an appropriate function of the court.[23]

Chief Justice Toal's majority opinion examined multiple angles of South Carolina's education system and how it affected students in the plaintiff districts. One important factor in the court's analysis was the input and output considerations also considered in *Abbeville I*. Inputs included "money, curriculum, teachers, and programming."[24] The court addressed how the state's current funding system was implemented, and found it "indicative of a comprehensive education regime."[25] The court concluded that looking at the General Assembly's inputs in the education system, the system *seemed* to provide South Carolina students with a minimally adequate education.[26]

However, the court then closely examined the outputs of the General Assembly's educational allocations. The results troubled the court, which stated, "While we acknowledge that the Defendants enacted a robust education scheme designed to address the critical aspects of public education, student performance in the Plaintiff Districts demonstrates an apparent disconnect between intentions and performance."[27] The court specifically considered the plaintiff districts' annual report cards, student test scores, graduation rates, transportation, teacher quality, and local district issues, such as district size.[28]

The court found the plaintiff districts' annual report cards and test scores to be particularly troubling. Annual report cards measure how prepared students in South Carolina schools are for testing and provide a broad picture of school district success. The plaintiff districts largely scored poorly on their annual report card ratings.[29] Similarly, in looking at students' standardized test scores, passage rates in the plaintiff districts "were consistently, alarmingly low."[30] The court acknowledged that while testing was not the only way to measure school success, test scores should still be used as a tool in that measurement.[31]

The court further examined the graduation rates of students in the plaintiff districts. This was one area in which the plaintiff districts saw significant improvement. However, the court reasoned that graduation rates only demonstrated that the plaintiff districts were allowing students to graduate, which did not necessarily indicate that their students received a minimally adequate education. Thus, though impressive, the court viewed the rising graduation rates in the plaintiff districts as insufficient to overcome other deficiencies.[32]

The court closely examined transportation issues as well, because "[s]chool children without access to adequate transportation cannot obtain constitutionally required opportunity."[33] South Carolina law splits the transportation burden, but in practice, most of the burden was placed on school districts. The court noted that this added burden on the plaintiff districts produced a number of issues, including overwhelming costs associated with providing transportation, long bus rides for students, and missed educational opportunities for students due to shortfalls in transportation. Testimony at trial indicated that students spent too much time on buses, making their school days excessively long. Buses often broke down, causing students to be late for class. Furthermore transportation costs were too high for the plaintiff districts to provide additional transportation to students needing extra academic instruction after school, requiring those students to find alternate transportation themselves. The court reasoned that these transportation problems further contributed to the constitutional violation.[34]

Teacher quality in the plaintiff districts also factored into the court's decision. A large percentage of teachers outside of the plaintiff districts— around 81.4 percent—held continuing contracts, meaning they "passed the Praxis examination, taught for three years, and successfully completed a formal evaluation process."[35] However, in the plaintiff districts, that percentage was much lower—a mere 62.2 percent. Funding likely contributed to the plaintiff districts' lower rate of continuing teacher contracts. During the economic recession of 2008, the General Assembly allowed districts to freeze teacher salaries. All but one of the plaintiff districts froze teacher salaries at that time, creating a continuing disadvantage in teacher wages compared to other school districts in the state that did not freeze salaries.[36]

The court also discussed two issues that none of the parties in the case raised—local legislative control and school district size. South Carolina has long given substantial control of local matters—including school districts—to the legislators who represent the various Senate and House districts within which school districts are located. The court noted that the Senate and House districts often covered more than one county; therefore local legislators who made local education decisions often had no direct interest in the school districts that their educational decision impacted.[37] The court concluded that "[t]he Defendants fail to address how the state-wide educational funding regime responds to fragmentary legislative control, and whether that control and resulting legislation has frustrated admirable education initiatives."[38]

Another significant and sensitive issue was school district size, and the administrative costs inherent in operating smaller districts. The court compared Allendale, which contained 1,250 students and received "Below Average" and "Unsatisfactory" annual report card ratings, to Lexington 5, which contained more than sixteen thousand students and achieved "Excellent" annual report card ratings during the same period. The court noted that smaller district size therefore did not necessarily correlate to higher report card ratings. However, here the court criticized the plaintiff districts for failing to reduce administrative costs, pointing out that "[i]nstead, the Plaintiff Districts have opted for a course of self-preservation, placing the blame for the blighted state of education in their districts at the feet of the Defendants."[39]

The court was also confronted with the General Assembly's legislative response to the trial court's order that the state address the issue of early childhood development. In the wake of *Abbeville I,* the General Assembly developed a program called the Child Development Education Pilot Program (CDEPP) to satisfy the trial court's ruling. CDEPP's goals included preparing children for formal education and educating parents. The court acknowledged CDEPP's moderate success but raised concerns about the program's funding, concluding that "it is unclear how the Defendants can effectively utilize the program absent full funding and implementation."[40]

After this thorough examination of how South Carolina's education regime specifically affected the plaintiff districts, the court concluded that

"South Carolina's educational funding scheme is a fractured formula denying students in the Plaintiff Districts the constitutionally required opportunity."[41] Thus the court's final task was to determine how to remedy the constitutional violation. The court was careful not to overstep judicial boundaries, noting that it would be inappropriate for it to determine educational policy on its own. Therefore, the court ordered both the plaintiff districts and the defendants to work together to find solutions to the violations and reappear before the court "within a reasonable time."[42]

In so holding the court set forth two cases from New York and Wyoming as examples.[43] First, the court examined a New York case, *Campaign for Fiscal Equality v. State (CFE II)*. In doing so the court noted that the New York Court of Appeals found that the New York constitution required the state to provide students with a "sound basic education."[44] The trial court found that students in New York City were denied a sound basic education and recommended sweeping education reforms.[45] The case was appealed to the New York Court of Appeals, and in *CFE II* the court halted the sweeping changes the trial court recommended. Instead the court ordered a three-step process: the state had to determine how much a sound basic education would cost in New York City, build a system that provided the needed resources to all the school districts so they could provide that education, and "ensure a system of accountability to measure whether the reforms provide the opportunity for a sound basic education."[46]

Next the court detailed a Wyoming case, *Campbell County School District v. State*. There the Wyoming Supreme Court considered the educational issue on an individual student level and found that the state legislature should first determine what constituted a "proper" education for each student and then determine how to fund that education.[47] The Wyoming court analogized a "proper education" to a basket that must be filled until it was constitutionally adequate. The *Campbell County* court directed that each school district should receive this basket, and before the legislature could consider any additional educational resources, the legislature should ensure that *all* school districts first received the constitutionally required basket.[48] While the court noted that the General Assembly was not bound to follow suggestions from either the New York case or Wyoming cases,[49] the cases provided two separate approaches that could serve as remedies for South Carolina's educational problems.

In conclusion the court recommended that the legislature look beyond funding as the sole mechanism to boost student performance and advised all parties work together to implement reforms.[50]

The *Abbeville II* decision drew praise from across the state.[51] Fred Carter, Francis Marion University president, called the decision a "monumental" one, stating, "We get one every 15 or 20 years. This is one of those decisions."[52] The *Times and Democrat* of Orangeburg reported, "This decision is an historic event that could put South Carolina on the path toward equal education opportunity for all public school students in the state."[53] The *Post and Courier* of Charleston called the decision a "landmark ruling" that "will amount to an historic rebuilding of the state's school funding formula and the policies."[54] The *State* newspaper even opined that the decision "could redefine South Carolina's public education system."[55]

Many South Carolinians viewed *Abbeville II* as a call to action for the state of South Carolina. Molly Spearman, state superintendent of education elect at the time the court reached its decision stated, "Today's Supreme Court ruling should be seen as a mandate that gives us the unique opportunity to resolve problems that will impact the future of our children and grandchildren for years to come and act to ensure every student has every opportunity regardless of where they happen to reside."[56] Senator Nikki Setzler commented, "I hope that instead of spending the 2015 session just talking, we seize the opportunity in the Senate and work in a bipartisan manner to meet the challenge give to us by the Supreme Court and give every child in South Carolina their chance to save the world."[57] Though hopeful the public also acknowledged the challenge the General Assembly faced in adhering to the court's decisions. One editorial stated, "It's a call for an overhaul of the way S.C. schools are funded. Talk about a tall order. But it's one we're pleased to see finally mandated."[58]

It remains to be seen what the enduring result of *Abbeville II* will be. However, it has taken more than twenty years to reach this point. Along the way there was one of the longest trials in the history of the state. The lawsuit inspired an award-winning film, *Corridor of Shame: The Neglect of South Carolina's Rural Schools,* and much publicity and controversy for the state. When South Carolina Educational Television (ETV) announced that the movie would air on its stations across the state, a legislator from Charleston was so offended that he filed a bill to fire the ETV board of directors.[59] During his presidential campaign, Barack Obama toured one of the schools featured in the film, and after his election he invited a student from one of the schools to be his guest during his State of the Union address in 2009.[60]

Recently Bud Ferillo, producer and director of *Corridor of Shame,* recognized Chief Justice Toal's role in *Abbeville II,* stating:

> Jean was an extraordinary legislator whom I met when she was elected to the House in 1974, also my first year as Research Director and chief of staff to the Speaker. She was a strong advocate for several issues that informed her judgment as a jurist: public education, social justice, home rule and the interests of rural communities. I heard her caution about not overstepping legislative prerogatives during oral arguments on the Abbeville case but I had faith that she wanted to be on the right side of history

and would ultimately write a strong decision for the plaintiff districts. And she sure did.[61]

Abbeville II is a significant decision for South Carolina education. Chief Justice Toal's majority opinion explored many factors in making this decision, including school resources and student performance. The court was careful to avoid legislating, acknowledging that education policy was best left to the General Assembly. The court's opinion balanced blame between the General Assembly and the plaintiff districts. It asserted that neither party was the winner or loser of this case; the only winner was South Carolina's students.[62] Though the case has not yet reached its conclusion, the South Carolina Supreme Court made clear in its opinion that it wants to see communication and solution making between the parties in the case. The court also made clear that it stands by its decision in *Abbeville II*. When the defendants requested the court rehear the case, Chief Justice Toal wrote in an order, "We are unable to discover that any material fact or principle of law has been either overlooked or disregarded, and hence, there is no basis for granting a rehearing."[63] Therefore, the court's decision in *Abbeville II* stands and will hopefully facilitate exciting changes in South Carolina's education system.

NOTES

1. *Abbeville Cnty. Sch. Dist. v. State (Abbeville II)*, No. 2007-065159, 2014 WL 5839956, at *1 (S.C. Nov. 12, 2014) (quoting *Brown v. Board of Education (Brown I)*, 347 U.S. 483, 493 [1954]).

2. *Id.* at *36 n. 2.

3. *Id.* at *1 (citing *Abbeville Cnty. Sch. Dist. v. State (Abbeville I)*, 335 S.C. 58, 68, 515 S.E.2d 535, 540 [1999]).

4. *State* (Columbia, S.C.), November 22, 2014.

5. *Abbeville II*, 2014 WL 5839956, at *1 (citing *Abbeville I*, 335 S.C. at 68, 515 S.E.2d at 540); *see also* S.C. Const. art. XI, § 3.

6. S.C. Const. art. XI, § 3.

7. The plaintiff districts also challenged the state's educational funding system as a violation of the Fourteenth Amendment.

8. *See Abbeville I*, 335 S.C. at 58, 515 S.E.2d at 535.

9. *Abbeville II*, 2014 WL 5839956, at *2 (citing *Abbeville I*, 335 S.C. at 68–69).

10. *State* (Columbia, S.C.), April 23, 1999.

11. *Abbeville II*, 2014 WL 5839956, at *3.

12. *Post & Courier* (Charleston, S.C.), August 23, 2014.

13. *Abbeville II*, 2014 WL 5839956, at *3.

14. *State* (Columbia, S.C.), November 22, 2014.

15. *Access Quality Education: South Carolina Litigation*, Nat'l Educ. Access Network, http://www.schoolfunding.info/states/sc/lit_sc.php3 (last updated July 2008).

16. *Abbeville II*, 2014 WL 5839956, at *2.

17. *Id.*

18. *Id.* at *3.

19. *Id.* at *2.

20. *Id.* at *5–6.

21. *Id.* at *5.

22. *Id.* at *6 (quoting *Marbury v. Madison,* 5 U.S. 137, 138 [1803]).

23. *Id.*

24. *Id.*

25. *Id.* at *9.

26. *Abbeville II,* 2014 WL 5839956, at *9.

27. *Id.* at *10.

28. *Id.* at *11, 13, 15.

29. *Id.* at *10.

30. *Id.* at *11.

31. *Id.*

32. *Id.*

33. *Id.* at *12.

34. *Id.* at *12–13.

35. *Id.* at *13.

36. *Abbeville II,* 2014 WL 5839956, at *14.

37. *Id.* at *15.

38. *Id.* at *15.

39. *Id.* at *16.

40. *Id.* at *19.

41. *Id.* at *16.

42. *Id.* at *22.

43. The cases were *Campaign for Fiscal Equity v. State* (CFE II), 801 N.E.2d 326 (N.Y. 2003), and *Campbell County School District v. State,* 907 P.2d 1238 (Wyo. 1995).

44. *Abbeville II,* 2014 WL 5839956, at *19 (quoting *CFE II,* 801 N.E.2d at 328).

45. *Id.* (citing *CFE II,* 801 N.E.2d at 328).

46. *Id.* (quoting *CFE II,* 801 N.E.2d at 348).

47. *Id.* (citing *Campbell Cnty.,* 907 P.2d at 1279–80).

48. *Id.*

49. *Id.*

50. *Id.* at *21.

51. For example see *Sun News* (Myrtle Beach), November 13, 2014; *Independent News* (Anderson, S.C.), November 26, 2014; *Journal* (Seneca, S.C.), December 3, 2014; *Greenville News,* December 9, 2014; and *Cheraw Chronicle,* January 6, 2015.

52. *Morning News* (Florence, S.C.), November 16, 2014.

53. *Times and Democrat* (Orangeburg, S.C.), November 25, 2014.

54. *Post and Courier* (Charleston, S.C.), November 13, 2014.

55. *State* (Columbia, S.C.), November 13, 2014.

56. *State* (Columbia, S.C.), November 16, 2014.

57. *State* (Columbia, S.C.), December 5, 2014.

58. *Island Packet* (Hilton Head, S.C.), November 23, 2014.

59. *State* (Columbia, S.C.), April 8, 2005.

60. *Independent Mail* (Anderson, S.C.), May 6, 2009.

61. Bud Ferillo, e-mail message to W. Lewis Burke, January 21, 2015.

62. *Abbeville II,* 2014 WL 5839956, at *22.

63. *State* (Columbia, S.C.), January 26, 2015.

TINA CUNDARI

Bringing the Courts into the Twenty-First Century

The State of Affairs

THE YEAR WAS 1999. The South Carolina General Assembly had just elected a new chief justice. A woman. The first in the state's history. It was a new day. Change was on the horizon.

Change was also on the horizon globally. Computer technology became increasingly present in our daily lives. The world was becoming smaller and more connected through the use of technology. Information could be shared almost instantly through e-mail. People could search for anything, anytime, and actually find it. The Internet was becoming bigger and faster.

South Carolina courts were behind. When Toal was elected chief justice, court personnel communicated by telephone and fax machine. No major courthouse in South Carolina had Internet access. There was a unified court system in principle but not in practice. Each of the forty-six counties had its own way of managing cases that were filed, with most using a paper system. Other counties used a self-funded electronic system. These systems did not communicate with one another, and all systems, whether paper or electronic, were outmoded.

Statewide practices or procedures for managing court business were non-existent. The clerks of court handled the enormous volume of documents, money, and notification requirements on their own, with little guidance or support from the South Carolina Judicial Department. The lack of uniformity among the counties made it virtually impossible to coordinate cases and dockets or even provide accurate information on a statewide basis.

For example many counties in South Carolina did not have the ability to do something as basic as group criminal, civil, family, probate, or magistrate filings to see an accurate picture of their caseload. Several counties could not determine how many cases a particular judge, a solicitor, or a public defender had assigned to them. Some counties kept track of their docket by using 5" × 7" note cards stored in shoeboxes.

Add to these inefficiencies the fact that the 1990s were a time of unparalleled economic and population growth for South Carolina. The growth in population naturally led to a growth in the number of court filings. Between 1988 and 1997, the total number of cases filed in the state trial courts rose from 1.3 million to more than 1.75 million. Unparalleled backlogs plagued the state.

Prior chief justices attempted to solve the problem by adding more judges and new courtrooms. But available resources limited the number of new judges and new courtrooms that could be added. At the time, Chief Justice Toal observed, "Right now our system is dying at the trial level. We can't just simply continue to add judges. There is a finite limit to the whole trial level system. We need to think smarter about how to get cases done."[1]

Late on a Friday evening in the summer of 2001, responding to an emergency, members of the South Carolina Supreme Court assembled in Chief Justice Toal's kitchen in person and by telephone to issue a stay against a video poker operator. This emergency meeting made an impression on the chief justice. A statewide judicial system should not be managed on a yellow legal pad from the kitchen table, without ready access to legal research, court records, and filings.

It was time for the state of affairs to change. It was time for the courts in South Carolina to come into the twenty-first century. It was time for there to be a unified court system not just in principle, but in practice. Chief Justice Toal understood this, and she strongly believed that technology was the answer.

The State of South Carolina operates under a unified judicial system led by the chief justice. Within the unified judicial system, there are eight levels of court: Supreme Court, court of appeals, circuit court, family court, masters-in-equity court, probate court, magistrate court, and municipal court. Personnel, facilities, and services are provided through the state, counties, and municipalities.

Technology is not just a matter of record keeping—it was a matter of justice. The human cost of justice delayed is justice denied for the victims and the accused alike. An unorganized and inefficient court system inevitably leads to a breakdown in the administration of justice. Technology would allow the Judicial Department to evaluate caseloads on a statewide basis, to evaluate inequities, and to allocate resources, such as additional judges, where needed. The free and timely exchange of information was essential to the administration of justice.

Technology is fundamentally about connection. Court personnel need to be able to communicate quickly and effectively. Technology is about uniformity. A person should be able to walk into any courthouse in the state and know that her or his case will be handled or managed the same as it would in any other county. Technology is about access. Access to the courts and court documents makes justice an evenhanded proposition, whether a citizen lives in a small county like Allendale with a population of 10,419 or a large county like Richland with a population of 384,504.[2]

The recognition of technology as the key to the effective and efficient administration of justice would become the hallmark of Chief Justice Toal's terms as chief justice. Although personally used to the "old way" of conducting business, Chief Justice Toal had a vision for how an effective, statewide system of justice could and should operate in the twenty-first century. She was willing to learn whatever she needed to learn to get the job done. The very system of justice depended on it.

Devising a Plan

Every major endeavor starts with a plan. In her first week in office, Chief Justice Toal met with the senior staff of the South Carolina Budget and Control Board to discuss the creation of a business plan for the management of South Carolina's court system. Her proposed thesis: the state's court system could be dramatically improved by the use of technology. The staff advised her that if she was indeed serious, she needed to make a detailed and comprehensive assessment of the technology needs of the entire court system, from magistrates and county clerks to the Supreme Court itself.[3]

Drawing on her years in private practice and in helping run the family sand mine, Chief Justice Toal approached the court system and her administrative responsibilities like a business. She started by retaining the services of IT managers and a private consulting firm, KPMG, to draft a business plan that outlined the goals, defined the mission, and established the potential revenue sources through which the system could be supported.

Three themes permeated the plan and continue to resonate today: connectivity, access, and standardization. For the system of justice to work, people needed to be able to connect to one another and to the court system. Second, people needed access to court records and greater transparency from the courts. Finally, how courts conducted business among the counties needed to be standardized.

The plan consisted of five basic initiatives: (1) provide the infrastructure to create high-speed connectivity everywhere in South Carolina where the courts do business; (2) create websites for each county clerk's office and for the state judicial branch; (3) develop and implement statewide uniform case management software; (4) establish a call center to provide support and training for each county; and (5) standardize the imaging of documents for the automated system.

In South Carolina the chief justice is not just the presiding judge for the Supreme Court. Under the Article V, section 4, of the South Carolina Constitution, the chief justice is also the CEO of the third branch of government, or the person charged with providing the administrative leadership for the entire judicial department. As the state's top judicial official, Chief Justice Toal assumed the responsibility of ensuring that the system ran well. If the system broke down, it was her job to fix it.

The stakes were high. The plan had to work.

Building Support

The South Carolina Judicial Department's primary source of funding is the state legislature. If the plan to bring technology to the courts was going to be successful, Chief Justice Toal knew that she had to get the support of the General Assembly.

Chief Justice Toal had to couch the push for technology as an initiative about more than simply resolving disputes, conducting trials, and speeding up dockets. Her plea to the legislature had to be about the value that accrued directly to all aspects of society, and not just to the court system itself. Chief Justice Toal was tasked with convincing members of the legislature that an improved and accelerated flow of information would benefit both the private and public sectors.

South Carolina was behind. Most states already had a judicial case management system in place and had already begun reaping the benefits from such connectivity. In the year 2000, South Carolina ranked dead last in the terms of total dollars—as well as per capita dollars—spent on the state court system. No one likes to be last. As a former legislator, Chief Justice Toal knew that she had to use the soundness of the plan as well as a little bit of shaming to persuade the members of the General Assembly.

The payout was simple: South Carolina would have a unified court system in name as well as in fact. Every citizen, including law enforcement, solicitors, defenders, witnesses, victims, litigants, and members of the business community, would have access to information seven days a week, twenty-four hours a day. There would be increased accuracy, efficiency, and timeliness of court information. When fully implemented, the technology plan would save time, money, and valuable state resources.

Historically, when it came to appropriations, the General Assembly treated the South Carolina Judicial Department as a state agency. Chief Justice Toal sought to change that way of thinking. She often reminded the General Assembly that the South Carolina Judicial Department was a third, coequal branch of government and deserved to be regarded as such.

In her pleas to the legislature year after year, Chief Justice Toal focused on the importance of funding the three branches of government, including the courts. She emphasized the essential nature of the constitutional function of the courts. She posited that underfunding the courts would result in a destabilization of state government because one of the three coequal branches of government would not be able to perform its core functions.

Making the Case

In the early 2000s, the South Carolina General Assembly, like legislatures across the country, was facing a financial crisis. When Toal was elected chief justice in 1999, the judicial system was funded with $43 million in legislative appropriations. By the time she became chief justice, midyear cuts had reduced that figure to $40 million, .0785 percent (or 4/5 of 1 percent) of the state's total budget, and that number continued to decline over the years.

For example in 2003 the general appropriation for the Judicial Department was reduced to $32 million, representing .0706 percent (or less than 3/4 of 1 percent) of the state's budget. In 2006, even if all requests were granted, the third branch of government would still receive less than 1 percent of state revenues.

On top of the budget cuts, South Carolina had the highest caseload per capita on the trial bench of any state court system in the country. South Carolina had not added any new trial judges in years, and yet the criminal caseload continued to grow exponentially. As of 2014 the average caseload per judge in South Carolina remained among the highest in the nation.

The real crisis affected the criminal and the family court dockets. South Carolina has ranked among the highest in the nation per capita for violent crime (such as murder, armed robbery, drug-related crimes, and gang violence) and criminal domestic violence. These cases caused increasing backlogs in the courts.

In a time of severe budget cuts and increasing caseloads, greater efficiency through the use of technology and innovative business processes was the key to keeping courthouses open in South Carolina. Year after year, through the annual State of the Judiciary address, Chief Justice Toal made the case for technology and appropriate funding to the General Assembly.

For example, in the State of Judiciary address delivered to the General Assembly on February 21, 2001, Chief Justice Toal stated: "Justice is not a luxury; it is not subject to the ebbs and flows of political fortune or economic success. It demands constant support and attention. Join me in bringing the powers of technology to bear on the needs of the state's court system. Join me in making a commitment to our future. Join me in assuring that justice will be an engine for fairness and equity."[4]

Looking Outside the State

Chief Justice Toal's quest to gain the support and funding for the technology initiative did not end at the borders of South Carolina. Owing to budget cuts and economic downturn, Chief Justice Toal was forced to search for funding beyond the borders of South Carolina and the traditional state legislative funding mechanism.

In 2002 Chief Justice Toal secured $3.2 million in funding through grants received from the United States Department of Justice, Bureau of Justice Assistance. This sum was crucial to bringing Internet access to the courts across the state. The grant would not have been possible without the leadership of Senator Ernest Hollings and the support of the South Carolina congressional delegation. Senator Hollings and his staff were able to build the support necessary to fund South Carolina's effort to introduce a unified technology system to its courts. It should be noted that federal dollars continued to be the primary source for funding South Carolina's court technology from 2002 to 2007.

Once the grant dollars were awarded, Chief Justice Toal primarily allocated resources to the counties that had the least ability to generate funds on their own. Thirty-one of South Carolina's forty-six counties have a population of one hundred thousand or fewer, with most of these counties having a population of fewer than forty thousand.[5] A truly connected system needed to include everyone.

The funds were primarily used to provide the basic hardware needed to implement high-speed connectivity, and to build websites for each of the forty-six clerks of court. The websites would serve as points of access for law enforcement, judges, attorneys, litigants, and members of the public, to court records, court decisions, and court information.

The federal funds provided the initial, critical boost needed for the technology initiative to take off. These funds also provided Chief Justice Toal with the leverage she needed to obtain funding from the state legislature.

Building a Team

Chief Justice Toal knew that she could not tackle the monumental task of modernizing the court system alone, even if it was her primary job. As a justice on the Supreme Court, she had a full caseload in addition to her obligations as the chief administrative officer. She needed a team, and she needed a good one.

Chief Justice Toal began by identifying a leader. She chose Joan Assey, a former school teacher with a doctorate degree and over thirty years of experience in education. During her time as an educator, Dr. Assey was instrumental in bringing T-1 Internet connectivity to every public school and library in Richland School District 2 in the mid-1990s through federally sponsored education grants. Dr. Assey also served as an advisor to Governor Jim Hodges regarding education and technology for distance learning in rural areas.

As the director of information technology, Dr. Assey built a team of managers and staff to lead Chief Justice Toal's technology initiative. Dr. Assey traveled all over the state introducing the initiative and promoting collaboration and local involvement. She attended county council meetings and meetings with local stakeholders, making presentations, answering questions, and building support.

Collaboration was critical. Chief Justice Toal and her team made sure to include judges, lawyers, county administrators, county IT managers, and law enforcement, to name a few, from the outset. Clerks of court, technology directors, and local officials helped design the new case management system. By involving these individuals and entities from the beginning, listening to their needs, and responding with ideas, a truly collaborative environment emerged.

Chief Justice Toal also realized that outside partnerships should be formed to ensure the project's success. The National Center for State Courts became a key partner. State courts across the country routinely turn to the center for information and guidance. The center helped South Carolina develop a statewide strategic plan for a comprehensive statewide case management system. The center's technology staff visited South Carolina numerous times, providing technical assistance and project management expertise.

In June 2000 Chief Justice Toal engaged KPMG as the systems integrator for the South Carolina Judicial Department. The firm was tasked with conducting a comprehensive examination of the current use and application of information technology by the Judicial Department. John Starmack was designated as the project manager and was tasked with developing the Strategic Technology Plan for the state courts that is still being used today.

Through grassroots efforts and leadership at every level, implementation of the plan was underway.

"Going for the Gold"

The cornerstone of Chief Justice Toal's technology plan was to use high-speed Internet-based connectivity to improve court operations and enhance public access to the court system. In 2001 there was no high-speed Internet access in any county courthouse. By 2003 twenty-five of the forty-six county courthouses had reliable, high-speed connectivity. In June 2004 all forty-six county courthouses had reliable, high-speed Internet connectivity.

The effort to bring reliable, high-speed Internet to the counties became known as "Going for the gold," a phrase coined by Joan Assey. Chief Justice

Toal maintained a map of the state of South Carolina and its counties, and she colored in gold the counties where high-speed connectivity had been installed. As one county and then the next became gold, other county officials began to say, "We want to be a gold county."

At the same time that high-speed connectivity was being installed in county courthouses throughout the state, the Judicial Department and the counties were each developing websites, which became portals through which members of the public could access information about cases and legal filings.

The Supreme Court website, which practically did not exist until 2001, became a point of access for a variety of valuable information, including court news, court calendars, orders and opinions, bar examination results, trial schedules, court rules and manuals, and standard court forms. In 2002, in honor of Freedom of Information Day, the South Carolina State Library recognized the Supreme Court website as one of the ten notable publications released in the past year.

By 2003 South Carolina became one of the few states in the country where every clerk of court's office had its own website. Clerks of court began posting their rosters online, saving thousands of dollars in serving notices by mail.

The savings and efficiencies promised through technology were becoming a reality.

A Case Study

In the summer of 2003, the Clarendon County courthouse braced for what would be one of the most significant trials in the state's history. The case was *Abbeville County School District v. State of South Carolina.*[6] The plaintiffs—school districts, students, parents, and taxpayers—challenged South Carolina's method of funding public schools. The case was historic not only because of the issues involved, but because of its size. Ultimately the trial would last 102 days, becoming the longest trial in the state's history, during which 112 witnesses would testify and approximately forty-four hundred documents would be entered into evidence.

In anticipation of the trial, the lawyers brought boxes full of documents with them to the courthouse. Unlike for most cases, the lawyers did not have five or ten boxes. They had 550 boxes. The weight of the boxes broke the courthouse elevator.

It did not take long to realize that a case this size could not be managed and tried using paper documents alone. The lawyers and the court needed electronic access to documents. Through major innovation and effort, the rural Clarendon County courthouse was transformed into a twenty-first-century courtroom within a matter of weeks. Christopher Rogers, network manager, and his staff as well as Scott Hayes, applications manager of the South Carolina Judicial Department recall having "all hands on deck" to finish the project. It was not unusual during the installation for the entire IT team to be on the floor pulling cable lines through walls and installing wire. By the time the trial began, Internet was available in the courtroom, and each law firm was able to access over eighteen thousand documents electronically as potential exhibits in the case. Even the local Holiday Inn Express, where some of the lawyers stayed, got on board. The hotel installed DSL lines to keep pace and to accommodate the lawyers' needs.

Having the right people in place was essential to transforming the courthouse into a state-of-the-art facility. Judge Thomas W. Cooper Jr. had the vision to realize that technology was essential to trying the case and to implement this vision in a rural locale. The clerk of court, Beulah G. Roberts, was willing to do whatever it took to make technology available in her courthouse. Even the court reporter, Kathleen Richardson, learned how to use real-time transcription in less than a month and used it for the first time during the trial.

The attorneys, all seasoned trial lawyers, had never tried a case in South Carolina in which they had electronic access to exhibits and Internet connectivity in the courtroom. One of the lawyers for the state, Robert E. "Bobby" Stepp, recalls, "It may seem commonplace today, but in 2003 it was groundbreaking to have Internet access in a courtroom in South Carolina, particularly in a courtroom in a small county like Clarendon. Having electronic access to the evidence and to the Internet fundamentally changed the way we prepared and tried the case."[7]

As the trier of fact, Judge Cooper had several resources at his fingertips. On one side of the bench, he had a computer that held a database of exhibits. On the other side, he had a computer showing real-time transcription of the testimony. He could stop the real time transcription at any moment and mark important areas of testimony. He could make notes in the margins, saving him hours of time when he later sat down to write the order.

The courtroom was also equipped with a large plasma television screen that projected the exhibits to the testifying witnesses as well as those who sat in the courtroom. Selected text could be highlighted and enlarged for everyone to see.

Carl B. Epps III, an attorney for the plaintiffs, said, "We made full use of the technology in the courtroom, which was novel at the time. We conducted Internet searches while witnesses were testifying and used websites or similar information that proved to be inconsistent with the witnesses' testimony on a regular basis. We created PowerPoints on the fly while witnesses were testifying for visual presentations of points we wanted to make. We had real-time transcripts for the lawyers and the court and relied on them heavily to confirm what we understood a witness to say when arguing points or examining the witness. The use of technology and the monitors made available to both parties, the court, and the witness enabled us to bring testimony and exhibits to life. Having the ability to use technology during the trial was a godsend in this complex and data driven case. It saved us an enormous amount of time, and all of us were able to tell our stories more effectively."

With the permission of the parties, Chief Justice Toal visited the trial one day and sat on the bench with Judge Cooper to see the implementation of the technology for herself. Elizabeth "Betsy" Van Doren Gray, a lawyer for the state, tells a story of the chief justice's visit to the courtroom that day: "I was in the middle of cross-examining one of the plaintiffs' key witnesses, and the examination was going very well. I was eliciting one admission after another from the witness. From time to time, I would look up at the bench to see if Chief Justice Toal and Judge Cooper were watching. They were whispering back and forth, marveling at the technology. Of course I wanted all the attention on my cross-examination, but the technology appeared to be stealing the show!"

The *Abbeville* case signified what was possible through the use of technology. South Carolina courts would be ready to handle the large, document-heavy trials that would become common in the modern era.

Owning It

During the time that the infrastructure for high-speed Internet access was being installed in courthouses across the state, work had begun on developing a case management system that would hold and track all the documents filed in a case, and that would allow the public to access court documents without stepping foot in the courthouse. Anyone, from attorneys to court personnel, to members of the public, could access a particular county's website and find out whether a case had been filed, and who the attorneys were, and view the filings.

Two key decisions were made early on. First, the Judicial Department decided to use an Internet-based system. This was risky business at the time. It was virtually unheard of for a government entity to have a website or to depend on the Internet to provide access to important documents. This decision was made in part based on innovation and in part on necessity. The Judicial Department did not have the funds to purchase large mainframe computers and to pay the hefty license fees it would take to support the system statewide. An Internet-based system would allow all forty-six counties in South Carolina, including the most rural, to afford to develop and maintain case information and court filings on their websites.

Second, the team determined that the Judicial Department needed to own the system. Initially the team worked with an outside vendor to develop the system. Over time it became apparent that an outside vendor would not be able to provide the level of service and expertise needed to operate the system over the long term, so the team took the bold step of acquiring the system from the vendor.

Although the acquisition of the system gave the Judicial Department more control, it also meant that the department had to become adept at servicing the system in-house. To do this the Judicial Department had to essentially create an in-house software company, a function not tradition-ally associated with a court system. Although the challenges were great, the benefits were many. Owning the system gave the Judicial Department the ability to modify and upgrade the system to reflect changes in the law, court rules, and procedure.

Once the system was developed, the Judicial Department gave the case management system to each county, at no cost to the county. Counties were responsible only for the maintenance fees.

Taking Off

Once Internet connectivity was established, the Judicial Department began deploying the case management system.

The first step was to identify the counties to pilot the system. Chief Justice Toal wanted to test the system in a small, rural county, and in a large county. Greenville County, the largest county in the state, was the first to volunteer. Greenville County already had a sophisticated informa-tion technology department in place. It also had a clerk of court, Paul Wickensimer, who had worked in the private sector for a utility company and could tap into that experience in working hand in hand with the Judi-cial Department staff. Another large county, Richland County, where the state capital is located, also volunteered. Pickens County, a relatively small county in the upper northwest corner of the state, adjacent to Greenville County, was the third county to volunteer. Because of their proximity to one another, Pickens and Greenville Counties partnered to host the sys-tem from a single platform.

These three counties began implementing the pilot program in 2002. In mid-2004 the case management system "went live" in these counties. By 2011 every county in South Carolina was using the Internet-based case management system.

The South Carolina Judicial Department gave the counties the system at no cost. The South Carolina Judicial Department provided around-the-clock support, a level of service not provided by previous private vendors.

As of 2015 the Judicial Department hosted forty-two of the forty-six counties, serving 3.1 million people. The only counties not hosted by the Judicial Department were the larger counties that already had an information technology infrastructure in place. The backup to the statewide server has been provided off-site through a partnership with Clemson University.

Chief Justice Toal's vision had been realized. A truly unified statewide system had been achieved. From 2002 to 2007 the South Carolina Judicial Department received 52 million dollars in federal grants to integrate technology within the South Carolina courts in all forty-six counties.

Leading the Way

South Carolina's technology journey is one of short duration. Within the first few years of Chief Justice Toal's administration, the South Carolina Judicial Department transitioned from an unknown entity using an archaic system to handle caseloads to a new role as a national leader in using an Internet-based platform to do the business of the court.

In 2002 the National Center for Digital Government, an international research and advisory institute on information technology for government and industry leaders, recognized the South Carolina Judicial Department with the "In the Arena Award." The award recognizes information technology leaders who strive for greatness, and whose devotion and enthusiasm have earned them a place "in the arena."

In 2003 Chief Justice Toal was recognized by *Government Technology* magazine with a "Top 25 Doers, Dreamers and Drivers Award." That same year she was the keynote speaker for the technology conference hosted by the National Center for State Courts. Chief Justice Toal told South Carolina's story of how a small, rural state with a tremendous caseload and limited resources became a technology leader. In 2004 Chief Justice Toal told the South Carolina story once again as the keynote speaker at the Kansas Judicial Conference.

In 2011 Chief Justice Toal was named the first recipient of the National Center for State Courts' Sandra Day O'Connor Award for the Advancement of Civics Education for her leadership in making South Carolina one of the first pilot states for Justice O'Connor's iCivics, a web-based interactive civics education program.

In 2013 the Forum for the Advancement of Court Technology recognized the South Carolina Judicial Department website as one of the top ten court websites in the country. The award honors courts that have extended and expanded access to public records, court services, and information online.

Today South Carolina is viewed by courts across the country as a national leader in its approach to court record management, based in large part by the decision made fourteen years ago to use an Internet-based platform for court records.

Looking back to the year 2000, it was improbable that a third branch of government, particularly a court system, would use an Internet-based system to manage its court records. No one could have predicted how integral the Internet would become in our lives and in world of business. Getting on board early was vital to the success story that is the South Carolina story.

For all this attention, Chief Justice Toal has given credit where credit is due: "The people who have made it work are the people in the smallest places in South Carolina in magistrates' offices and clerks' offices because that's where automation starts. It doesn't start in the big shot offices in Columbia."

The Present

As of 2015 the South Carolina Judicial Department is unified in principle and in practice.

The South Carolina Judicial Department currently uses four statewide court software systems.

- The Case Management System (CMS) provides standardized record keeping and business processes in circuit court and magistrates courts for all forty-six counties. The South Carolina Judicial Department hosts, maintains, and supports the systems in forty-two of the counties, serving 1,729 users and benefitting 3.1 million people statewide.
- The Appellate Case Management System (C-Track) manages the Supreme Court and court of appeals records and provides public access to briefs, records, orders, opinions, and documents filed in the appellate courts.
- The Attorney Information System (AIS) serves as a central repository of contact information for the approximately fifteen thousand licensed lawyers in South Carolina. This system was a necessary first step for establishing an electronic filing system in South Carolina.
- Electronic filing (e-Flex) remains the crown jewel. In 2012 the General Assembly invested $5 million to launch the development of an electronic filing system. The system is currently under development and is expected to be piloted in 2015.

Except for the C-Track system, the State of South Carolina owns each of these systems. Owning the systems gives the state the ability to support and modify the systems in-house, on an ongoing basis. It also gives the state control over the security and stability of the systems.

Ownership has paid off in other ways. Ordinarily outside vendors share in the user fees generated by a software system. Because the State of South

Carolina owns the CMS and other systems, the fees generated from the use of the systems go back to the state.

Today members of the public can watch an oral argument at the South Carolina Supreme Court from the comfort of their home or office. The arguments are available online at the South Carolina Judicial Department website. Citizens can track any case from start to finish, without having to spend the time and incur the expense of traveling to Columbia, where the Supreme Court sits.

The presence of technology in the courtroom is obvious when you step foot into any courtroom in South Carolina. Judges and their law clerks typically have laptop computers on the bench. Court reporters and court personnel can also be seen working on computers. Lawyers bring computers and handheld devices to court. Information can be accessed with the touch of a button. Digital monitors are available to display documents, exhibits, videos, and any other manner of digital presentation.

Even in the appellate courts, where the use of technology in the courtroom has traditionally not been so obvious, large digital screens are permanently affixed to the courtroom walls, allowing attorneys or the judges to call up a document from the court record at any time for demonstrative purposes.

Perhaps most important, the public can access documents filed in circuit courts throughout the state without cost through the individual county websites. Members of the public can also access documents filed in cases on appeal through the C-Track system on the Judicial Department website. The courthouse doors are truly open and accessible to everyone.

What began as an aspirational idea has become intricately woven into the fabric of the judicial system in South Carolina. Every time the chief justice writes an administrative order, technology is part of the conversation. For example in 2007 when Chief Justice Toal ordered the creation of a pilot program for the business courts in the circuit courts of South Carolina, technology played a key role. Business courts, which are now available statewide, are courts designed to handle complex business, corporate, and commercial matters. Cases pending in the business courts are assigned to a single judge who manages the case from start to finish. Business court judges are required to issue written orders on dispositive motions. The written orders are sent to Court Administration, which publishes the orders online, creating a body of law on complex business matters that did not exist before.

This is just one example of how technology has become an integral part of the court system and how the Judicial Department has evolved with the times and with the demands of the people it serves. Businesses need reliable courts where they can seek relief. The development of a first-class court system and the creation of business courts has been a critical piece in building the state's economy.

Technology has been a game changer for South Carolina courts and for the citizens of South Carolina. Technology has brought a level of sophistication, efficiency, and uniformity to the South Carolina's judicial system that had never before existed.

The Future

Electronic filing is the future of the South Carolina court system. Electronic filing will provide lawyers and parties the ability to file, serve, and view legal documents over the Internet at any time, even when the court is closed, revolutionizing the way that business is conducted in the state courts of South Carolina. Once again the primary benefit is access. Members of the public will have the ability to access court documents at every level—trial or appellate—from anywhere using a computer.

The integration of technology into the court system and the modern era have brought with them new challenges that the Judicial Department will continue to address. For example enhanced security is and will continue to be a main priority. The Judicial Department will continue to dedicate resources to data protection and training centered on security awareness.

Another priority is disaster recovery. In 2014 the Judicial Department requested funding for a disaster recovery system to ensure that all forty-six counties are able to continue essential functions should disaster strike. The Judicial Department has also partnered with Clemson University to develop a disaster recovery or backup center outside of Columbia. Whether there be a natural disaster, a health pandemic, or a terrorist act, the business of the courts must keep going.

Finally the same themes identified early on—connectivity, uniformity, and access—will continue to inform refinements to the current systems. Until the day she retires from the bench, Chief Justice Toal will continue to make technology a priority, finding ways to make the courts in this state more accessible, more efficient, and easier to navigate by citizens, attorneys, and all who use the court system.

Madam Chief Justice

The significance of Jean Hoefer Toal's tenure as chief justice and the impact that her vision and leadership have had on South Carolina cannot be overstated. When she was sworn into office, the courts in South Carolina were years behind courts in other states in terms of technology and how caseloads were tracked and managed. Today technology in the courtroom is as much a fixture as the American flag, thanks to the vision and leadership of Chief Justice Toal.

Chief Justice Toal distinctly remembers the day she was sworn in as the state's first female chief justice. As the swearing-in ceremony was taking place inside the courtroom, Chief Justice Toal could hear the murmur of voices coming from the lobby, just beyond the doors to the courtroom. Hundreds of women lawyers from across the state had gathered in the courtroom lobby and stood on the courtroom steps to be a part of this significant moment in South Carolina history.

After taking the oath and addressing the audience, Chief Justice Toal did not retreat to the privacy of her home or chambers. Instead she made her way to the lobby and out to the courthouse steps to join those who had assembled, recognizing that it was their moment too. There is a famous photograph capturing the momentous occasion. It was then that the name that would be written large in the history of South Carolina became known: Madam Chief Justice.

NOTES

1. "Jean Toal Poised to Become Chief Justice," *Post & Courier*, February 27, 2000.
2. 2010 Census.
3. Chief Justice Toal, State of the Judiciary address, Joint Session of the General Assembly, February 21, 2001.
4. Chief Justice Toal, State of the Judiciary address, February 21, 2001.
5. 2010 Census.
6. *Abbeville Cnty. Sch. Dist. v. State (Abbeville II)*, 2014 WL 5839956, November 12, 2014; *Abbeville Cnty. Sch. Dist. v. State (Abbeville I)*, 335 S.C. 58, 515 S.E.2d 535 (1999).
7. Interview by Tina Cundari, December 7, 2014.

Family, Friends, and Community

Jean Toal, Family at the Center

BEFORE SHE WAS THE senior member of the five-member Supreme Court—
her brothers and sisters on the bench—Jean Toal was the eldest of the five
Hoefer children. She is known politically for her aggressive leadership of
the South Carolina judicial system, but the judges, clerks, and lawyers
don't know the half of it. She's been bossing her family around for our
entire lives. Either because she has worn us down or because it is true, we
love being along for the ride when she's in charge.

Family has always been central to Toal. Her three sisters and brother,
along with cousins, were her earliest circle of confidants and companions.
The summoning together of family for forced fun and food is a long-standing
Toal tradition. When the Toal daughters, Jean and Lilla, were young, the
week really began on Sunday morning with the smell of pork roast, twined
in rosemary. If our mom is cooking for a crowd, she is a blur of action,
chopping, stirring, rattling the cabinets with only the occasional "God-
damn it, Jean" flying around the kitchen if the knife dares get too close to
her fingers. By the time our grandmothers, Margaret "Pat" Toal and Lilla
Hoefer, and some subset of aunts, uncles, and cousins arrived in the afternoon, the whole feast would be close to finished. The pork roast with its
parade of sides like lima beans, creamed corn, double-stuffed potatoes,
and sweet tea were made only more delicious by the rule that children were
allowed to go through the line first. To finish the meal, there was usually
apple pie with ice cream, cheddar cheese, or both.

While the meal was delicious, it wasn't the point. The meal was simply
the method of gathering friends and family. Everyone's activities were a
subject of freewheeling conversation that might touch on the latest
goings-on at the Garden Club, the courthouse, the State House, and even
A. C. Moore Elementary School. Then the storytelling would begin. Family members would tell stories about Mom's father and his brothers starting

the sand mine, or Mom and her sister Lilla cutting up with cousin Sophie, vacations at Sea Island, and stories of the terrifying nuns of St. Peter's. That weekly touchstone was a mixing of generations, a time to share oral history, and an opportunity for family to be together.

Loud, opinionated, and driven in public, in private Toal has a fierceness that translates as something closer to loyalty. History will probably remember her reelection as chief justice in 2014 as her most difficult political race, but her family remembers the many House races, unsuccessful bids for the court, and successful judicial elections that preceded it. In the winter of 1995, our mother was the first sitting Supreme Court justice to be challenged for reelection in over one hundred years. The election coincided with other challenges closer to home.

Bill Toal's mother, Pat, a constant, lively companion for Sunday dinners and family vacations, was less and less able to care for herself. Bill had been dutifully traveling to her Forest Acres home daily to check on her, but even morning and night visits didn't seem like enough. Seeing that Bill's constant worry and back-and-forth was unsustainable, Jean was sure she had a solution. The decision to invite Pat to move in, and to build the "Granny House," an addition that would accommodate her wheelchair, was easy. Jean never thought twice about tearing out her rose garden or bringing her mother-in-law into her home.

Jean's younger daughter, Lilla, watched both events unfold—her mother's contentious 1995 election and her grandmother's decline—and she still remembers that winter with the bitterness of a disillusioned fifteen-year-old. Even as her parents showed so much compassion under stress at home, all the public saw was article after article about how aggressive and "abusive" her mother was in her role at the court. When Lilla asked her mom, "Why don't you fight back? I think you should show them what real aggression looks like." Jean's simple reply was, "I've got to take the high road."

As unpleasant as the crucible of South Carolina politics can be, in some ways it's unsurprising that our mother has thrived. When others are worried and frustrated, when the right way is unclear, when crisis seems like it is lurking around the corner, our mother is in her element. She leans hard on the principles that are important to her and the people that are important to her, and she is able to help us see the world as it should be instead of dwelling on the world as it is.

Family, Friends, and Community

Family for Jean Toal includes more than those related directly by blood. It includes the whole circle of "the people" she has acquired over time. She is particularly fond of telling the story of meeting Jim Assey and his family at Camp St. Mary's at age eleven. She'll begin, "He was the head of his family and I was the head of mine," as though they were tiny adolescent feudal lords meeting to sign a land deal. She talks in similarly glowing terms about all her friends, as if it is her fate to meet the most wonderful people, in the most wonderful places, and to shoulder the responsibility of showering them with her own brand of force-feeding, drill sergeanting, elaborate merry-making love.

When Jean and her husband, Bill, moved back to Columbia as a young couple, they began to cultivate a circle of friends that would also become their family. They reconnected with law school friends and Jean's fellow Dreher High School alumni and neighbors Martha and John Bryan. Together with three other young families—the Asseys, the Groses, and the Waites—the four couples formed the "Table for Eight." Their families socialized and vacationed together in Saluda, North Carolina, Litchfield, South Carolina, and Swans Island, Maine, where their children always put on shows for their parents; the most memorable was a patriotic bicentennial extravaganza. In later years they joined with other Columbia families to form the ChamberPots, an irreverently named social club devoted to sharing a love of food and chamber music with a younger, not immediately appreciative, generation. As Toal's daughters age, we have come to appreciate so much more than the explicit lessons of culture these adults gave us. They are more than casual friends; they call each other to celebrate and commiserate. They are the first people to show up for a funeral or a wedding, and they end up in the kitchen and in charge because they know exactly where everything is and exactly what is needed. They have taught us that part of living a good life is having others to share in that bounty.

Behind a woman who seems to have it all is a partner who is getting it all, whether he wants it or not. None of our fond memories of Mom's service and our family would have been possible without the patience and support of one man: Bill Toal. Bill and Jean met in law school and married between their second and third years. Like the law students they were, they still "renew their contract" each year on their anniversary. But that joking belies the deep and abiding partnership between two people who share not just a love of the law but a view of what it means to live a good life—surrounded by family and friends and serving the community. They share values, but their personalities are complimentary. Where Mom is a blur of motion, Dad is so calm we sometimes don't know if he is awake until he cracks a joke.

Their partnership started officially as a young married couple editing the *South Carolina Law Review,* he as editor in chief and she as a managing editor, but we like to imagine what might have attracted them to each other. Imagine two driven, absolutely brilliant, undoubtedly somewhat romantically awkward law students, in thick-rimmed 1960s glasses and one with groovy sideburns. Whatever smooth lines were or were not exchanged to kick off their courtship, it was clear they had both found someone who was a true equal. Someone to stand toe-to-toe with. A worthy opponent for debate and a devoted sidekick for fun. No one knows how to get on Jean's nerves more than Bill, and no one makes her laugh as hard. Bill brings out her tender side, but he is also unfailing in his support of her initiatives, small and large.

Jean and Bill's ability to work together on what is important has become an abiding part of their marriage and family life. They were equally enthusiastic partners in raising us, their daughters. Dad was just as likely to scoop us up for a pizza dinner as Mom was to take us out in the backyard to run around. From reading stories to us, to patiently listening to our explanations of what we were learning at school, to schlepping all over the state for sports and academic competitions, they were deeply involved in our lives. Because they knew our needs so well, they were also comfortable inviting other adults to help share the responsibility for caring for us. The influence of other adults—our nannies, Viola Patrick and Pansy Baskett, our grandmothers, Lilla and Pat, our aunts and uncles, and their incredible network of friends—was profound. Beyond broadening our perspective, having contact with so many different adults with strong character helped us understand that leaning on others is a sign of strength, not weakness.

Beyond a strong circle of family and friends, Jean Toal is fiercely loyal to Columbia, its many communities, and its institutions. A tour of downtown with her takes forever because she wants you to understand the significance of each building, not only in its present form, but also for who lived there and worked there twenty, sixty, or hundreds of years ago. As a sidewalk historian, she is just as likely to let you in on childhood secrets—that the post office building that became the Supreme Court was the best place to roller skate or that the librarian at the Caroliniana granted her check-out privileges at the age of eight—as she is to highlight South Carolina's colorful past of protest, assassination, and legislative shenanigans. From serving as a founding member of the Shandon Neighborhood Council, to being a vocal member of the A. C. Moore PTA long before her daughter Jean was a student there, to attending events at both her husband's and her own home parishes, Shandon Presbyterian and St. Joseph's Catholic Church, Jean gives her energy back to a city that provided her abundant opportunities to explore and learn as a child.

Jean Toal, Builder of the Cathedral of Life

The U.S. government class at Dreher High School used to take a field trip to the state Supreme Court. When Lilla was a freshman, she got cornered after the visit. "Man, your mom is tough. Does she question you like that?" The answer is that Jean Toal is discerning and decisive in every aspect of her life. When Mom is passionate about something, she is "all in." When she gets her mind set on making or doing something, she wants it to be the very best.

A family friend, Jusef Assi, coined a phrase that is perfect for describing this phenomenon. When the very first Publix grocery store opened in his town, he told us in reverent tones, "It's Beautiful. Everything you could want. Like a palace. So clean. Like a cathedral." Not long after, "like a cathedral" found its way into Toalese, the strange non-idiomatic language our mother uses to communicate. The often illogical and convoluted pursuit of the very best, most cathedralesque experience is a hallmark of the way Jean Toal lives her life, whether she's remodeling her kitchen to be just the way she wants ("like a palace") or driving a van full of bricks to Washington, D.C., so that her daughter's garden can achieve near-palace status.

The pursuit of Toal-standard "excellence" frequently takes time and a less than straightforward path to achieve. No one makes a better companion on this journey than Toal's longtime friend Joan Assey, one of the few women whose standards are even more exacting than her own. By way of illustration, Joan and Jean decided that Jean's front yard needed an extreme makeover. The sloped hill leading to the street was a mess of weeds and roots. "Wouldn't it be beautiful if it were terraced and planted with ivy?" Armed with their vision, Joan made plans, and Jean got out the shovel. When the job was too big for the two of them, they recruited their children and their friends' children, Tom Sawyer–style, to weed, terrace, and replant the banks. Joan's high school–aged son, James, did most of the work, with his sister Elizabeth and little Jean pitching in. Even elementary-aged Lilla earned money that summer hauling and digging in the front yard.

Joan and Jean tackle problems with gusto. Conference audiences all over the country know they transformed court technology in South Carolina. But before they did that, they transformed yards from Wheat Street to Saluda Avenue, to Athens, Georgia, to Washington, D.C. Joan draws elaborate plans. She has a meticulously organized and labeled notebook full of examples for inspiration. The very finest purveyors are found. Each plant has a place. Jean is the foreman, getting the job over the finish line. In her younger days, she was the hauler, the hole digger, the muscle. She taught all of us that if you have a $5 plant, you need a $10 hole.

Gardening is only one example of Jean's philosophy that anything worth doing is worth doing in the biggest, boldest way possible. In sports she does not just root for a team, she adopts them for life. The chief who has mentored generations of Gamecock women hoopsters is the consummate fan in the stands. She loves baseball, but whether it's the Braves, the Gamecocks, or little Jean's softball team, she always has a scorebook in hand. It makes her feel involved in the game. At home she keeps a "shrine" full of talismans that bring good luck to her various teams. A neon Braves sign lights up her kitchen.

Mom always believes that anything worth doing, including watching or playing a sport, is worth doing well. Even if you love a sport and are dedicated to practice and playing, that does not mean you will actually excel at playing that sport. For Jean that is extremely vexing. In golf she's perfectly willing to buy the latest and greatest club or gadget in pursuit of shaving off a few strokes. Bill always says, "If you could buy a golf game, Jean would have one." Her daughters and even their friends have generations of discarded clubs, passed down to make room for the latest and greatest.

Her willingness to lose herself in a passion goes beyond sports. When she becomes interested in a topic, she immerses herself. And if she is not an expert going in, she will learn: reading books, talking to those in the field, and emulating the very best. Sometimes that produces amazing results. She can tell you the strengths and weaknesses of every Teddy Roosevelt biographer, explain the intricacies of developing a sand mine, compare the merits of early twentieth-century cowgirl yodelers, and quote "Tintern Abbey" from memory. Our family benefited most from her decision to take up biscuit-making, using Bill's grandfather's recipe. Even after many rounds of inedible hockey pucks, she was determined to become the family champ. Today her biscuits are the lightest and fluffiest, but she has set her sights on besting her grandson Patrick, whose biscuits won reserve champion at the Arlington County fair, and Bill, against whom she enters biscuits in head-to-head State Fair competition each fall.

We hesitate to share one of our best examples of Mom's pursuit of excellence at all costs, but we're hoping that the statute of limitations for minor customs violations is short. In 1988 the Toals and the Asseys took a Christmas vacation to England to join James, who was studying in Oxford at the time. Mom and Joan had scouted out the perfect flat and the perfect itinerary; all that was left was to plan the perfect Christmas dinner. We would start the day by listening to Queen Elizabeth's Christmas address. For dessert a traditional English figgy pudding would be served before we headed out to enjoy carols and services at a lovely village church. The difficult part to figure out was the proper English feast. If you have exacting tastes, and you have been known to drive hours out of your way to get the best barbeque, peaches, or produce in a state you know well, settling for the unknowns of the beef of the British Isles just isn't going to cut it. So, unbeknownst to most of us, into our checked baggage went a Lexington County country ham, just in case. This was pre-9/11 and pre–mad cow, so regulations and questioning weren't incredibly tight. Even though the ham turned out to be too large for our small English oven (and had to be cooked with the door propped open), as expected, the country ham from Four Oaks Farm was indeed delicious.

A Gathering Place

Many of Toal's finest schemes start with an idea that is already close to her heart. Her parents' house on Adger Road was special to Toal not just as her childhood home, but also as the place where she played the role of Sergeant York to her four siblings, the place where her ambition and intellect matured together. It was a gathering place where sisters, brothers, and cousins shared relaxing afternoons at the pool, Easter egg hunts, and Christmas cheer. She had marked milestones in those halls—births, deaths, graduations, joining and leading the court, birthdays, weddings, and anniversaries. As her own mother aged, our mom knew that her family needed a gathering place for the time after the Hoefers left Adger Road. They needed a beach house.

The Hoefers love the Isle of Palms. Cousins had a house on Sullivan's Island, and Jean spent many summer nights on the Charleston barrier islands as a child and teenager. Every August she reminds us how she spent her sweet sixteenth birthday mere yards down the beach. They bought property in the late 1990s, but it took until 2006 before the perfect beach house was ready for fun. Mom sweated every detail of the construction. She made sure there were enough bedrooms for her mother and siblings. The house had to be wheelchair accessible for her mother, and there needed to be a porch—a big porch with a railing that holds a beverage and another at foot height, so you can rock your rocker while watching beach-goers and Charleston Harbor traffic.

Today the "Sand Pit" is ground zero for family fun. Like Adger Road before it, the beach house has seen weddings, birthdays, anniversaries, holidays, and reunions. More than anything, it is a gathering place to stay connected to siblings and their families and to make new memories, one beach week at a time.

But do not imagine Toal actually relaxes at the beach. Beach week days begin early with Mom in the kitchen. Regardless of whether anyone else is awake or hungry, she cooks "the full Hunt Club breakfast" of bacon, sausage, grits, eggs (scrambled or fried), and, of course, biscuits every morning. An assortment of jams and jellies is produced. Many pots of coffee are consumed. Throughout the day there will be activities, golf, mini-golf, visits to historic sites, tennis, and beach going. Then, in the evening, everyone will gather, relax, and recount their day. Begrudgingly Mom will now allow her sons-in-law to cook the dinner, often for more than twenty gathered friends and family from three generations.

Jean Toal, the Nontraditional Traditionalist

Leo Tolstoy's oft-quoted line "all happy families are alike; each unhappy family is unhappy in its own way" provides a quick diagnosis, yet it ignores a whole category of families common worldwide and endemic to the American South. The family that is just a little . . . strange. The realization that your family is strange, not just unique or quirky, but maybe only a hair's breadth away from full on crazy, is no sudden epiphany. Only when you get out into the world on your own can you gradually see that the routines, vocabulary, mannerisms, and compulsions you assumed were within the realm of normal are not that normal after all.

When we were both living at home, we did not think anything was strange about having a mother who worked as a lawyer and a legislator. Our mother isn't known as a cutting-edge fashionista (this is the same woman who wore full slips under her suits under her robes until at least 1996), but to us, she had an amazing closet for playing dress up. Inside the doors waited a rainbow of perfumed suits, jackets, blouses, and an army of stiff Ferragamo heels she wore to stomp up and down the marble halls of the General Assembly. When we tied her "feminine" 1980s bow ties around our heads and laughed, Mom would take the joke and change the subject. Only when we grew up and continued to give her grief did she explain that her closet was strange for a reason. When she began her career, she was one of ten women in the state of South Carolina practicing law. There was not a booming market for court-appropriate attire. Those silly lady bow ties, along with the suits and heels, and we suspect some of the cussing and bravado she is known for, were all parts of a costume that might convince skeptical male judges and legislators to pay attention to her arguments rather than her gender. We were just fortunate enough to grow up in a household where our parents taught us that the idea that someone would not take your ideas seriously because of your age, gender, or race was as silly as those paisley rosettes.

It also dawned on us slowly that all the traditions and rituals we took for granted were not actually traditional. When we were children, nothing seemed more normal than beginning each day by coming down the staircase and greeting the portrait of Teddy Roosevelt with "Good Morning, Mr. President." We thought it was pretty normal to ensure good luck by saying "Rabbit, rabbit!" on the first day of the month before anyone else chimed in. Maybe it comes from being raised as a Catholic, a religion filled with novenas, saints' days, stations, and other repetitive rituals, but our Mom loves to repeat funny, quirky things until they become traditions. A cauliflower put in a stocking at Christmas instead of traditional fruit now is decorated to commemorate the year's victories (the Outback-Bowl-iflower), births (Baby Ruth-iflower), and even deaths (Michael Jackson-iflower, complete with sparkly glove). A pot of spaghetti sauce put on to make Sunday night's meal easier becomes a never-to-be-varied tradition of eating pasta while watching the *Wonderful World of Disney,* even when Mom really wanted to be watching *60 Minutes.*

As law students and as a young couple, Jean and Bill loved to host oyster roasts in the backyard. Over the years those gatherings transformed into a Christmas tradition: Wheat Street Irregulars. Sometime in the early 1980s, a caroling party that roamed the neighborhood spreading Christmas cheer became housebound. Bill says it was because the neighbors asked them not to sing in public. Friends and family gather. Carols are sung around the piano in the living room. There are songbooks. Silly hats are worn. The menu never changes—big salad, lasagna, bread, a turkey from Bob and Judy Felix, and lots and lots of cookies. Grandchildren have replaced children as the small people running through legs and stealing just one more cookie. Now this party has a northern version as well. Jean has replicated it in the Washington, D.C., suburbs. But Bill still has to play the piano.

For as long as we can remember, our mother has driven giant vans. Volkswagen buses, a series of Chryslers, and now a Gamecock-garnet Honda. One purpose is clear: the woman likes the option to haul—gardening supplies, grandchildren, and groceries. Although she has made electronic filing a professional passion, somehow she still needs plenty of room for plastic post office crates full of briefs and opinions. Most people leave for vacation with a full cooler and a suitcase. Mom carts her mobile law library along, just in case. It's not unusual for her to be up at 5:00 A.M. on a weekend or "vacation," drinking the first morning cup of coffee and carefully annotating memos with a veritable armada of multicolored highlighters and adhesive flags. Just as her clerks can "follow the yellow brick road" to see her thinking, her daughter Lilla has enjoyed learning more about the chief's youthful literary interpretation by reading her rainbow-colored copies of Faulkner and Shakespeare.

All these varied traditions are more than quirky fun. For Mom they are a way to unite and honor the community of family and friends she has gathered. A living room "shrine" is a way to keep everyone and everything close to your heart front and center on a shelf where you can see them. It makes her happy to know that whether they are in South Carolina, California, or Jerusalem, on the first day of the month, her daughters and grandchildren are racing to say "Rabbit, rabbit" just as she did during her youth.

Jean Toal, Inventor of Grandchildren

Anyone who has seen the annual State of the Judiciary speech or been to any other presentation by Chief Justice Jean Toal knows how it will end. The closing will feature photos of her beloved grandchildren, Patrick Jacob Eisen and Ruth Margaret Mandsager. Patrick and Ruthie have grown up in her presentations, leading Lilla and Jean to comment, more than once, "you know my mother invented grandchildren."

Before she turned seventy, Toal looked out at the beach from the porch of her family's beach house and saw the paragliders being pulled by the boat in the air. She decided she wanted to do that, and the next day, Mom, Joan, Jean, and Patrick were headed to the Isle of Palms marina to try it themselves while the rest of their families watched in shock. Patrick and his grandmother, known to him as "Big Mama," loved soaring high above the Atlantic and waving to the beach house as they passed it.

Whatever Patrick and Ruth love at any given moment, their "Big Mama" loves too. She is perfectly willing to listen to all the kinds of trucks and trains there are and even build a front-end loader on the beach. She will sing and read. She loves to watch a movie with them but will often request they also watch one of her favorites, *Babe* or *Charlotte's Web*. When Patrick took up hockey, she learned about the blue line and offside. When the family visited Disney World, she ran ahead to get "fast pass" tickets to rides she did not want to go on for Patrick. She is constantly buying those children bigger shoes.

Toal believes her grandchildren, like all her passions, are the greatest (and the authors of this essay agree). Of course having grandchildren has also laid bare another Toal personality trait—she has the sleeping habits of a toddler. Patrick and Ruth are early risers. They are full of boundless energy and are incredibly active throughout the day. But when it is time for bed, they are ready, regardless of whether the time has reached double digits. We know that when Mom is ready to "hit the upper deck," which is her code for going to bed at 8:30, usually with the Braves game blaring in the background, it is because she's had a day that she packed fuller than any of us, and that her brain and body will probably be ready to go again far before anyone else in the house would think is reasonable.

Conclusion

Exuberance, determination, loyalty, pursuit of excellence, and persistence are not just hallmarks of Jean Toal's professional life. They are essential parts of her personality. The traits she brought to bear on the court are the same traits she shows in her personal and family life. The public knows she loves the law and the state of South Carolina deeply and passionately. Her family and friends know she pursues all her interests with gusto. She loves her community, friends, and family deeply and passionately. Her pursuit of excellence can be exhausting to witness but is an essential part of her that makes our lives richer. We see it every day in our gardens, in our kitchens, and in our children. We are glad South Carolina has also benefited from Jean Toal's desire to make it "like a cathedral."

SUE ERWIN HARPER AND ELIZABETH VAN DOREN GRAY

The Sisterhood of the Ladder

The Impact of Chief Justice Toal on the Rise in Participation of Women in the Legal Profession in South Carolina

As a well-regarded trial lawyer, a successful and skilled political leader, and, later, a highly esteemed appellate judge, Jean Toal has single-handedly done more than anyone else in South Carolina to open doors for women to enter the legal profession, to remain in the legal profession, to achieve success in the legal profession, and to meet the inimitable challenges they face in the legal profession. Jean Toal has been a constant cheerleader and mentor for women lawyers. She is a role model and catalyst. Just as she helped, encouraged, and mentored women lawyers, she has expected and challenged each of those she mentored to help, encourage, and mentor other women lawyers who follow them. This may well be one of the most significant and meaningful contributions she has given to South Carolina women.

Before It Was Merely Difficult

Gaining entry into the legal profession was not easy for women. Myra Bradwell (1831–94) was the first woman to be eligible for admission to the Illinois Bar yet was barred from admission by the Illinois Supreme Court.[1] That Illinois decision was affirmed by the United States Supreme Court, deferring to the state court's right to control and regulate the practice of law. In a concurring opinion joined by three other justices, Justice Bradley concurred in result but articulated his logic that women should not be allowed to be admitted to practice law:

> Man is, or should be, woman's protector and defender. The natural and proper timidity and delicacy which belongs to the female sex evidently unfits it for many of the occupations of civil life.
>
> The humane movements of modern society, which have for their object the multiplication of avenues for woman's advancement, and of

occupations adapted to her condition and sex, have my heartiest concurrence. But I am not prepared to say that it is one of her fundamental
rights and privileges to be admitted into every office and position, including those which require highly special qualifications and demanding special responsibilities. In the nature of things it is not every citizen of every
age, sex, and condition that is qualified for every calling and position. It
is the prerogative of the legislator to prescribe regulations founded on
nature, reason, and experience for the due admission of qualified persons to professions and callings demanding special skill and confidence.
This fairly belongs to the police power of the State; and, in my opinion,
in view of the peculiar characteristics, destiny, and mission of woman, it
is within the province of the legislature to ordain what offices, positions,
and callings shall be filled and discharged by men, and shall receive the
benefit of those energies and responsibilities, and that decision and firm-
ness which are presumed to predominate in the sterner sex.[2]

In 1879, less than one hundred years before Jean Toal became a South Carolina lawyer, Belva Lockwood (1830–1917), became the first woman ever to
gain admission to the United States Supreme Court following a legislative
mandate[3] that allowed all qualified women attorneys to practice in any federal court. In 1880 Lockwood became the first woman lawyer to argue a case
before the U.S. Supreme Court.[4] A century later, in 1988, Jean Toal was
elected to the South Carolina Supreme Court. A March 1999 article published in the *Journal of Supreme Court History* about Belva Lockwood's journey in the law was entitled "Before It Was Merely Difficult: Belva Lockwood's
Life in Law and Politics."[5] That title could be applied aptly to Jean Toal's
journey in the law as a woman in South Carolina in the last four decades.
She entered the profession in 1968 "before it was merely difficult." She was
one of only a handful of women lawyers and became a trial lawyer in a profession that had only just started allowing women on its juries. There were no
women judges, and virtually no women trial lawyers. She excelled.

Instead of simply observing the "sea change" that has occurred in the
legal profession in the last forty years, Jean Toal has been a catalyst.
Instead of keeping the accolades to herself as she gained the reputation as
an exceptional legal mind, a skilled advocate, and a scholarly jurist, she
has selflessly brought other women along. Not only did she encourage
other women to join her in the profession, she mentored these new lawyers
on how to become excellent lawyers. Had she opted to be a sole, successful
woman lawyer, the sea change would not have occurred. Instead she wel-
comed, encouraged, taught, and mentored her "sisters in the law," and
women and the profession are better for it.

Jean Toal's legacy of mentoring has led, among other things, to the creation of the South Carolina Women Lawyers Association (SCWLA), an

organization moving into its third decade, and grounded on the principle of advancing women in the legal profession. Her abiding lesson to those women lawyers, which is now referred to as the "ladder principle," is quite simple. The ladder principle is this: As you climb the ladder of success, do not stop to bask in the spotlight of your own success alone; do not "pull up the ladder" once you are aboard. Instead leave it down for those who come behind you and offer them a hand in achieving the same success that you enjoy. Jean Toal has lived this lesson her entire career, and literally hundreds of women lawyers across the state and the nation have benefited from her guidance. Moreover she never misses an opportunity, whether publicly before a group of women, or simply in a private conversation, to remind them how important this is, and the importance of passing the concept on to others. As a result hundreds of women in South Carolina and elsewhere now actively mentor other young female lawyers. The lesson is self-perpetuating.

The Lawyer

Jean Toal has always had the rare ability to turn adversity and challenge to her advantage. She was one of four women among the two hundred students in her class when she started law school in 1965. The proportion of women in law schools nationwide in the 1960s was about 4 percent.[6] When she graduated from the University Of South Carolina School of Law in 1968, Toal entered a profession where less than 1 percent of the members of the South Carolina Bar were women.[7] Only a few were in active practice. In fact, when Jean Toal was admitted to the bar, she was only the ninetieth woman ever admitted.[8]

The numbers nationwide were not much different. As Toal was entering law school in the 1960s, women constituted 3.5 percent of the profession, or about 6,348 members, according to the American Bar Foundation.[9] In the decade after Toal entered the practice, a completely different story unfolded. In 1970 there were 13,000 women lawyers (4 percent); by 1980 that number had grown to 62,000 (12.45 percent).[10] Women like Toal were instrumental in effecting that change.

In the 1970s as the barriers to women's legal education were lifted, as more and more young women looked to law careers as a way of acquiring competence and effectiveness, and as older women encouraged and provided models for younger women to emulate, an extraordinary development occurred: law progressively became a favored field for women. After decades of virtually no movement, the number of women lawyers grew radically in the decade from 1970 to 1980, and the proportion of women in the law schools rose from 4 percent in the 1960s to 8 percent by 1970 and then to 33 percent by 1980.[11]

While most law firms had offered her only legal secretarial positions,[12] Jean Toal was hired as an associate by the Greenville law firm of Haynsworth, Perry, Bryant, Marion, and Johnstone—at the time, with sixteen lawyers[13]—the largest in the state and one of the most prestigious. United States circuit judge Clement Haynsworth, later nominated for the United States Supreme Court, had been a member of the firm. Toal's husband, Bill, was a law clerk to Judge Haynsworth. But it was not only prestige and size that set this firm apart from the others; it was different also because it had had not one, but *two* rare women partners.

The first was James Marjory Perry, "Miss Jim,"[14] one of the founding partners of the firm. Admitted to the South Carolina Bar in 1918, she was the first licensed female attorney in the state.[15] She was active in the National Association of Women Lawyers and served a term as vice president of that organization.[16]

The other woman partner in the firm was Jean Galloway Bissell. When she joined the firm in 1958, Perry was still practicing. Bissell enjoyed a business practice, later serving as general counsel of South Carolina National Bank. In 1984 Jean Galloway Bissell became the first South Carolina woman to serve as a federal judge when President Reagan appointed her to be a United States Circuit Court judge on the federal circuit court of appeals. She served until her death in 1990. Just as Jean Bissell was mentored by "Miss Jim" Perry, Jean Toal routinely credits Judge Bissell as *her* mentor in the early days of her career.

When Toal joined the firm, she became one of only forty women who were licensed to practice law in the state, only ten of those whom were actively practicing.[17] Toal undertook an office practice, as support not only for Jean Bissell, but also for the lawyers at the Haynsworth firm who had trial practices. Because women were not permitted to serve on state court juries in South Carolina, there were only two women in the state routinely trying jury cases.[18] After passage of the 1957 Civil Rights Act, however, women did have the right to sit on federal juries in the state.[19] Ironically South Carolina senator Strom Thurmond still holds the record for the longest one-person filibuster in history—twenty-four hours and eighteen minutes—in an attempt to keep this bill from becoming law.[20] Shortly after Toal's arrival at the firm in 1968, however, women were allowed to sit on state juries for the first time. "This historic milestone created a great opportunity for Toal."[21] As Toal herself explains it, "because so many men had job-related exemptions and women did not, many juries were female."[22] Her male litigator colleagues were eager to utilize "this rare female lawyer to impress their new 'feminine juries.'"[23] Jean Toal not only met the challenge of trial work—she flourished. Soon her reputation as a bright, diligent, and well-prepared lawyer was widespread, and she became a highly sought after litigator.

Throughout her successful law practice, she exhibited absolute profes-
sionalism and by her conduct set the example for other members of the bar.
Male leaders of law firms held her up to the young women entering their
firms as the kind of lawyer they all could be.[24]

But all was not well. By the 1970s a study of sex discrimination in the
legal profession by an NYU women's rights group reported remarks that
had been made to women applicants for positions at New York law firms:

- "We don't like to hire women."
- "We hire some women, but not many."
- "We just hired a woman and couldn't hire another."
- "We don't expect the same kind of work from women
  as we do from men."
- "Women don't receive more than $____ salary."
- "Women don't become partners here."
- "Are you planning on having children?"[25]

Upon completion of its study in 1971, the NYU group filed a complaint
with the New York Commission on Human Rights against ten major New
York law firms. A few years after the litigation was filed, the firms agreed
to guidelines that would assure the hiring of women associates.[26] With the
exception of the Haynsworth firm's role in the employment of Miss Jim
Perry,[27] Jean Galloway Bissell, and later Toal, other established, larger
South Carolina law firms were slower to hire women lawyers.[28]

During this same period, an analogous situation developed in South
Carolina. By 1971 Jean Toal had returned to Columbia and joined Belser,
Belser, and Baker law firm, an all-male law firm. With her return to Columbia, Toal had begun to take on more cutting-edge civil rights cases.[29] She
was approached by a female law student, Victoria Eslinger, who had been
denied a job as a page for the South Carolina Senate because she was a
woman.[30] At the time no women had ever been allowed to hold these prestigious jobs, which were reserved for male law students. The jobs paid well
and generally resulted in a network of contacts for the pages, who benefited from these contacts in their future legal careers. Ostensibly as justi-
fication for the otherwise blatant discrimination, the South Carolina
Senate expressed concern about the reputations of potential female pages
who might be asked to run errands at night to deliver documents to senators in their hotel rooms.[31]

Jean Toal called on the Center for Study of Women, a joint venture of
Columbia and Rutgers law schools headed by law professor Ruth Bader Ginsburg,[32] for assistance. They filed a class action lawsuit on behalf of named
plaintiff Victoria Eslinger, alleging the refusal by the state Senate to hire
women as pages was an unconstitutional denial on the basis of gender.[33]

Although the district court ruled against Toal and Eslinger, they prevailed in the United States Court of Appeals for the Fourth Circuit.[34] Since then countless other women, many of whom became lawyers, have served as pages in the Senate. By her legal skills and tenacity, Jean Toal broke down that long-standing barrier to women law students. The *Eslinger* case "was the highlight of her early legal career and demonstrated Toal's commitment to helping other women in the profession."[35]

Jean Toal's practice was wide and varied: she handled civil cases and criminal cases, including murder cases and a death penalty appeal, as well as complex business transactions. She represented the Catawba Indian Tribe in what was then one of the largest eastern Indian land claims in the country.[36] She regularly appeared at all levels of the South Carolina state and federal courts. In many instances she was the first female lawyer to enter an appearance in these courts.

The Legislator

With the assistance of the national "Win with Women '74" campaign, sponsored by the National Women's Political Caucus, Jean Toal ran for and was elected as a Democrat to the House of Representatives in 1974. Three Republican women returned to the House, and four Democratic women were elected, including Juanita Goggins, the first African American woman.[37]

Toal served with distinction in the House for thirteen years, while also practicing law full time. During much of her tenure in the state legislature she worked tirelessly for the Equal Rights Amendment. Although the amendment was approved by the United States Congress in 1972, it fell three states short of ratification. "Even before her election, Jean Toal had been an advocate for the proposed amendment on the grounds that it would make 'women first-class citizens.'"[38] Representative Toal distinguished herself as an eloquent orator and skilled floor leader for the legislation and candidates she supported. As the floor leader for the Equal Rights Amendment in South Carolina, her inspired advocacy for women's rights is ingrained on each of those who were present in the State House the day she lead the fight. Many of those present that day were the founders of SCWLA. During her legislative years, Toal also sponsored and fought for other legislation designed to improve conditions for women in South Carolina, including a sex crime law, a bill expanding the application of the South Carolina Human Affairs Law (S.C. Code §§ 1-13-10, *et seq.*) and a law that established a Victim's Compensation Program (S.C. Code §§ 16-3-1610, *et seq.*) Her message of the importance of equal rights and opportunities for women continued to be heard outside the State House by women as they were considering the legal profession. From her position of leadership she was able to open doors for women to be hired as professional legal staff for the House and Senate. It is now commonplace for women to serve in legal staff positions not only in the State House but also throughout state government. However, despite her efforts and visibility in the legislature, Representative Toal was only one of seven women out of 124 total House members in 1975, and there were no women serving in the South Carolina Senate. A woman did not serve in the Senate until 1981, when two women senators were outnumbered by forty-four men. When Toal left the House in 1987, those numbers were not measurably better.[39]

As a legislator Toal also used her considerable political skills to place women on the judiciary in South Carolina. In 1983 Toal was the floor leader in the South Carolina legislature and was the major force behind the election by the South Carolina General Assembly of Judge Judy Bridges to the family court, the very first female judge in South Carolina's history. Without Toal's skilled support, the election could not have taken place. Bridges credited Toal with her successful election: "Jean Toal's energy was boundless, and her ability to persuade and cajole her male colleagues to vote for a woman (who at the time was pregnant) as a Family Court Judge turned the tide."[40] Toal eventually became chairman of the House Rules Committee, the first woman to head a standing committee in the legislature's history.[41] That was the first, but there were many other such elections guided by Jean Toal, including the election of the late court of appeals judge Carol Connor as the first woman to sit as a circuit court judge. The election was noteworthy, because Jean Toal served as Judge Connor's floor leader even as Toal was running her own race to be the first woman justice of the South Carolina Supreme Court. Both were successful on January 27, 1988, and the face of the judiciary in South Carolina was forever changed. Not only had Jean Toal encouraged women as lawyers, she began her days as a role model for women judges that day.

Since 1988 at least thirty-four women have been elected to judgeships in South Carolina's administrative law court, family court, circuit court, court of appeals, and Supreme Court. Karen LeCraft Henderson was nominated and confirmed as the first female United States district judge for the District of South Carolina in 1986,[42] and in 1992 Orangeburg native Karen Williams was appointed to the United States Court of Appeals for the Fourth Circuit; she later became the first woman to serve as that court's chief judge.[43] In 2014 five of the sixteen United States district judges in the state in active or senior status were female.[44] On a national level, women hold 33.3 percent of the seats on the United States Supreme Court, and 33.1 percent of the seats on the circuit courts of appeals.[45] Overall, 24.1 percent of the federal court judges in the country are female,[46] and women hold 27.1 percent of federal and state court judgeships combined.[47]

The Judge

In 1988 Jean Toal was elected the first female, the first Roman Catholic, and the first native Columbian to serve on the South Carolina Supreme Court. She became the first woman elected chief justice in 2000. During her more than twenty-seven years on the court, she has written more than 895 published majority opinions and 236 published concurring or dissenting opinions.[48] In those years she has distinguished herself as an exceptional leader and brilliant jurist while continuing to mentor women lawyers. She is well known throughout the state and elsewhere for her scholarly opinions on a wide range of topics and her rapid-fire and tough questions during oral arguments in the Supreme Court. Appellate lawyers anticipate that Justice Toal will know their record as well as they do (or better) and prepare their arguments accordingly. While recognized as an authority on a number of issues, she is widely regarded as an expert on constitutional issues and has authored many groundbreaking decisions.

Her presence on the bench has prompted greater sensitivity by other justices to gender issues. In fact in 1994 the Supreme Court ruled that demeaning sexist remarks directed toward a female litigator will not be tolerated in any court in South Carolina.[49]

In 1995 SCWLA presented its Jean Galloway Bissell Award for the first time. This award, named after Toal's mentor, the late federal circuit judge Jean Galloway Bissell, is presented in recognition of distinguished and noteworthy service to the public and to the legal profession and achievement of professional excellence, as well as participation in activities that have paved the way to success for women lawyers on the national, state, or local level. The award's criteria include activities that have influenced women to pursue legal careers or that have opened doors in settings historically closed to women lawyers. It was fitting that Justice Jean Hoefer Toal was the first recipient of this award. When she accepted the award, she reflected on her own mentor and the great influence Judge Bissell had on her life. She then reiterated the importance of her own familiar message of supporting other women as they meet the challenges of the legal profession.

In 1998 SCWLA sponsored its first trip to Washington, D.C., for South Carolina women lawyers to be sworn into the Supreme Court of the United States. Justice Toal quickly offered to participate at her own expense, and to sponsor the admission of approximately fifty women lawyers. On the morning of their swearing-in, Justice Toal stood at the podium and individually moved for the admission of each one. Across the bench was Justice Ruth Bader Ginsburg. At a reception following the admission ceremony in one of the halls of the Supreme Court, Justices Ginsburg and Toal reminisced about the circumstances of the *Eslinger* case they had worked on together years before. Since that time SCWLA has sent several groups to

Washington for this purpose, and each time Justice Toal has accompanied and sponsored the group of women for admission to the court.

At Chief Justice Toal's swearing-in as chief justice of the South Carolina Supreme Court, hundreds of women attended, and because the swearing-in took place in the small Supreme Court courtroom, many waited outside the courtroom to share the joy with their new "Chief." After the oath was taken, a roar of cheers resounded from the marble halls outside of the courtroom, as South Carolina women lawyers celebrated the culmination of the career of their mentor Jean Toal. Instead of greeting the group of powerful governors, senators, and distinguished guests inside the courtroom, at the conclusion of the ceremony, Chief Justice Toal immediately joined in celebrating her new role with the women lawyers in attendance, and posed with them on the Supreme Court steps. Her recognition of South Carolina women lawyers at a time when she might have understandably delayed her appearance is an example of her unwavering effort to support and include women lawyers in her story, career, and ascension.

Since becoming head of the court, Chief Justice Toal has been a pioneer in the area of technology in the judicial system in South Carolina. She has obtained federal grants to bring the courts throughout the state into the computer age. Each of the forty-six county clerks of court in South Carolina now have access to Internet-based, statewide case management systems. In recognition of her groundbreaking achievements in this area, Chief Justice Toal was the keynote speaker in the fall of 2003 at the National Center for State Courts "Court Technology Conference" in Kansas City, Missouri, and received the *Government Technology,* "Top 25 Doers, Dreamers and Drivers Award" in 2002. She has challenged all the judges in the state to become "connected" via e-mail and the Internet and has, through her wit and cajoling, brought many otherwise unwilling, technologically challenged judges into the twenty-first century.

In 2004 the American Bar Association awarded Toal the Margaret Brent Women Lawyers of Achievement Award. Margaret Brent was the first woman lawyer in America, arriving in the colonies in 1638 and achieving much success thereafter. In 1648 she formally demanded a "vote and voice" in the Maryland Assembly, which the governor denied. Over 250 years later, *Harper's Magazine* noted: "By this action, Margaret Brent undoubtedly placed herself as the first woman in America to make a stand for the rights of her sex."[50] Honorees receiving this award have achieved professional excellence in their field and have paved the way to success for other women lawyers. Given the criteria for the award and the qualities of the woman for whom it is named, it is most fitting that Toal received the national recognition that goes along with the Margaret Brent Women Lawyers of Achievement Award.

Today Chief Justice Toal continues to tackle difficult questions involving women, including the issue of domestic violence, a critical issue in a state that ranks first in the nation in the rate of women killed by men. Chief Justice Toal has called for the creation of a blue ribbon commission to study issues involving domestic violence and sentencing patterns for poor and minority defendants.

The Person

As a lawyer, legislator, and judge, Toal continues to counsel, advise, and encourage women by word and example that it is possible to have a successful legal career and a rewarding family life. When asked about her achievements, she is quick to point to her proudest achievement—her loving family. She married a fellow law student, William Thomas Toal, during law school, on August 28, 1967. She is the proud mother of two daughters, Jean Hoefer Toal Eisen and Lilla Patrick Toal Mandsager, and is a grandmother of two, a grandson, Patrick Jacob Eisen, and a granddaughter, Ruth Margaret Mandsager.

Justice Toal's concern for women lawyers extends well beyond the professional realm. Each year in South Carolina, the governor sponsors a "Walk for Life" to raise money and awareness for breast cancer issues. During that walk, in honor and support of those who have had breast cancer, names of friends who have had the disease are pinned on the backs of participant's shirts. Jean Toal faithfully participates in this walk with those names on her back.

As an individual she goes out of her way to follow and encourage women lawyers who have attained positions of leadership, such as state bar presidents, elected and appointed officials, and corporate executives. But her message, which she sets by example every day, is constant: Support other women; be their cheerleader and advocate; help them where you can; pick them up when they fall; correct them quietly when they need it; and share your success with them.

SCWLA was founded in 1993 by a group of women lawyers, each of whom was mentored by Jean Toal. Vickie Eslinger and Ann Furr called together about seventy-five women for the first gathering in the summer. Sue ("Corky") Erwin Harper was the first president, presiding over the first board meeting of the organization on September 23, 1993. Among those serving on the first board were Janet Butcher, Betsy Carpentier, and Pamela Roberts. SCWLA Board service proved to be a training ground: Elizabeth Van Doren Gray and Alice Paylor were two early SCWLA board members who went on to hold the office of president of the South Carolina Bar.

In those early days, when SCWLA was a fledgling organization struggling to increase membership and to gain stature in the legal community, Justice Toal gave credibility to the organization by willingly speaking to the group at every opportunity, being visible at each annual meeting and seminar, accompanying members on their annual pilgrimage to Washington, and even graciously opening her family home for SCWLA receptions. Because her brilliant legal mind and tenacity had long earned her the respect of the bench and the bar, her embrace of SCWLA gave the new organization, and its members, instant credibility. Today SCWLA boasts over nine hundred members statewide.

Then and Now

In the forty-six years since Jean Toal joined the bar, the legal profession has undergone a sea change. In the fall of 2014, women constituted 43.78 percent of the students at the school.[51] Nationally the change is even more remarkable, with women constituting over 47 percent of total law school enrollment.[52] Whereas women were less than 1 percent of the South Carolina Bar when Jean Toal became a member in 1968, today women constitute almost 20 percent of its membership. Nationally women made up 31.1 percent of all lawyers in the country in 2012.[53]

Conclusion

As another notable South Carolina woman once put it, "You can't be what you can't see."[54] Throughout her career, women lawyers in South Carolina have "seen" Jean Toal in high relief—as a leading trial lawyer, a devoted wife and mother, a skilled politician, and an esteemed appellate judge. But she has provided much more than someone for women lawyers to "see" and to "be." In her inimitable way Jean Toal has pushed, pulled, cajoled, and challenged women to enter and to excel in the legal profession in South Carolina. Moreover she has encouraged women to "pay it forward" by doing the same for those who follow them. The impact Jean Toal has had on the growth and success of women lawyers in South Carolina is profound, and her influence will be felt for generations to come.

NOTES

1. The Illinois Supreme Court ruled that because Bradwell was a woman, she should be denied admission, noting that "we are certainly warranted in saying that when the legislature gave to this court the power of granting licenses to practice law, it was with not the slightest expectation that this privilege would be extended to women." *Bradwell v. Illinois*, 83 U.S. (16 Wall.) 130, 132–33 (1872).

2. *Id.* at 141–42.

3. On February 15, 1879, Congress passed "An Act to Relieve Certain Legal Disabilities" that allowed all qualified women attorneys to practice in any federal court.

4. Jill Norgren, "Belva Lockwood: Blazing the Trail for Women in Law," *Prologue*, vol. 37, no. 1 (Spring 2005).

5. Jill Norgren, "Before It Was Merely Difficult: Belva Lockwood's Life in Law and Politics," *Journal of Supreme Court History*, vol. 24, issue 1 (March 1999): 16–21.

6. Pamela Paxton and Melanie Hughes, *Women, Politics, and Power: A Global Perspective* (New York: Sage, 2007) at 279; A. Susan Owen, Sarah R. Stein, and Leah R. Vande Berg, *Bad Girls: Cultural Politics and Media Representations of Transgressive Women* (New York: P. Lang, 2007) at 100.

7. W. Lewis Burke and Bakari T. Sellers, *Jean Hoefer Toal: The Rise of Women in the Legal Profession* in 3 *South Carolina Women* 416 (2012).

8. Ruth Williams Culp, *Portia Steps Up to the Bar* (Raleigh, N.C.: Ivy House, 2003) 153.

9. Cynthia Fuchs Epstein, *Women in Law* (2nd ed. University of Illinois Press, 1993) at 2.

10. *Id.* at 3.

11. *Id.*

12. Years earlier Supreme Court justice Sandra Day O'Connor had faced similar difficulties when she graduated third in her class from Stanford Law School in 1950. Only one law firm offered her a position, and that was as a legal secretary. *Sandra Day O'Connor,* The Oyez Project at IIT Chicago-Kent College of Law, www.oyez.org/justices/sandra_day_oconnor (last visited August 10, 2015).

13. Burke and Sellers, *supra* note 7, at 416.

14. Miss Jim's father, James Margrave Perry, wanted a son to bear his name. So "[w]hen his wife delivered their third daughter in May 1894 . . . [s]he was named James. Her middle name, Marjory, was about as close to Margrave as it was possible for a female name to be, but this baby would be known as 'Jim.'" Judith Bainbridge, "'Miss Jim' Blazed New Trail for Women in State," Ms. JD (June 8, 2011), http://ms-jd.org/blog/article/miss-jim-blazed-new-trail-women-state.

15. Culp, *supra* note 8, at 14.

16. *Id.* at 17.

17. Burke and Sellers, *supra* note 7, at 416.

18. *Id.*

19. Civil Rights Act of 1957, Pub. L. 85–315, 71 Stat. 634 (1957) (codified as amended at 42 U.S.C. §§ 1975–1975d [2006]).

20. *Filibuster and Cloture,* U.S. Senate, www.senate.gov/artandhistory/history/common/briefing/Filibuster_Cloture. htm (last visited November 17, 2014).

21. Burke and Sellers, *supra* note 7, at 417.

22. *Id.* at 416; Culp, *supra* note 8, at 154.

23. *Id.*

24. For example, the late governor Robert E. McNair frequently commented on the strength Toal as a lawyer and legislator, as told to Elizabeth Van Doren Gray.

25. Cynthia Grant Bowman, *Women in the Legal Profession from the 1920s to the 1970s: What Can We Learn From Their Experience About Law and Social Change?,* Cornell Law Faculty Publications, 13–14 (2009), http://scholarship.law.cornell.edu/facpub/12.

26. *Id.* at 14–15.

27. The next woman to be hired at the Haynsworth firm was Elizabeth Blair Haynsworth Taylor, who was admitted to the South Carolina Bar in 1947. After graduating from the University of Virginia Law School (she had applied to Harvard Law School, too, but it did not admit women) and practicing with a Wall Street law firm in New York for a short time, she became associated with the Haynsworth firm. Culp, *supra* note 8, at 92.

28. The entry of women as other than token hires in South Carolina did not begin in earnest until the mid to late 1970s, when the big law firms in Columbia and elsewhere

slowly began to hire women: *e.g.,* Adele Jeffords Pope (hired by McKay, McKay, Sherrill, Townsend, and Wilkins in Columbia in 1975); Elaine Beckham Fowler (hired by Turner, Padget, Graham, and Laney in Columbia in 1975); Sheryl Cudd Blennis (hired by Nelson, Mullins, Grier, and Scarborough in Columbia in 1976); Elizabeth Van Doren Gray (hired by McNair, Konduros, Corley, Singletary, and Dibble in Columbia in 1977); and Susan Mackall Smythe (hired by Buist, Moore, Smythe, and McGee in 1977).

29. Burke and Sellers, *supra* note 7, at 417.

30. *Id.* Another law student, Darra Williamson (now Cothran), was also denied a Senate page position at the same time and for the same reason. See *Index Journal* (Greenwood, S.C.), Feb. 17, 1971, at 16.

31. Burke and Sellers, *supra* note 7, at 417.

32. By coincidence, now United States Supreme Court justice Ruth Bader Ginsburg assisted Toal in the *Eslinger* case. At the time Justice Ginsburg was teaching at Rutgers University Law School (1963–72) and Columbia (1972–80) and was serving as the director of the Women's Rights Project of the American Civil Liberties Union.

33. Burke and Sellers, *supra* note 7, at 416.

34. See *Eslinger v. Thomas,* 324 F. Supp. 1329 (D.S.C. 1971), *aff'd and rev'd,* 476 F.2d 225 (4th Cir. 1973).

35. Burke and Sellers, *supra* note 7, at 418.

36. *South Carolina v. Catawba Indian Tribe,* 476 U.S. 598 (1986).

37. Burke and Sellers, *supra* note 7, at 419.

38. *Id.*

39. In 1987, of the forty-six member Senate, two were women, whereas eleven women served in the House. http://www.projectxxsc.com/sc_facts (last visited December 12, 2014).

40. Burke and Sellers, *supra* note 7, at 420.

41. *Id.*

42. *Karen Henderson,* Ballotpedia, http://judgepedia.org/Karen_Henderson (last visited Aug. 10, 2015). Since 1990, Judge Henderson has been a federal appeals judge on the United States Court of Appeals for the District of Columbia Circuit. *Id.*

43. Judge Williams served as chief judge of the Fourth Circuit from 2007 until her retirement in 2009. She died in 2013. *State* (Columbia, S.C.), November 2, 2013.

44. They are Cameron McGowan Currie, Margaret B. Seymour, J. Michelle Childs, Mary G. Lewis, and Bruce Howe Hendricks.

45. *Women in the Federal Judiciary: Still a Long Way to Go,* Nat'l Women's Law Ctr. (Aug. 4, 2015), www.nwlc.org/resource/women-federal-judiciary-still-long-way-go-1.

46. Dina Refki et al., *Women in Federal and State-Level Judgeships: A Report by the Center for Women in Government & Civil Society,* Univ. at Albany, State Univ. of New York, 1 (2012), www.albany.edu/womeningov/publications/summer2012_judgeships.pdf.

47. *Id.*

48. LexisAdvance, South Carolina Cases, Query: Written by (Toal) published (SE Reporter) 1395 Opinions; Query: Concur by (Toal) published (SE Reporter) 58 Opinions; Query: Dissent by (Toal) published (SE Reporter) 158 Opinions (December 11, 2014).

49. *State v. Pace,* 316 S.C. 71, 447 S.E.2d 186 (1994).

50. Caroline Sherman Bansemer, "A Colonial Dame: Neglected Records of the Life of Mistress Margaret Brent, the Earliest American Woman to Demand the Right of Suffrage," *Harper's,* vol. 97, no. 577 (July 1898): 230.

51. The source for this number is "ABA reports" per Susan Palmer, associate dean for Student Affairs, University of South Carolina School of Law (e-mail to Lewis Burke on Nov. 14, 2014).

52. ABA Chart: "First Year and Total J.D. Enrollment by Gender 1947–2010."

53. Bureau of Labor Statistics, Current Population Survey, "Table 11: Employed Persons by Detailed Occupation, Sex, Race, and Hispanic or Latino Ethnicity," *Annual Averages 2012* (2013).

54. *Marian Wright Edelman,* Goodreads, http://www.goodreads.com/quotes/536048 (last visited Aug. 10, 2015).

Personal Reflections

RICHARD W. RILEY, FORMER UNITED STATES SECRETARY
OF EDUCATION AND GOVERNOR OF SOUTH CAROLINA

The Lady's a Leader

Jean and I first became acquainted as members of the South Carolina General Assembly. I was serving in the Senate when Jean began her service in the South Carolina House in 1975. She was one of fifty-two newly elected members when single-member districts were first instituted. She was recognized immediately for her keen intellect and leadership abilities. Jean and I developed a close friendship in 1976 when we were leaders in President Jimmy Carter's successful campaign.

I had hoped to have Jean's support when I entered the race for governor in 1978. However, Jean had already committed to support Lieutenant Governor Brantley Harvey. While Brantley was my opponent, he was an honorable candidate, and Jean was his very effective campaign chair. With strong support from my large Greenville County, I defeated Brantley in a run-off election. It was an honorable, but hard-fought, campaign.

After my election Jean immediately volunteered to help with my progressive legislative agenda and became my House floor leader on many legislative initiatives. Our first real test in the House was legislation reforming the Public Service Commission. Jean, still a junior House member at that time, teamed with our friend and later Speaker Bob Sheheen and passed our bill despite the opposition of the House leadership.

Jean's leadership ability was recognized by her colleagues when she was elected as chair of the Rules Committee. She continued her support for my legislative program, and it became clear to all that she was a real leader in the House for progressive reform.

As governor, in 1982 and 1983, I devoted my efforts to major education reform. South Carolina was so far behind other states, especially in education funding. Working with educators, business leaders, and parents, we developed the comprehensive Education Improvement Act. The proposal included a one-cent increase in the sales tax to fund teacher pay and the other important components of the act. While I was never able to convince Jean to support the tax increase (she favored funding the EIA by eliminating the sales tax exemptions), she strongly supported the other important elements of the bill and was key to the ultimate passage of the act.

Jean was an active supporter of the substantive initiatives of the act in the House during many weeks of debate. With the help of our grassroots lobbying efforts, we gained enough support for passage of the act, including the penny tax, but were blocked procedurally from its consideration. Despite her opposition to the penny tax, Jean exercised her tactical skills and brought the bill to a vote over the opposition of the House leadership. This effort on her part definitely ensured EIA consideration and passage. That is real leadership, in my view. I was so grateful to her then, as I am now.

Jean was never an "in your pocket" vote. She always fought for what she thought was right. She was the campaign chair for my opponent for governor—but became one of my strongest supporters when I won. She was opposed to the penny sales tax increase—but was a key leader in getting the comprehensive EIA passed.

Jean also was a strong advocate for judicial reform, and she worked tirelessly in the legislature for the creation of our unified judicial system. She has continued that effort throughout her twenty-five years on the Supreme Court. Her efforts have brought South Carolina's judiciary from its somewhat closed, quill-and-ink operations to the forefront in technology, in addition to providing greater access to justice for the people of South Carolina.

Jean brought her vast legislative experience to the South Carolina Supreme Court in 1988. Her many political struggles and government experiences as a progressive leader in the House have contributed to the outstanding skills she used so effectively as chief justice of our Supreme Court. This was never clearer than in the recent court ruling in the *Abbeville* case. Jean was a strong, effective leader of the court in this significant decision. She wrote the majority opinion which declared that the General Assembly did not meet the constitutional requirement of "minimally adequate" education for all in the poor, rural plaintiff school districts. This decision will prove to be a positive driver for better education for all South Carolina children in the future.

I know of no other leader who has made such a lasting and positive impact on the future of our state in both the legislative and judicial arenas. South Carolina has been fortunate indeed to have Jean Toal's leadership, and I am fortunate to count her as my friend.

The Hoefer Girls

My first exposure to Jean Hoefer Toal came early. I was eleven, and visiting Jean's home to pick up her younger sister, Ann, for a trip to horseback riding camp at Converse College in Spartanburg. Converse had advised Ann needed a ride, and we were driving through Columbia on our way from Florence.

The Hoefer home had a pool and a pool house, but they were off limits. Why? Because big sister Jean said so. She was explicit in her direction that we were not to trespass on her territory (I believe she was living in the pool house at that time). Jean addressed her younger sister in language I had never heard before. I was terrified. Ann was not. Her vocabulary was at least as colorful as Jean's.

Off we went to camp, where I spent time with Ann, who was a great and fearless rider but was "excused" from the dining room after uttering expletives overheard by the "ladies" of Converse. My time with the Hoefer girls taught me one thing at an early age: they were tough and knew how to cuss. (I later learned the proper term is "curse," but this was "cussing.")

The next time I encountered Jean was twenty years later in a Columbia courtroom of the United States District Court circa 1980. The occasion was my first roster meeting as a new assistant United States attorney. The courtroom was packed, and Jean and I were the only female attorneys present. At that time roster meetings were a tradition in South Carolina, but not in the District of Columbia, where I had gone to law school and practiced law. At these roster meetings, all lawyers with cases on the trial roster were required to gather and report to a federal judge on the status of their cases so that a roster of cases could be set for trial. I hardly knew Jean and certainly knew no one else, including the judge. Again I was terrified. And again Jean was in command, but this time through the strength of her personality and the force of her intellect. I simply watched and listened to her and copied what she did. It seemed to work.

After court we reintroduced ourselves and laughed about sister Ann (now a respected New Haven physician) and the Converse story. Having a connection with Jean brought immediate respect from the male members of the bar. There began a personal and professional friendship that has lasted over three decades.

Although we never served on the same court, Jean and I frequently worked together on committees, in associations, and through our legal and judicial positions. We shared responsibilities during the formation and early years of the South Carolina state grand jury, as Jean was tasked by Chief Justice George Gregory with overseeing the South Carolina Supreme Court's role regarding that new institution. We served on many continuing legal education panels together. We participated together in the early years of the Justice John Belton O'Neall Inn of Court and the South Carolina Women Lawyers Association. We worked together on the biography of our common mentor, Judge Matthew J. Perry Jr.

Through the years we have shared family news and professional support. During the confirmation process for my nomination to the federal bench, she was there to provide accurate information to those doing the vetting. When the going was tough, Jean "had my back," and I will never forget it. But she also had the backs of many women, like Judy Bridges, Carol Connor, and Vicki Eslinger, and others too numerous to name here. She is a loyal ally, and a tireless advocate for fairness and equality.

There was a time when being a female lawyer or judge was a lonely vocation. Jean provided backbone, strength, and inspiration to the growing numbers of female lawyers and proved to doubters that women are strong, capable, and tireless legal advocates. She gave us a model to which to aspire. She continued across the years to provide leadership to countless women in the profession. She encouraged, supported, and protected us.

The tough-as-nails sixteen-year-old I first encountered over half a century ago used her strengths in so many ways for the people of South Carolina. She dragged the courts of South Carolina into the twenty-first century and lifted and championed the status of women in the profession along the way.

I guess it takes a little colorful language to get folks' attention sometimes. Once Jean got it, she used it for good. Isn't that what matters in the end?

ROBERT J. SHEHEEN

Observations of Chief Justice Jean Hoefer Toal

When I was first asked to provide a vignette concerning my history with the chief justice, I was eager to participate. When I began to review my fifty-year history and association with Mrs. Toal, it became much harder than I expected. Our association began at the University of South Carolina School of Law, and it has continued to this day. The friendship has encompassed every element: personal friend; colleague at the bar; colleague in the General Assembly; subordinate attorney under her presiding over the South Carolina Bar.

What is remarkable about all these associations is that she has never varied in any way from the personal loyalty that comes from treating me as a friend and colleague in any way. So I have chosen to write about her attitude in all these endeavors and not tell you a personal story about her or her family. She has two wonderful children and a devoted husband, all of whom are friends.

She has participated with me as a lawyer, and she was a loyal ally on every occasion even when we disagreed. She has been an adversary who respected me and my clients at every level of each case in which we were adversarial. She has presided over arguments in cases before the Supreme Court in which I have represented clients, and she is demanding and unyielding in her consideration of all points of view before participating in the court's decisions. All the while she is a close friend, who has been there when a member of my family died, when trouble has accompanied my family's activities, and when I have faced hardships.

The one sterling and enduring characteristic that accompanies all her public activities, even when we have been adversaries in those activities, is her total commitment to the institution in which she has participated. She meets the most stringent test of public service: Does she respect the institution in which she participates and has that institution become a better place because of her participation? In every case of her public activities and participation, the answer is a resounding yes. As an example, when she served as chairman of the House Rules Committee, she crafted a rule that helped the South Carolina House, when I was Speaker, to endure the problems encountered by the FBI sting known as "Lost Trust." After a particularly rancorous debate in the South Carolina Senate about whether to expel a member after his conviction of voter fraud, she led the way to absolve the South Carolina House from such a debate by crafting a rule that would provide for suspension upon indictment and automatic expulsion upon conviction. Administration and application of that rule allowed me as Speaker to help preserve and restore the reputation of South Carolina during the "Lost Trust" debacle.

During our time together in the General Assembly, while I was chairman of the Judiciary Committee in the House, and she chaired the Constitutional Law Subcommittee, we encountered a particularly "sticky" problem about the legislature's participation in the rule-making process with the Supreme Court. We were caught between Chief Justice Woodrow Lewis and Senator Marion Gressette, chairman of the Senate Judiciary Committee. She presided over a hearing at which Chief Justice Lewis appeared and testified at her request. He was less than cordial and dressed down the subcommittee for "interfering," as he saw it, with the court's authority under the constitution. We were less than happy about the confrontation, but she insisted that we arrange a meeting with the chief justice several weeks later at his office in Darlington County so that he would have the advantage of the group of legislators appearing on his "turf," and not feel that we were there to transgress on his authority under the Judicial Article. We concluded the meeting with a joint decision to pursue settlement of the controversy and headed back to Columbia celebrating our resolution of the controversy. Little did we know that Senator Gressette would accuse the House group of selling out to the chief justice and reject our compromise as diluting the legislative authority. Our victory was short-lived, and we could not resolve the rule-making controversy until Chief Justice Lewis retired shortly thereafter. We resolved the matter with the new chief justice, Bruce Littlejohn, after we had cleared the new resolution with Senator Gressette before introducing the resolution that still remains in place. Being caught between those two legendary giants in South Carolina government didn't deter Jean. The controversy made her work harder to get it resolved while maintaining her credibility with both sides: the Supreme Court and its assertion of its administrative authority on one side and Senator Gressette with his firm commitment to legislative supremacy on the other.

Finally, in all her public endeavors, she has always remained approachable and "convenient" to the citizens of South Carolina. Arrogance and aloofness have never been in her dictionary. In her private associations, she has been loyal to her faith, her family, and her friends and does not let either of those arenas affect the other.

I. S. LEEVY JOHNSON

From My Vantage Point

Most people know Chief Justice Jean Hoefer Toal for her love of the law, her advocacy for justice, and her compassion for equal rights. But what most people do not know is all these attributes are derived from her love for her family and all mankind.

I have had a view of Chief Justice Toal reserved for few people. This is especially significant in light of our backgrounds. We both grew up in segregated communities. She attended the all-white, highly rated Dreher High School, and I attended the underrated, all-black C. A. Johnson High School. She is Catholic, and I am Baptist. She is white, and I am black. In spite of these areas of separation, our lives merged in 1965 when we enrolled as first-year law students at the University of South Carolina School of Law. Since that time our lives have been inseparable.

From my vantage point I have witnessed her endearing love for her family. Her husband, Bill, and I have been law partners for over forty years. This partnership has afforded me a window of opportunity to view her sustaining love for her family. She is a devoted wife, a mentoring mother of her two daughters, and a doting grandmother of her two grandchildren. Although she has unimaginable demands on her time, she has never defaulted on her commitment to her family. She has the remarkable ability to manage her schedule so she can spend quality time with each of them.

A perfect example of her relationship with her family was on full display when she was sworn in as an associate justice on the South Carolina Supreme Court. Bill presented her to the court, and her daughters had the honor of assisting her with the robing. It was a touching moment to observe history being made with the full participation of her husband and daughters.

It is no secret that much of Jean's time now is devoted to her grandchildren. She has received almost every award accorded a person of her stature. But she will be the first to admit that the gift of her two grandchildren exceeds any award or honor she has ever received. Patrick, the son of Jean and Peter, and Ruth, the daughter of Lilla and John, have added a dimension of joy to her life that is reflected in her treatment of everyone who comes in contact with her. She has a public image of being tough; but when it comes to her grandchildren, it is not an exaggeration to describe her as a "softie."

Her advocacy for justice is mirrored in her consistent promotion of family values. She and Bill have been married for over forty-seven years. During this time they have maintained a loving, supportive relationship. She is the consummate wife. She has always been supportive of him and her entire family. This supportive spirit was never more evident than when Bill's mother became seriously ill. Bill and Jean constructed an addition onto their home to house Bill's ailing mother. Jean provided nursing care on the level of a trained health professional. Mrs. Toal was a loving, warm person, and Jean reciprocated in kind.

Jean does not have a prejudiced bone in her body. While we unfortunately live in a racially polarized society, it is comforting to know that a person in her position is color-blind. She does not believe in diversity; she believes in inclusion. I read once, "diversity is inviting you to the dance; inclusion is being asked to dance." All throughout Jean's life she has danced and paved the way for others to dance. Being a trailblazer and role model for women lawyers has propelled her to unprecedented heights in the legal profession. At every stage of her career she has extended a helping hand to help others who would not otherwise have the benefit of her wisdom, intelligence, and work ethic. She has a comfort level with the "man and woman on the street and the man and woman in the suite."

JUSTICE JOHN W. KITTREDGE

Destined for the Records Book

It was the spring of 2000. I was a circuit judge, serving as the chief administrative judge for the court of common pleas in the thirteenth judicial circuit. It was about 10:00 A.M. when I was summoned from the bench because the chief justice was on the phone. Jean Toal had only recently been sworn in as the chief justice of South Carolina. "What in the world does the chief justice want to talk with me about?" I wondered. I remember the call well. It went something like this:

Good morning, Madam Chief Justice. How may I help you?
Kittredge, are you the admin judge up there?
Well, yes ma'am, I am.
Where is Choppy's court reporter?
I am not sure, ma'am. Is there a problem?
You bet there is a problem, Kittredge. Choppy Patterson is holding court—or is supposed to be holding court—and I hear his court reporter has not shown up. What are you going to do about it?
I will get right on it, ma'am.
Good. Call me back when the problem is resolved.

As I said goodbye, thoughts were racing through my mind as I sunk into my chair. In no particular order, I thought: "It is a new day in South Carolina. I don't believe she wants to be a ceremonial chief justice. How in the world am I going to find Judge Patterson's court reporter? Will I be a circuit judge tomorrow?" It was 10:20 when a bailiff came in and announced that Judge Patterson's court reporter had just arrived. I regained my senses and called the chief justice to report the good news. She thanked me for my prompt handling and resolution of the "crisis." Before I could tell her I didn't do anything, she was gone. Yes, it *was* a new day in the South Carolina judiciary.

I have always been a friend and admirer of Jean Toal. She cares so profoundly and passionately about the law in general and the South Carolina judicial system in particular. It is that passion that drives her as our chief justice.

My contact with Jean became more frequent when I was elected to the court of appeals in 2003. And my election to the state Supreme Court in 2008 allowed us to serve together as colleagues on the same court. I have observed her in action day in and day out. Jean handles her position as a justice wonderfully; she has such a remarkable legal mind, and she quickly grasps complicated and nuanced legal issues. Similarly Jean has served superbly as chief justice.

Jean's leadership in bringing technology to the state court system has been recognized nationally, and deservedly so. I have often heard that Jean's technological contributions are the hallmark of her tenure as chief justice. That may be a true statement, but it is woefully inadequate in recognizing the breadth of her tremendous leadership impact on all fronts. Permit me to briefly share a few personal insights that reflect a fuller view of Jean's leadership of the third branch of government, observations that resonated and remained with me through the years.

Serving as a judge is not easy. Moreover, at the appellate level, the degree of collaboration among the judges is a good barometer of the general success or failure of an appellate court. As with most things in life, maintaining collegiality and a genuine spirit of collaboration among appellate judges is easier said than done.

Jean is a master in patiently guiding the Supreme Court justices through some hard issues and discussions, often involving disputes between the other two branches of government. I have often wondered if the legislative and executive branches in other states find as much joy in suing each other as they do in South Carolina. Whatever the controversy, everyone is fully heard, and contrary views are respected. Jean's leadership models this fine quality. It manifests itself in a collegial atmosphere where difficult issues are freely debated, free of any agenda, and where all share the common desire to achieve the correct result under the law.

Fast forward with me to the end of the process, when a divided court issues majority and dissenting opinions. When Jean and I have disagreed, she immediately reaches out and expresses respect for my point of view. It illustrates the adage that members of a court can disagree without being disagreeable.

Truth be told, published decisions of the Supreme Court represent only the tip of the iceberg of the court's workload. In addition to reviewing matters in its original and appellate jurisdiction, the Supreme Court handles attorney and judicial grievances, character and fitness concerns regarding bar applicants, rule changes, appointments to a wide variety of commissions, court of appeals certiorari petitions, postconviction relief certiorari petitions, and the list goes on. The duties of the chief justice go even further and include the administrative oversight of all courts within the unified judicial system, assignment and rotation of the trial court judges, the preparation and presentation of the judiciary's budget to the General Assembly, and I could go on.

I guess the point I want to make is that many of Jean's considerable leadership skills pass below the radar. As time passes it is my strong sense that the many contributions Chief Justice Jean Hoefer Toal has made to our beloved state's legal system will become more well-known and appreciated. Her opinions are well-crafted, substantive expositions on a myriad of legal matters vital to the rule of law and the citizens of South Carolina—indeed many of her writings have acquired the status of landmark decisions. That alone would seem enough to qualify as an extraordinary career. But there is more. Add fifteen amazing years as head of the South Carolina judicial branch, as our chief justice, and the end result is a career of public service destined for the record books. I am pleased to call Jean Toal my friend and chief justice.

My First Glimpse

My first glimpse of my future chief justice was in the early 1970s when I, along with several other law students, decided to go to the South Carolina State House to watch debates on the Equal Rights Amendment. That amendment, which provided simply that women should have "equal rights under the law" unleashed a firestorm of opposition. The forces opposing the amendment had engaged a nationally known conservative activist named Phyllis Schlafly, from Illinois to argue the case against ratification. Ms. Schlafly recited the "parade of horribles" that would ensue if the amendment were passed, including women being rendered penniless because their husbands would no longer have to support them and unisex bathrooms being the norm. The young woman lawyer-legislator chosen to debate Ms. Schlafly was none other than Jean Hoefer Toal. A champion debater in both high school and college, she deftly turned the focus of the conversation away from the specious arguments put forth by Ms. Schlafly and focused on the main goal of the amendment: to provide women equal pay for equal work.

Jean Toal certainly persuaded me that night, and she clearly convinced her fellow House members because they voted unanimously in favor of ratification. Sadly the South Carolina Senate did not follow suit so the amendment did not pass here in South Carolina and ultimately failed to garner enough votes nationwide for ratification. However, I came away from that night with great respect and admiration for Jean Toal. Little did I know that many years later, in June 1999, Jean Toal and I would be elected chief justice and chief judge, respectively, of the two highest courts in this state, or that I would one day serve with her on the Supreme Court of South Carolina.

I graduated from law school in the 1970s at a time when older women lawyers were scarce. My mentors were my first two employers, Justice J. B. "Bubba" Ness and James P. Stevens Sr. While they could not have done more to inspire me and to steer my career toward the bench, it has been a special blessing to serve with Jean Toal on the Supreme Court and to have her as my mentor and chief justice. I continue to learn from her daily. Although I delight in the opportunity to observe her formidable legal prowess, it is the tone with which she conducts the court that I most appreciate. She consistently models what leadership should look like. Her special gift is the ability to incorporate other's ideas and viewpoints into a discussion or an opinion; she knows exactly how to make a junior justice feel that his or her contributions are valuable and integral to the cauldron of justice.

Ours is a special relationship. We share cooking secrets and family stories, we host parties together, and we laugh and cry together. Although we may sometimes vehemently disagree with one another, we always have each other's backs. And when we are in agreement, we are a force to be reckoned with. If it sounds like Jean Toal and I are sisters, that's because we are!

JUSTICE JAMES E. MOORE

An Amazing Lady

I have been privileged to know Jean Toal since 1975 when she first served as a legislator. As one of the few female attorneys, she learned early on not only how to survive, but how to compete successfully in the male-dominated world of politics and the practice of law.

The same energy and enthusiasm exhibited then continued when she served as a justice and later as chief justice of the Supreme Court. Jean has always amazed me in the following ways:

- Her careful and thorough preparation of every case presented;
- Her vast legal knowledge and ability to recall the names and dates of previous cases;
- Her ability to ask the penetrating questions;
- Her ability to recognize the issues and persuade others to her position;
- Her attention to detail in the administration of the judicial system;
- Her knowledge, not only of the law but also of sports, gardening, cooking, and other innumerable activities;
- Her willingness to attend and speak at local, state, and national bar-related functions and conferences; and
- Her vision and farsightedness in developing and implementing technology for the judicial system.

The leadership Jean Hoefer Toal has provided and the many contributions she has made to the judicial system will long be remembered.

BLAKE HEWITT

Reflections of a Law Clerk

The thing that I will always remember about Chief Justice Toal is how hard she worked.

We used to joke among the law clerks that there were two jobs in the Supreme Court building that nobody wanted. One was Dan Shearouse's job, because there are a multitude of little-known but extremely important tasks that come with being the clerk of the Supreme Court. The other job nobody wanted was the chief justice's job. I was constantly in awe of how she managed everything.

The position of chief justice carries tremendous responsibility. I think everyone expects this to be the case, but I am not sure that most people understand just how big an undertaking this job involves. The governor has cabinet officials and an alphabet soup of executive agencies. In the General Assembly, the responsibility for drafting and scrutinizing legislation is allocated first to specialized committees and then equally among the 170 members of the legislature.

The chief justice does not have a cabinet, and there is no network of agencies to help implement the rule of law. The Supreme Court sits in supervision of all other courts in the state, and the administrative head of that court is the chief justice. If anything went wrong somewhere in the court system, it seemed like the phone call of complaint eventually made its way to the chief's chambers. On top of dealing with those sorts of tasks, the chief had to spend the first part of each year assembling the judicial department's budget in order to ask the General Assembly for funding so that the court system could be open. A lot of the load is carried by the local clerks of court and the Supreme Court's Office of Court Administration, but because the chief is the head of the judicial department, she ultimately answered for all of it.

I have never encountered someone who had a stronger work ethic than Chief Justice Toal. You would try to beat her in to the office, and you would try to stay after she had left for the day, but you quickly discovered that your effort was pointless because she would sometimes stay until seven or eight o'clock at night (yes, on Fridays too). And even when she was not "at" work, she was still working. She went to bed late, she woke up early, and she was always in motion. No time of hers was idle or wasted. I have never known such persistent diligence, such serial focus, and such relentless determination to succeed. She was truly a force of nature. She never stopped.

Some of my favorite experiences involved the chief's State of the Judiciary speeches. Each year, the General Assembly invites the chief justice to address a joint assembly of the House and the Senate to talk about issues that are important to the South Carolina court system. Our usual workday in chambers began at 8 A.M., but on State of the Judiciary day, the chief asked us to be at work by seven, and she always brought Krispy Kreme doughnuts. She would have been working on the speech for weeks, but she liked to move items in the speech around until the very end. And it was only at the end that she liked for the clerks to divide up the speech and type it out. This was a lot of fun. We were working on a short deadline, we were constantly interacting with each other and offering the chief suggestions, and by the time we walked across Gervais Street to watch the speech, we were in the middle of the biggest sugar rush you can imagine.

In the tribute that ETV put together for the former House Speaker Bob Sheheen, Chief Justice Toal spoke of the bond that she and Representative Sheheen shared in the fact that both of them had spent many years being committed to "absolute engagement" in the political life of South Carolina. I think that the term "absolute engagement" perfectly captures Chief Justice Toal and her approach to her work and to public service. The job of chief justice was not something that she did until she went home each day. She lived it. Her commitment was twenty-four hours a day. She spent weeks going to event after event on the road, she worked constantly, she was a master coalition builder, and she was fully devoted to South Carolina and its future.

She was a profound influence on my development as a person and as a lawyer. I will always treasure the time that I spent working for her.

MARY CAMPBELL MCQUEEN

National Leader

In his article from the Harvard *Executive Session for State Court Leaders in the 21st Century* then chief justice Wallace B. Jefferson from Texas chose to title his perspective on state court leadership as "herding lions." As a national and state judicial leader, Chief Justice Jean Hoefer Toal definitely embodies the requisite skills of a successful ringmaster: collaborative while in control; compassionate yet demanding; tireless and energetic; mentor and supervisor; and leader of the mighty. My first encounter with the new chief justice from South Carolina occurred in 2001 at the annual Conference of Chief Justices (CCJ) in Seattle, Washington, while I was serving as the Washington administrator for the courts. While a good listener, Chief Justice Toal came to her first national meeting of the chief justices with a vision and resolve to make a difference.

A "difference" according to Chief Justice Toal was improving justice including access to vulnerable populations, leveraging technology to increase court efficiency, preserving fair and impartial courts through public education, and enhancing the profession of judging in her state and the nation. The CCJ are the leaders of the state courts throughout the nation and our territories. While sharing common visions the "lions of our state courts" also share differing opinions about how justice should be defined and provided. Chief Justice Jean Toal was indomitable in her vision to tame the energy of these lions into a pride of effective leaders who could represent and protect the interests of the various states and preserve their independence.

Relying on her experience as a lawyer and a legislative leader, Chief Justice Toal encouraged, intimidated, and transformed CCJ into a "pride of lions" with a single purpose and national voice. During her term as president of CCJ, Chief Justice Toal worked collaboratively with her colleagues to achieve 100 percent participation of all fifty states as well as all U.S. territories, an achievement that had never before been accomplished nor repeated. Her inclusive leadership style coupled with her sincere commitment to service were the cornerstones of that success.

Chief Justice Toal's experience as a state legislator contributed to her effective development of national partnerships among the CCJ, Congress, and national leaders. During her tenure as CCJ president, she forged lasting relationships that led to hosting a major national conference on the Role of State Court Leaders in Advancing Public Policy and presided over the opening of the Center House on Capitol Hill in Washington, D.C., as the national headquarters for the state courts.

Recognizing the shared leadership responsibilities between trial court judges and state court chief justices, Chief Justice Toal advanced the shared leadership partnerships by launching the first national Forum for Presiding Judges that drafted *Guidelines on Roles and Responsibilities of Trial Judges,* to advance the effective administration of justice. That commitment to state court leadership resulted in support for the Fourth National Symposium on Court Management hosted by the National Center for State Courts in 2010. Later that year, under Chief Justice Toal's leadership, CCJ and the Conference of State Court Administrators (COSCA) completed a white paper, *Court Interpretation: Fundamental to Access to Justice,* which established the first national policy on the importance of language access in the state courts. That landmark paper is the basis for current efforts to expand language access across the nation recognizing her vision that all persons regardless of national origin or race should be provided meaningful access to justice.

Chief Justice Toal's conviction that "justice" is really "for all" can be demonstrated by her support for the National Consortium on Racial and Ethnic Fairness and the creation of state court Fairness Commissions across the country. Her belief that the public's trust and confidence in the courts is essential to justice resulted in the creation of a graphic novel series titled *The Justice Case Files,* designed to explain how courts protect and support citizens in their daily lives based on story lines from daily experiences. In 2010 South Carolina's civic education program launched by Chief Justice Toal was awarded the inaugural Sandra Day O'Connor Award for Civic Education conferred annually on a court or state for exemplary commitment to civic education regarding the American justice system.

Her vision for the future established Chief Justice Toal as a national leader in court technology and South Carolina's state court technology project as a national best practice. Speaking at state, national, and international court technology conferences, her leadership model has been embraced by colleagues around the world.

"Taming lions" requires courage, stamina, confidence, wisdom, experience, and credibility. Chief Justice Toal has used all these skills merged with her sense of honesty, commitment to transparency, and ability to forge genuine partnerships to tame our state courts most revered lions— the chief justices of our country.

BRADISH J. WARING

Heeding the Call

"Brad, I need to talk to you . . . and bring Fred." That's how Jean Toal greeted me at the January 2010 South Carolina Bar Convention at Kiawah Island. Knowing that one ignores such a directive at one's own peril, Fred Suggs (bar president) and I readily complied. What followed was a sobering two-hour discussion of the judicial funding crisis the court was facing. What came out of that meeting was a new and novel strategy to fundamentally change the annual conversation with the legislature about the need for adequate judicial funding.

It is a national tragedy that the third branch of government is so inadequately funded on both a state and federal level. In South Carolina it is a sad reality that the judicial branch is forced to seek funding from the state legislature in a manner much like a state agency. Adequate judicial appropriations have perennially been a problem for our judicial branch, but few (including most members of the South Carolina Bar) realize how perilous the state of judicial funding had gotten by the time of our meeting that January morning. From 2000 to 2010, state appropriations for the judiciary had been cut by 51 percent. According to a September 2009 survey conducted by the Conference of State Court Administrators, South Carolina's budget cut was the most of any state in the country. Despite yearly pleas to the legislature and significant belt-tightening measures to cut expense and conserve money, by the time the legislature convened in 2010, the court was facing a serious funding crisis, and an $11.5 million deficit. The relatively modest but carefully built reserve that the chief justice had set aside for a rainy day was gone, spent to repair the worsening roof leaks on the buildings that house our two appellate courts. Significant layoffs of key personnel (including law clerks and critical staff) as well as limited court sessions were a real likelihood. In a warning to fellow judges in early 2010 the chief stated, "If I must operate our court next year without [increased funding] I will be forced to direct massive layoffs and drastic curtailment of terms of family and circuit court." The situation was indeed dire.

Ironically, in the face of the ongoing national economic crisis at the time, South Carolina's economic development initiatives were beginning to pay off. In October 2009 Boeing announced its decision to locate a new assembly line for its 787 Dreamliner aircraft in Charleston instead of Everett, Washington. The decision was hailed as a "game changer" and, as predicted, has spurred significant associated economic development statewide.

It was against this backdrop that our conversation took place. It was time, she said, to refocus the strategy and to engage the business community in our efforts to call attention to the seriousness of the problem and the chaos that would result from a failure to at least fund the core needs of the court. She solicited our assistance in bringing the resources of the bar and its membership to the campaign. Fred and I quickly agreed (as if we had a choice)! We were no strangers to some of the prevailing legislative attitudes toward the funding of legal initiatives at that time. Indeed since 2006 every bar president had appeared before legislative committees seeking funding for unfunded or underfunded criminal and civil court appointments. With fewer lawyers in the legislature, we were used to hearing from committee members that funding for such appointments would only serve to assist "criminals." While the chief had certainly not met with that kind of resistance to her funding requests, it was nonetheless evident to her that some members of the General Assembly needed to fully grasp the consequences of a nonfunctioning court system.

I recall the determination in the chief's voice. It was clear to me that she had resolved to use all available resources to fix the immediate problem. However, what struck me most was the realization that she had hit on *the* very thing that would universally resonate with all members of the legislature, regardless of any negative predispositions or attitudes about judicial funding. Her goal was to send the message that an efficient and fully functional statewide judicial system is as important to attracting business to the state as any other infrastructure consideration. We needed, she said, to persuade members of the General Assembly that a properly funded and efficient legal system was not only good for business; it was an essential in attracting new business. Here was something near and dear to all South Carolinians. While it sounds so simple today, the idea was indeed novel. Thus began a new effort, which continues to this day, to engage the business community as allies in the fight to adequately fund our state courts.

With the help of a host of bar members, business leaders, and business organizations too numerous to mention, the 2010 judicial funding crisis was narrowly averted in June of that year. According to the *State* newspaper, "only massive lobbying by business, conservative and legal groups won a final narrow vote in the Legislature for full funding." Quoting the chief, the paper went on to say, "Business groups realized 'if you lose your court system, you lose public order. And then you lose the ability to attract any kind of new industry to South Carolina.'"

One can only wonder what would have happened without the prescience of Jean Toal.

WALTER B. EDGAR AND JUDGE JOSEPH F. ANDERSON JR.

All Hail the Chief!

Quintessential South Carolinian

Animis Opibusque Parati

Dum Spiro Spero

WHEN WE WERE ASKED to write an epilogue for this tribute to our state's chief justice, it was very easy to agree to do so. Both of us have known Jean Toal for many years both personally and professionally. In addition we have followed with interest and admiration her nearly half-century of public service to the people and state of South Carolina.

In selecting the title for the epilogue, we pondered a number of possibilities: "Trail-Blazer," "Lasting Legacy," "Champion of Equality," and "A Progressive Voice." Each of these spoke to one or more aspects of Jean as a person and a public figure. However, each of them spoke to just one facet of her career and diminished the others. In essence they pigeonholed her. And if there were ever an individual who would not appreciate being categorized or stereotyped, it would be Jean Hoefer Toal. In selecting "Quintessential South Carolinian," we determined that there are or have been very few individuals in the history of the state who have better exemplified South Carolina's mottoes: "Prepared in Mind and Resources" and "While I Breathe, I Hope."

The previous pieces and essays chronicle a remarkable career. Who would have expected the graduate of a silk-stocking, all-white Columbia high school to become a civil rights activist before she graduated from Agnes Scott College? That she did so is a reflection of her personality and her desire to fight for the underdog. She might have come from a privileged background, but she was willing to help those who had hope, but needed help. This persistent willingness and desire to champion the cause of South Carolinians sometimes neglected or ignored by the state's power structure is a recurring theme over the years: helping African Americans register to vote; assisting young women as both counsel and mentor; righting a centuries-old wrong for the Catawba people; supporting the right of all school children in South Carolina to a decent education.

Championing a cause—be it civil rights, women in the law, or court reform—is one thing. Making a difference, making changes happen, is quite another. Throughout her career Jean has been able to make a difference because she has always done her homework. She has been prepared whether it was a case for trial or mapping legislative strategy. She possesses a rare combination of intellect and "street savvy." Some people are gifted intellectually, and some have keen political instincts. Jean has both in abundance. These two qualities, along with a dynamic and determined personality, have enabled her to make a difference in the lives of South Carolinians.

When the Toals moved back to Columbia in the 1970s, they bought a house in the Shandon neighborhood. Shandon and several other in-town neighborhoods were attracting young professionals who soon became involved in the political and civic life of the city. During that decade so many residents sat on city council and served on the boards of cultural and community organizations that the local media began to refer to the "Shandon Mafia." Jean was one of the organizing forces behind the formation of neighborhood councils. In turn these groups became a political force and advocates for schools, historic preservation, and cultural agencies. They made a difference in Columbia.

Before the neighborhood councils came into existence, there really were no public forums for civic debate and political action. There was a vacuum—and just as nature abhors a vacuum and fills it—Jean Toal saw a civic vacuum and through her determination and skill created a force for positive change in the capital city. In many ways the example of the neighborhood councils was a template for her public career: (1) see a need, (2) propose a solution, and (3) make sure that the solution is a beginning, not an end in itself.

In 1974, when the General Assembly was reapportioned into single-member districts—essentially neighborhoods—Jean was elected to represent House District 75, based in Shandon. Because of reapportionment, there were fifty-two new legislators in the 124-member House. Representative Toal took it on herself to organize the group into the first freshman caucus—and was elected its chair.

Despite the changes wrought by reapportionment, the House still operated pretty much under a seniority system. Seniority meant that while there was a passel of freshmen legislators, mere numbers would not ensure effectiveness. However, knowledge of the rules of the House and how to use them in the legislative process would give the freshmen some clout. Jean took it on herself to learn not just the rules under which the House, but those under which the Senate, operated.

The Freshman Caucus filled a need, and it was led by someone who knew how to make it an effective voice for change in the House. As Jean has often been quoted, "I did my homework on the issues and I knew each of the 123 other members of the House." She was prepared.

While nature abhors a vacuum, there is another law of physics that can be applied to politics and government: "For every action, there is an equal and opposite reaction."

The push for progressive legislation and the shift in power and alliances within the House upset a number of more traditional legislators. In 1978 they formed what was called the "Fat and Ugly Caucus" to block, amend, or delay bills that dealt with modernization and reform. In reaction a coalition of progressive legislators formed the "Crazy Caucus." Representative Toal along with Representative Bob McFadden were the recognized leaders of this group.

During the next decade, the General Assembly passed significant legislation that dealt with a variety of reform issues necessary to make South Carolina a better place in which to live. Almost all of these originated in the House, where Jean often served as the floor leader for reform legislation. She and her fellow members of the "Crazy Caucus" had hope. They did not prevail on every issue; sometimes there were compromises, but they persevered in their desire to improve the quality of life for all South Carolinians. Because Representative Toal always did her homework, because she utilized the research staff of the House effectively, she was prepared to lead the fight for reform legislation.

In 1988 Representative Jean Toal was elected to the South Carolina Supreme Court. She was the court's first woman jurist, but that is not for what she should be remembered. When she assumed her seat, the general procedures were very traditional. We know from her colleagues on the bench and her former law clerks that she kind of shook things up. She insisted on having her law clerks research and brief her for every case that came before the court, not just those for which she was assigned to write an opinion. This practice, which she instituted in 1989, has now become the standard for all justices. By being prepared she altered the nature of the oral arguments before the court. No longer were they simply a presentation by the attorneys in the case. Instead they became a lively exchange between the members of the court and opposing counsel.

In the first years of the new millennium, South Carolina's court system was anything but a "system." Record keeping and procedures were antiquated. Courts were overburdened, and there was a tremendous backlog of cases. The state's new chief justice viewed the morass with dismay and saw that in South Carolina the constitutional right to a speedy trial was something of a non sequitur. That right had been enshrined in the Magna Carta and cited by a colonial South Carolina court in 1765 during the Stamp Act Crisis before it became the sixth amendment to the United States Constitution.

Increasing the number of trial judges was not the answer, but making use of modern technology was. In 2001 Chief Justice Toal initiated a plan that would within a few years make the state's court system truly a system—and a nationally recognized leader in the use of technology.

During her twenty-seven years on the Supreme Court, Toal has written many opinions that affected the lives of South Carolinians. If you were to ask any South Carolina judge or attorney to list the significant opinions that Jean Toal authored while on the court, the lists would, no doubt, be lengthy. If asked to name the single most significant case, there would be little doubt that many would cite *Abbeville County School District v. State*. On November 12, 2014, the South Carolina Supreme Court rendered its verdict in favor of the plaintiff school districts. Chief Justice Toal wrote the opinion for the majority of the court.

In the foreword, introduction, ten essays, and ten personal reflections in this book, the myriad aspects of the life and career of the chief justice have been ably chronicled. There are many "firsts." She has represented our state superbly on the national stage. She is a luminary in the legal profession who will leave a lasting legacy to her native state in such things as progressive legislation, careful stewardship of the judicial branch, increased participation by women in all segments of society, and scholarly, well-reasoned judicial opinions. Her impact on her state and the nation may be difficult to quantify, but most assuredly Jean Hoefer Toal will leave South Carolina much better than she found it.

Contributors

JOSEPH F. ANDERSON JR. received his B.A. degree from Clemson University and his J.D. degree from the University of South Carolina School of Law. He served for one year as a law clerk to the Honorable Clement F. Haynsworth Jr., chief judge of the United States Court of Appeals for the Fourth Circuit. In 1976 he began the practice of law with his father in Edgefield, South Carolina, and also represented Edgefield and Aiken Counties in the South Carolina General Assembly. In 1986 President Ronald Reagan appointed him to be a United States district judge, a position he holds today. From 2000 to 2007, Judge Anderson served as chief judge of the district.

JOAN P. ASSEY is the director of technology for the South Carolina Judicial Department. Previously she served as the technology advisor for education in the office of Governor James Hodges. Dr. Assey began her professional career as an English teacher in Richland County School District 2. In addition she served as the district's director of technology. Under Dr. Assey's leadership, the South Carolina Judicial Department has been awarded $52 million in federal grants to use in developing technology for its court system. Her leadership led to the development of the judicial branch's website providing access to court records to the legal community and the public.

JAY BENDER holds the Reid H. Montgomery Freedom of Information Chair at the University of South Carolina, where he has had a joint appointment to the faculties of the School of Journalism and Mass Communications and the School of Law. Bender is of counsel to the Columbia, South Carolina, law firm of Baker, Ravenel, and Bender, L.L.P. The firm is a successor to the firm of Belser, Belser, Baker, and Barwick, where Bender started his law career in 1974 as a law clerk working primarily with a young associate named Jean Hoefer Toal. Toal became a partner in the firm, and Bender became an associate upon his admission to the South Carolina Bar in 1975. Bender and Toal continued to work together until, as he says, "She found other work" with her election to the Supreme Court of South Carolina.

C. MITCHELL BROWN is the leader of the appellate practice group at Nelson, Mullins, Riley, and Scarborough, L.L.P., in Columbia, South Carolina. He has served on the Executive Committee of Nelson Mullins for a number of years. He has orally argued over eighty cases in appellate courts, including in various state supreme courts and federal circuit courts of appeal. He has argued in many cases involving constitutional questions and multimillion-dollar verdicts. Mr. Brown has published several articles and given a number of national- and state-level presentations on appellate practice. He is a graduate of the University of South Carolina School of Law. Mr. Brown proudly served as one of the first law clerks for Chief Justice Jean Toal when she was an associate justice in 1989.

W. LEWIS BURKE JR. is Distinguished Professor Emeritus at the University of South Carolina School of Law, where he taught clinics, alternative dispute resolution, trial advocacy, and South Carolina legal history. He is the author or editor of four books, including *Dawn of Religious Freedom,* coedited with James L. Underwood; *Matthew J. Perry: The Man, His Times and His Legacy,* coedited with Belinda Gergel; and *At Freedom's Door: African American Founding Fathers in Reconstruction South Carolina,* coedited with James Lowell Underwood. He is the author of numerous chapters and articles on legal history. Presently he is working on a book on the history of South Carolina's black lawyers to be published by the University of Georgia Press.

M. ELIZABETH (LIZ) CRUM earned her B.A. from Agnes Scott College in 1970 and her J.D. from the University of South Carolina in 1973. She was one of the first women hired as an assistant attorney general for South Carolina in 1973, practicing in the Special Litigation Unit. In 1977 she became the director of research and staff counsel for the South Carolina House of Representatives Judiciary Committee. Crum joined the McNair law firm in 1981 and is a shareholder with the firm. Crum has been actively involved with the South Carolina Women Lawyers Association, serving on the board and as its president.

TINA CUNDARI is a member of the law firm Sowell, Gray, Stepp, and Laffitte, L.L.C., in Columbia, where she has practiced since 2005. Cundari is a graduate of the Honors Program of the College of Charleston and the University of North Carolina at Chapel Hill School of Law. From 2003 to 2005, she had the privilege of serving as a law clerk for the Honorable Jean Hoefer Toal. While clerking Cundari taught legal writing to first-year students at the University of South Carolina School of Law. She practices in the areas of commercial litigation, professional liability and ethics, and appellate advocacy.

CAMERON MCGOWAN CURRIE was appointed United States district judge for the District of South Carolina by President Clinton in March 1994. Prior to that she served as chief deputy attorney general and director of the state

Grand Jury Division of the South Carolina Attorney General's Office, as a United States magistrate judge, and as an assistant United States attorney in the District of Columbia and the District of South Carolina. She also engaged in private practice in the District of Columbia and in Columbia, South Carolina. Judge Currie was born and raised in Florence, South Carolina, and is a graduate of the University of South Carolina. She received her law degree, with honors, from George Washington University School of Law.

WALTER B. EDGAR is Claude H. Neuffer Professor of Southern Studies Emeritus and Distinguished Professor Emeritus of History at the University of South Carolina. Before his retirement he was director of the Institute for Southern Studies for thirty-two years and held four named professorships. He is the author or editor of more than a dozen books on South Carolina and the American South, including *South Carolina: A History, The South Carolina Encyclopedia,* and *Partisans and Redcoats: The Southern Campaign That Turned the Tide of the American Revolution.* He is the author of numerous articles and essays that have appeared in publications on both sides of the Atlantic. In 2008 he was inducted into the South Carolina Hall of Fame.

JEAN TOAL EISEN is the deputy staff director of the Senate Appropriations Committee. A native South Carolinian, Toal Eisen began her Senate career working for Senator Ernest F. Hollings. She earned her B.A. in mathematics and philosophy from Yale University. Toal Eisen lives in Arlington, Virginia, with her husband, Peter, and her son, Patrick. Her mother is the chief justice of South Carolina.

ROBERT L. FELIX is the James P. Mozingo III Professor Emeritus of Legal Research at the University of South Carolina School of Law. From 1967 to 2006 he taught torts, conflict of laws, products liability, and law and literature. He received his A.B. and LL.B. degrees from the University of Cincinnati; M.A. degree from the University of British Columbia; and LL.M. degree from Harvard University. He has studied at Oxford University and been a Fulbright Visiting Professor in France and Belgium. Professor Felix is coauthor of *The South Carolina Law of Torts* and a treatise and a casebook on the conflict of laws. He is a member of the Richland County Bar Association and a member of the International Law Committee of the South Carolina Bar. Having assumed emeritus status in 2006, he teaches courses in Roman law, law and literature, and conflict of laws.

RICHARD MARK GERGEL is a United States District Court judge for the District of South Carolina. He is a native of Columbia, South Carolina, and graduated from Duke University, summa cum laude, in 1975 and the Duke University School of Law in 1979. He returned to Columbia to practice in 1979. He opened his own law firm in 1983 and specialized in complex civil litigation. He is also an avid historian and has authored and coauthored numerous articles and a book on South Carolina history. He is the founding president of the South Carolina Supreme Court Historical Society. In December 2009 he was nominated to the United States District Court bench by President Barak Obama and was unanimously confirmed by the United States Senate in August 2010. Judge Gergel sits in the Charleston federal courthouse.

RUTH BADER GINSBURG is a United States Supreme Court justice, the second woman to be appointed to the position and the first Jewish female justice. She graduated from Columbia Law School and became a staunch courtroom advocate for the fair treatment of women. She worked with the ACLU's Women's Rights Project, for which she argued six landmark gender equality cases before the U.S. Supreme Court. Ginsburg was appointed by President Carter to the U.S. Court of Appeals for the D.C. Circuit in 1980 and was appointed to the Supreme Court by President Clinton in 1993. As a judge Ruth Ginsburg favors caution, moderation, and restraint. She is considered part of the Supreme Court's moderate-liberal bloc, presenting a strong voice in favor of gender equality, the rights of workers, and the separation of church and state.

ELIZABETH (BETSY) VAN DOREN GRAY has concentrated her law practice in litigation matters since 1977. She is a 1970 graduate of the University of South Carolina and earned her J.D., cum laude, from the University of South Carolina School of Law in 1976. Among other positions she has served as president of the South Carolina Bar, is a member of the South Carolina Women Lawyers Association, is a fellow of the American College of Trial Lawyers, and has been a recipient of the South Carolina Women Lawyers Association Jean Galloway Bissell Award. Starting her career as the first woman attorney hired by the McNair Law Firm, P.A., in 1977, she is currently a member of Sowell, Gray, Stepp, and Laffitte, L.L.C., in Columbia.

SUE (CORKY) ERWIN HARPER is a partner in the firm of Nelson, Mullins, Riley, and Scarborough, L.L.P., in Columbia, South Carolina. She is a graduate of Queens College and the University of South Carolina School of Law, where she was an editor of the *South Carolina Law Review*. She clerked for the Honorable Robert F. Chapman, United States District Court judge for the District of South Carolina. A founder and the first president of the South Carolina Women Lawyers Association, she received that organization's Jean Galloway Bissell Award in 2004. She is certified by the South Carolina Supreme Court as specialist in employment and labor law and is a fellow in the College of Labor and Employment Lawyers.

JESSICA CHILDERS HARRINGTON graduated from the University of South Carolina School of Law in 2015 with a Children's Law Certificate. She was a member of Women in Law and the Children's Advocacy Law Society. During law school she was the research assistant for Professor Lewis Burke. She received a B.A. in history, with honors, from the University of North Carolina at Charlotte.

KAYE G. HEARN, a justice of the South Carolina Supreme Court, received her B.A., cum laude, from Bethany College in 1972 and her J.D., cum laude, from the University of South Carolina School of Law in 1977. She received an LL.M. from the University of Virginia's Graduate Program for Judges in May 1998. Hearn served as a family court judge from 1986 until 1995, when she was elected to the South Carolina Court of Appeals, serving as its chief judge for ten years. Hearn was elected to the South Carolina Supreme Court in May 2009, becoming only the second woman member in the court's history.

BLAKE HEWITT is a graduate of the Georgia Institute of Technology and the University of South Carolina School of Law. He clerked for the chief justice for three years, and he subsequently clerked a fourth year with United States district judge Joseph F. Anderson Jr. He is a practicing lawyer with the Bluestein, Nichols, Thompson, and Delgado law firm. His principal area of practice is appeals.

I. S. LEEVY JOHNSON assumed the presidency of the South Carolina Bar in 1985, the first African American to do so. His legal career has included service as a trial lawyer, legislator, bar leader, and community servant. After graduating from C. A. Johnson High School in 1960, he received an associate of mortuary science degree from the University of Minnesota in 1962 and a bachelor of science degree in 1965. From the University of South Carolina School of Law he was awarded a juris doctor degree in 1968. Embarking on a career in public service, in 1970 he made history by becoming one of the first African Americans elected to the South Carolina General Assembly since Reconstruction. In 1999 Governor Jim Hodges bestowed on him the state's highest civilian award, the Order of the Palmetto.

JOHN W. KITTREDGE of Greenville, South Carolina, began his legal career as a law clerk to the Honorable William W. Wilkins Jr. He practiced law in the firm of Wilkins, Nelson, and Kittredge. Justice Kittredge was elected as a family court judge in 1991 and then elected a circuit court judge in 1996. He was elected to the South Carolina Court of Appeals in 2003 and then elected as a justice to the South Carolina Supreme Court in 2008.

LILLA TOAL MANDSAGER is an adult learning specialist for Summit Public Schools, a network of nine public, heterogeneous, college prep charter schools in California and Washington. Since receiving her M.A. in secondary English teaching from Stanford University, she has worked as an English teacher, a college mentor, a teacher coach, and a school administrator. She believes that high-quality, public education is the shortest path to social justice. She lives in Columbia, South Carolina, with her husband, John, and daughter, Ruth.

MARY CAMPBELL MCQUEEN has served as president of the National Center for State Courts since August 2004. Previously McQueen served as Washington State court administrator from 1987 to 2004 and director of Judicial Services for the Washington State Office of the Administrator for the Courts, 1979–87, president of the Conference of State Court Administrators in 1995–96, and chair of the Lawyer's Committee of the American Bar Association/Judicial Administration Division. She is a member of the Washington and U.S. Supreme Court Bars and Recipient of the American Judicature Society's Herbert Harley Award in 2004.

JAMES E. MOORE received his bachelor of arts degree from Duke University and his juris doctor degree from Duke University School of Law. Upon graduation from law school, Justice Moore engaged in the private practice of law for fifteen years in Greenwood, South Carolina, and served four terms in the South Carolina House of Representatives. After being elected resident circuit court judge of the Eight Judicial Circuit in 1976 and during his fifteen-year tenure, Justice Moore served on numerous state and national committees. Justice Moore was elected to the Supreme Court of South Carolina in 1991, where he served for seventeen years. He now serves South Carolina as an active/retired justice.

SANDRA DAY O'CONNOR received her B.A. and LL.B. from Stanford University, where she served as editor for the *Stanford Law Review*. After being turned down by law firms who refused to hire women, she embarked on a distinguished prosecutorial career that led her to the Arizona Court of Appeals. In 1981 Ronald Reagan nominated her as a justice of the United States Supreme Court, and she received unanimous Senate approval. O'Connor made history as the first woman justice to serve on the Supreme Court. As a justice O'Connor was involved in many important cases, on issues ranging from abortion and affirmative action to property and voter rights. She retired January 31, 2006, after serving for twenty-five years. Following her retirement from the court, Justice O'Connor founded iCivics, Inc., a nonprofit organization that prepares young Americans to become knowledgeable, engaged twenty-first-century citizens by creating free and innovative educational materials. In recognition of her lifetime accomplishments, President Barack Obama awarded Justice O'Connor with the nation's highest civilian honor, the Presidential Medal of Freedom, on August 12, 2009.

RICHARD W. RILEY served for four years in the South Carolina House and ten years in the Senate. He was the first two-term governor of South Carolina (1979–87) in modern times and the longest-serving U.S. secretary of education (1993–2001). As governor of South Carolina, his landmark accomplishment was the comprehensive Education Improvement Act. As U.S. secretary of education, he helped President Clinton launch historic initiatives to improve the quality of and access to early childhood, K–12, undergraduate, technical, and advanced education to prepare all students for college, career, and citizenship. After leaving public office, Riley returned to his law firm, Nelson, Mullins, Riley, and Scarborough, and has remained a public ambassador for education improvement.

BAKARI T. SELLERS is the son of civil rights activist Cleveland Sellers, is an attorney, and represented House District 90 from 2006 to 2014. Sellers was twenty-two when elected. He is a 2005 graduate of Morehouse College and a 2008 graduate of the University of South Carolina School of Law. Bakari Sellers has worked with the Strom Law Firm, L.L.C., since 2007.

ROBERT (BOB) J. SHEHEEN was born and raised in Camden, South Carolina. He attended Camden public schools; Duke University (1961–65); and the University of South Carolina School of Law (1965–68). He has practiced law since October 3, 1968. He served in the South Carolina House from 1977 through 2000, where he served as chairman of the House Judiciary Committee, and as Speaker of the House from 1986 through 1994.

AMELIA WARING WALKER has served as a law clerk to the Honorable Jean Hoefer Toal since 2011. She received a B.A. in art history from Washington and Lee University in 2004, and a J.D. from the University of South Carolina School of Law in 2009.

BRADISH J. WARING is a past president of the South Carolina Bar and a former two-term state bar delegate to the American Bar Association. He is a member of the prestigious National Center for State Courts' Lawyers Committee, and the Chief Justice's Commission on the Profession. As part of his mission to assist in increasing judicial funding in the Palmetto State, Waring is serving a second term on the South Carolina Judicial Council. He is a member of the Nexsen Pruet law firm's board of directors and represents a diverse mix of clients in complex commercial litigation including products liability, insurance coverage, business disputes, and admiralty.

Index

House Committees' officer election
procedures, 70n8
House District 75, 46, 179
House Education and Public Works
(Education) Committee, 48, 61
House Interstate Cooperation Com-
mittee, 48
House Journal, 67
House Judiciary Committee, 16, 17,
42, 46, 48, 49, 53, 54, 56, 60, 62,
63, 70n11, 70n16, 165
House Labor, Commerce, and In-
dustry (LCI) Committee, 48, 67
House Legislative Ethics Commit-
tee, 48
House Medical, Military, Public,
and Municipal Affairs (3M)
Committee, 48
House Rules Committee, 46, 48–
49, 68–69, 153, 162, 165
House standing committees,
speaker and speaker pro tempore
not serving on, 70n10
House Subcommittee on Constitu-
tional Laws (Con Laws), 48, 53–
54, 63, 165
House Subcommittee on Criminal
Laws, 48
House Subcommittee on Election
Laws, 48
House Subcommittee on General
Laws, 48
House Subcommittee on Special
Laws, 48
House Ways and Means Commit-
tee, 48, 49, 68
Hughston, Thomas L. (Tommy), 49,
66, 70n14
Humana, 42–43
"Hunt Club breakfast," 143
Hutson, Doris Camille, 11

iCivics, 132, 174–75

Illinois, 170
Illinois Bar, 147–48
Illinois Supreme Court, 147–48,
157n1
improved real estate, 96–98, 108n2
in favorem vitae, doctrine of, 80–81
"In the Arena Award," 132
"irresistible impulse" test for insanity, 82
Isle of Palms, 143, 146
Italian prisoners of war, 10

Jackson, Michael, 144
Jackson, Robert H., 86n4
Jasper County, 94
Jasper County courthouse, 94
Jasper County School District, 112
Jean Galloway Bissell Award, 154
Jefferson, Wallace B., 173
*Jefferson's Manual of Parliamentary
Practice,* 70n12
*Jensen v. Anderson County Depart-
ment of Social Services,* 104–5,
106, 110n65, 110n74
Jerusalem, 145
Jim Crow, 10
John Belton O'Neall Inn of Court,
164
Johnson, I. S. Leevy, 12, 16,
166–67
Johnson, Toal, and Battiste, 44
*Johnson v. Collins Entertainment Co.,
Inc.,* 85–86, 91–92, 93, 95n23
Journal of Supreme Court History,
148
*Joytime Distributors and Amusement
Co., Inc. v. State,* 93–94
J. P. Stevens, 13, 41
Judicial Adjustment Act of 1979,
62–63
Judicial Reform Committee, 73n127
Judicial Screening Committee, 18,
20–21, 62

Orangeburg Massacre, 13
Orangeburg *Times and Democrat,* 118
Outback Bowl, 144
Owen Martin v. National Railroad Passenger Corporation 'AMTRAK,' 15
Oxford University, 142

Patient's Compensation Fund, 69
Patrick, Viola, 140
Patterson, Grady, 65
Patterson, Larry R. (Choppy), 168
Paylor, Alice, 156
Peeples, Rodney, 18, 20, 23
Pennsylvania, 33, 34
Perry, James Marjory (Miss Jim), 9, 13, 150, 151, 158n14
Perry, Matthew J., Jr., 10–11, 11–12, 16, 24, 46, 164
Perry Mason (television show), 37
Philadelphia Newspapers, Inc. v. Hepps, 101, 102
Pickens County, 54, 131
Platt v. CSX Transportation, Inc., 107, 111n86
Poe, Hazel Collings, 11
Pope, Adele Jeffords, 159n28
Portee, Larry, 39
post conviction relief, 81
Powell, Lewis F., Jr., 101, 109n35
Powell, Warren C., Jr., 37, 75
Praxis examination, 115–16
products liability, 108n2, 108n20
public duty doctrine, 105
public duty rule, 103–7, 110n58, 110n60
Public Service Commission Merit Selection Act of 1979, 63–65
Publix grocery store, 141
punitive damages, 85, 100, 102

Quinn, Frank I., 90

Racketeer Influenced and Corrupt Organizations Act (RICO), 91, 92, 93
Rainey, John S., 84
Ravenel, Cravens, 75
Rawl, A. Victor, 66
Reagan, Ronald Wilson, 150
reapportionment, 55, 70n2, 71n30, 179
Reed v. Reed, 4–5
referendum on video poker (November 1999), 93
Republican Party, 51
Reserve Fund. *See* Constitutional 5 Percent Legislative Reserve Fund—Article III, section 36
Reyelt v. South Carolina Tax Commission, 90
Reynolds v. Sims, 46
Richardson, Kathleen, 129
Richland County, 22, 31, 32, 38, 39, 40, 54, 56, 67, 123, 131
Richland County Bar Association, 39
Richland County Court of Common Pleas, 91
Richland County Education Association, 38
Richland County School District 1 Board of Trustees, 38, 56
Richland School District 2, 126–27
RICO. *See* Racketeer Influenced and Corrupt Organizations Act (RICO)
Riley, Richard W., 17, 64, 67, 68, 161–63
Roberts, Beulah G., 129
Roberts, Pamela, 156
Robert's Rules of Order, 70n12
Rock Hill, 34, 36
Rogers, Christopher, 128–29
Rogers, John I., 71n20
Rogers, Tim, 28n101